T0387681

Research on College Stress and Coping

A Volume in
Research on Stress and Coping in Education

Series Editors

Christopher J. McCarthy
University of Texas at Austin

Richard G. Lambert
University of North Carolina at Charlotte

Research on Stress and Coping in Education

Christopher J. McCarthy and Richard G. Lambert, Series Editors

Research on College Stress and Coping:
Implications From the COVID-19 Pandemic and Beyond (2024)
edited by Christopher J. McCarthy,
R. Jason Lynch, and Stephen DiDonato

Research on Teacher Stress:
Implications for the COVID-19 Pandemic and Beyond (2023)
edited by Christopher J. McCarthy and Richard G. Lambert

Higher Education for the People:
Critical Contemplative Methods of Liberatory Practice (2022)
by Maryann Krikorian

Stress and Coping of English Learners (2018)
edited by Teresa Rishel and Paul Chamness Miller

Mindfulness for Educational Practice:
A Path to Resilience for Challenging Work (2015)
edited by Gordon S. Gates

International Perspectives on Teacher Stress (2012)
edited by Christopher J. McCarthy,
Richard G. Lambert, and Annette Ullrich

Personality, Stress, and Coping: Implications for Education (2011)
edited by Gretchen M. Reevy and Erica Frydenberg

Toward a Broader Understanding of Stress and Coping:
Mixed Methods Approaches (2010)
edited by Kathleen M. T. Collins,
Anthony J. Onwuegbuzie, and Qun G. Jiao

Emerging Thought and Research on Student,
Teacher, and Administrator Stress and Coping (2007)
edited by Gordon S. Gates

Thriving, Surviving or Going Under: Coping with Everyday Lives (2006)
by Erica Frydenberg

Understanding Teacher Stress in an Age of Accountability (2006)
edited by Richard G. Lambert and Christopher J. McCarthy

Toward Wellness: Prevention, Coping, and Stress (2003)
edited by Gordon S. Gates and Mimi Wolverton

Research on College Stress and Coping

Implications From the COVID-19 Pandemic and Beyond

Edited by

Christopher J. McCarthy
University of Texas at Austin

R. Jason Lynch
Appalachian State University

Stephen DiDonato
Thomas Jefferson University

INFORMATION AGE PUBLISHING, INC.
Charlotte, NC • www.infoagepub.com

Library of Congress Cataloging-in-Publication Data

CIP record for this book is available from the Library of Congress
http://www.loc.gov

ISBNs: 979-8-88730-732-9 (Paperback)

979-8-88730-733-6 (Hardcover)

979-8-88730-734-3 (ebook)

Copyright © 2024 Information Age Publishing Inc.

All rights reserved. No part of this publication may be reproduced, stored in
a retrieval system, or transmitted, in any form or by any means, electronic,
mechanical, photocopying, microfilming, recording or otherwise, without written
permission from the publisher.

Printed in the United States of America

DEDICATION

This book is dedicated to the faculty and staff working in higher education during the COVID-19 pandemic, who dedicated themselves to the well-being of college students during a world-wide crisis.

CONTENTS

Acknowledgments .... *ix*

Introduction—College Stress and Coping During the Pandemic:
　　What Can We Learn and How Could We Move Forward?
　　Christopher J. McCarthy, R. Jason Lynch, and Stephen DiDonato ....*xi*

1.　Invisible on the Front Lines: A Post-Intentional
　　Phenomenological Investigation of COVID-19 Trauma
　　in College Student Affairs Professionals
　　R. Jason Lynch, Chelsea Gilbert, Libby Clary,
　　and Bethany Gonzalez *1*

2.　Asian International PhD Students' Perceived Challenges,
　　Stress, Coping Strategies, and Resilience During and Beyond
　　the COVID-19 Pandemic
　　Jun Ai, Ankita Bhattashali, Ming-Tso Chien, Hyesun Cho,
　　and Yi Zhang *27*

3.　A Descriptive Phenomenological Study of the Factors
　　Influencing Multinational Female Graduate Students'
　　Academic Productivity During the COVID-19 Pandemic:
　　A Feminist Perspective
　　Nuchelle L. Chance and Tricia M. Farwell *53*

4.　First Generation College Students' Health and Well-Being,
　　Academic Engagement, and Sense of Self During the COVID-
　　19 Global Pandemic
　　Megan K. Rauch Griffard, Rex A. Long,
　　and Cassandra R. Davis *79*

viii   CONTENTS

5. Relationships Between Study Conditions, Stress, and
   Perceived Health: Studying at University After the COVID-19
   Lockdown
   *Knut Inge Fostervold, Silje Endresen Reme, Helge I. Strømsø,
   and Sten R. Ludvigsen* 109

6. College Students, Stress, and COVID: Lessons and Potential
   for the Future
   Shannon C. Mulhearn, Megan Adkins, and Stefanie Neal 135

7. Struggles and Stress: Impact of the COVID-19 Pandemic on
   STEM Preservice-Teachers
   *Seema Rivera, Preethi Titu, Katie Kavanagh, Jan DeWaters,
   Ben Galluzzo, and Mike Ramsdell* 161

8. A Rapid Scoping Review of Collegiate Student's Stress,
   Coping, and Help-Seeking During COVID-19
   *Caroline Weppner, Christopher J. McCarthy, Trisha Miller,
   Yijie Tian, Francesca Di Rienzo, R. Jason Lynch, and
   Stephen DiDonato* 183

9. Conclusion—Higher Education in the Aftermath: Obstacles
   and Opportunities
   R. Jason Lynch, Christopher McCarthy, and Stephen DiDonato......... 225

About the Authors.. *231*

ACKNOWLEDGMENTS

The editors gratefully acknowledge the contribution of the following external reviewers to this volume:

Madison Blaydes
Francesca Di Rienzo
Trisha Miller
Yijie Tian
Caroline Weppner
University of Texas at Austin

Dr. Lyra L'Estrange
School of Early Childhood & Inclusive Education
Queensland University of Technology
Brisbane, Australia

Research on College Stress and Coping: Implications From the COVID-19 Pandemic and Beyond, pp. ix–ix
Copyright © 2024 by Information Age Publishing
www.infoagepub.com
All rights of reproduction in any form reserved.

INTRODUCTION

COLLEGE STRESS AND COPING DURING THE PANDEMIC

What Can We Learn and How Could We Move Forward?

Christopher J. McCarthy
University of Texas at Austin

R. Jason Lynch
Appalachian State University

Stephen DiDonato
Thomas Jefferson University

Yale University's unofficial anthem *Bright College Years* extols higher education experience as a time of growth and happiness with the phrase, *"with pleasure rife, The shortest, gladdest years of life; How swiftly are ye gliding by! Oh, why doth time so quickly fly?"* This sentiment might have been true for some, but for most students the undeniable benefits of college come at a cost. There are many reasons that students experience stress and turmoil during their college experience: students coming directly from high school are developmentally in transition as they navigate the transition from adolescence to adulthood, they must adjust to new relationships, and a new academic environment (Weppner et al., this volume). So, it is widely recognized that the college years, from undergraduate through graduate, can be stressful.

Research on College Stress and Coping: Implications From the COVID-19 Pandemic and Beyond, pp. xi–xiii
Copyright © 2024 by Information Age Publishing
www.infoagepub.com
All rights of reproduction in any form reserved.

Moreover, stress is experienced by staff, faculty, and administrators in higher education. Not coincidentally, the financial landscape of higher education has changed in recent decades, with less public funding and higher costs for students. Many academic budgets are strapped as well, leading to flattening of employee salaries and tight academic budgets. Two- and four-year institutions have increased their efforts to increase diversity, but in some cases, are unable to support the varied needs of a more diverse student body. And the mental health of students is an ongoing need: as colleges become more inclusive, they also become more a part of the frontlines of mental health care.

We developed this book because the COVID-19 pandemic created new challenges for when an international public health emergency was declared in early spring 2020, with social distancing measures put in place for several semesters. While the pandemic had a universal, while uneven, impact on everyone, it uniquely impacted certain sectors, most particularly including education at the K–12 and college level. The extra demands levels associated with such measures led to the previous book in this series for Information Age Publishing in 2023 (McCarthy & Lambert, 2023) focused on K–12 educational settings, but there was clearly a need to account for the unique impacts of COVID on higher education.

Our goal in this book was to organize a volume that documented the many ways in which stress and coping played out during the height of the COVID pandemic. The first study in this book was conducted by one of us (Lynch) and addresses the impact of trauma on college student affairs professionals. Following are several numbers of studies addressing the impact of COVID on Asian international students (Ai et al., this volume), multinational female graduate students (Chance & Farwell, this volume), first-generation students (Griffard et al., this volume), undergraduate students (chapters by Fostervold et al., this volume; Mulhearn et al., this volume), and STEM preservice teachers (Rivera et al., this volume). The book concludes with a scoping review of literature on existing stress and college students, which has already been published and a conclusion by us as editors.

In addition to presenting their studies, we also asked authors to describe paths forward in college settings for supporting students and workers in higher education. As we go to press with this book, the prevailing zeitgeist is relief that the immediate impacts of the pandemic are behind us. Yet, its impact will be felt for years to come, including sources of stress and trauma that will likely manifest over time. It is essential that higher education use this time as an opportunity to create a healthy environment for all students.

In concluding this introduction, we note that stress is a ubiquitous but poorly defined construct, and each chapter takes a somewhat different approach to how it is defined and measured. While this has advantages, it can also create a muddled picture for those seeking interventions to offset the effects of stress. We hope this book further defines the nature and scope of stress for future investigation and intervention.

REFERENCE

McCarthy, C. J., & Lambert, R. G. (2023). *Research on teacher stress: Implications for the COVID-19 pandemic and beyond*. Information Age Publishing.

CHAPTER 1

INVISIBLE ON THE FRONT LINES

A Post-Intentional Phenomenological Investigation of COVID-19 Trauma in College Student Affairs Professionals

R. Jason Lynch
Appalachian State University

Chelsea Gilbert
The Ohio State University

Libby Clary
Appalachian State University

Bethany Gonzalez
Appalachian State University

ABSTRACT

Trauma may be defined as "any disturbing experience that results in significant fear, helplessness, dissociation, confusion, or other disruptive feelings intense enough to have a long-lasting negative effect on a person's attitudes, behavior, and other aspects of functioning" (American Psychological Association, 2020, para. 1). As the COVID-19 pandemic upended the operations of college student affairs divisions across the United States, many practitioners found themselves navigating both direct and indirect experiences of trauma and stress. This study sought to better understand how student

Research on College Stress and Coping: Implications From the COVID-19 Pandemic and Beyond, pp. 1–26
Copyright © 2024 by Information Age Publishing
www.infoagepub.com
All rights of reproduction in any form reserved.

affairs practitioners described their experiences of trauma and stress during the pandemic, as well as how they made meaning of these experiences. Using a post-intentional phenomenological approach, 36 student affairs practitioners served as co-researchers, and each completed a one-hour virtual interview. Phenomenological reduction and imaginative variation analytical techniques were used to create a composite narrative of practitioner experiences, revealing four key themes, including: (1) Chronic stress, anger, and fear related to opaque and callous leadership, (2) Reconceptualizations of self and community care, and (3) Insidious neoliberal logics driving environmental stressors in student affairs, and (4) Social identity and positionality as drivers of stress and trauma. Implications for policy, practice, and future scholarship are discussed.

College student affairs professionals (SAPs) are helping professionals who are on the front lines of college and university student support services (Reynolds, 2010). The importance of their roles was heightened as a result of the novel coronavirus (COVID-19) pandemic, when the lives of college students across the United States were upended as institutions rapidly shifted to remote curricular and co-curricular learning and engagement (Burke, 2020b). The mental health challenges faced by students in the months that followed skyrocketed (Copeland et al., 2021), and were further exacerbated for many minoritized students by continued incidences of anti-Black and anti-Asian racial violence (Choo & Diaz, 2021; Philimon, 2020). Meanwhile, the professionals supporting these students faced growing uncertainty regarding their own job security, safety, and well-being (Douglas-Gabriel & Flowers, 2020; Smith, 2020). Over time, this uncertainty, coupled with the emotional weight of supporting others, can manifest itself as trauma (Knight, 2013; Silver, 2020). To date, much of the research on the impact of the COVID-19 pandemic on college student affairs professionals has centered on issues of burnout (Chessman, 2021; Connor, 2021; Kunk-Czaplicki, 2023; Vega & Coon, 2022). While this is a useful and appropriate lens through which to view SAP experiences, it does not provide a holistic view of the experiences of these professionals, the potential long-term impacts of surviving such trauma, and may lead senior student affairs leaders to treating the wrong symptoms. Thus, the purpose of this study was to investigate the experiences of trauma as described by college student affairs professionals during the first months of the COVID-19 pandemic. As such, our research questions asked: (1) how do college student affairs professionals describe the trauma and stress they experienced during the COVID-19 pandemic? (2) how did college student affairs professionals come to their experiences of trauma and stress during the COVID-19 pandemic?, and (3) How did the co-researchers' social and environmental context shape their experiences of trauma and stress?

LITERATURE REVIEW

The construct of trauma originated in the discipline of psychology (Jones & Cureton, 2014), and has been critiqued by some scholars for being overly restrictive (May & Wisco, 2016) or lacking attention to social context (Stevens, 2009). In this study, we define trauma as "any disturbing experience that results in significant fear, helplessness, dissociation, confusion, or other disruptive feelings intense enough to have a long-lasting negative effect on a person's attitudes, behavior, and other aspects of functioning" (American Psychological Association, 2020, para. 1) and are intentionally attentive to the ways that trauma's impact can fall outside conventional diagnostic criteria, especially for minoritized individuals (e.g., Brown, 1991; Szymanski & Balsam, 2011; Yehuda et al., 1998).

Differentiating Trauma and Burnout

As cited, studies exploring the experiences of SAPs during the COVID-19 pandemic have overly focused on burnout as a primary result of the global crisis. However, often these authors may conflate, or diminish, the role of trauma as a precursor or result of extreme burnout. While both constructs share overlapping symptomologies, they are indeed distinct phenomena. Using the definition of trauma described above, we know that trauma results from highly disturbing experiences that impact our long-term ability to cope and function. On the other hand, Galek et al. (2011) describe burnout as, "the confluence of interpersonal and institutional sources of occupational stress" (p. 634). This is a distinct outcome of difficult work environments. Newell and MacNeil (2011) describe three symptom domains of burnout: emotional exhaustion, depersonalization, and reduced sense of personal accomplishment. Table 1.1 provides a comparison of the characteristics of trauma to burnout. With these considerations in mind, we next summarize literature regarding college student affairs professionals and trauma, as well as trauma and the COVID-19 pandemic.

College Student Affairs Professionals and Trauma

College student affairs professionals experience both direct and indirect forms of trauma as a result of their day-to-day work. In one study, 44% of a sample ($n = 617$), met all four symptom criteria for PTSD (Lynch, 2022). Direct trauma experienced by those working at colleges and universities include, but are not limited to, instances of workplace racism (Burke,

Table 1.1

Differentiating Trauma and Burnout

Trauma and Secondary Trauma	Burnout
• Can occur within or outside of occupational settings and may originate from an expansive variety of events or circumstances. • Results from a direct or indirect threat to life or sanity (American Psychiatric Association, 2013), or simply an event or circumstance that is so disturbing it overwhelms one's capacity to cope (American Psychological Association, 2020). • Wide range of symptomatology to include, but not limited to fear, anger, hopelessness, exhaustion, hypervigilance, avoidance, withdrawal, minimization, sleep disturbance, intrusive thoughts, jumpiness, dualism, short-temperedness, etc. (American Psychiatric Association, 2013; van Dernoot Lipsky, 2009).	• Most often attributed to occupational hazards, low job resources, and high job demands (Galek et al., 2011). • Results from role conflict, work structure, role ambiguity, etc. (Maslach et al. 2001) • Symptoms include exhaustion, depersonalization, and reduced sense of accomplishment (Newell & McNeil, 2010).

2020), living through a natural disaster (Davis et al., 2010), or experiences of campus violence (Flynn & Heitzmann, 2008).

Secondary trauma, or indirect trauma, on the other hand, refers to "the stress resulting from helping or wanting to help a traumatized or suffering person" (Figley, 1999, p. 10); individuals in helping professions are at an increased risk of indirect trauma (Newell & MacNeil, 2010). Because student support work is often emotionally demanding, indirect trauma in college student affairs professionals is endemic within higher education and impacts educators' well-being, self-efficacy, and job satisfaction (Lynch, 2017; Lynch & Glass, 2019; Stoves, 2014). Studies have attributed unhealthy professional socialization, lack of social support, and shortfalls in professional preparation as antecedents to the development of secondary trauma in this population (Lynch & Glass, 2020). Within some marginalized groups in student affairs, such as Black men, scholars have found that age, supervisory support, and trauma type (ex: student deaths) also greatly impact the experience of secondary trauma (Clark, 2022). For college student affairs professionals, both direct and indirect traumatic exposure has increased significantly as a result of the COVID-19 pandemic.

Trauma and COVID-19 in Student Affairs

The global pandemic of COVID-19 and its ensuing aftermath placed many college student affairs professionals in challenging—and potentially traumatic—workplace circumstances (Benhamou & Piedra, 2020; Turk et al., 2020), from campuses with high numbers of COVID-19 cases, to a lack of personal protective equipment, to chronic stress as a result of unclear and rapidly changing guidance from senior leadership (Douglas-Gabriel & Flowers, 2020; Smith, W., 2020). Some student affairs professionals also experienced a form of potentially traumatic stress known as *moral injury* when asked by institutional administrators to engage in actions that were misaligned with their values (Williamson et al., 2020), such as continuing to hold in-person programming despite increasing rates of COVID-19. Beyond this, as college student depression, anxiety, and stress increased (Copeland et al., 2021), college student affairs professionals also had increased responsibility to engage in emotional support, placing them at further risk of secondary trauma and its associated negative impacts (Newell & MacNeil, 2010).

METHODS

The purpose of this study was to better understand how U.S. college student affairs professionals described their experiences of trauma and stress during the COVID-19 pandemic, how they made meaning of these experiences, and how their social and environmental contexts shaped their experiences. To that end, we employed the use of post-intentional phenomenological methods. Specifically, phenomenology may be described as a method of "[determining] what an experience means for the persons who have had the experience and are able to provide a comprehensive experience of it" (Moustakas, 1994, p. 13). Yet, contemporary poststructuralists have critiqued phenomenological approaches as overly centering the voice and interpretation of the primary researcher, privileging their voice as a definitive and fixed account of co-researcher experiences (Soule & Freeman, 2019; Vagle, 2014). Within the philosophy of post-intentional phenomenology, co-researcher experiences are explored within social and environmental contexts, and co-researchers' experiences are emphasized as "partial, multiple, and always in the process of becoming" (Soule & Freeman, 2019, p. 858). More simply put, human interpretations of their lived experiences are complex, ever-changing, and often informed by the context in which they find themselves. For example, as one ages they are often able to make more sense of events that happened to them in the past and may often come to a different conclusion about past events than

6   R. J. LYNCH, C. GILBERT, L. CLARY, and B. GONZALEZ

their younger self may have. To that end, while we aimed to interpret co-researcher's lived experiences with them, we know that these interpretations represent a point in time and space that may evolve in the future.

Co-Researcher Recruitment and Selection

Co-researchers were selected using criterion-based sampling (Merriam, 2009). Criteria for participation included being a full-time employee in a college student affairs functional area, identified within the Council for the Advancement of Standards in Higher Education (Wells, 2015), since March 2020 (i.e., when much of U.S. higher education transitioned to emergency remote operations). Co-researchers were recruited using an existing pool of participants who completed a previous survey which sought to measure the prevalence and extent to which U.S. educators and educational leaders self-reported patterns of trauma exposure during the onset of COVID-19 (Lynch, 2020). At the end of the survey, participants had the option of indicating their interest in participating in a follow-up qualitative study. From this pool, participants were sent emails detailing the purpose and requirements of the study, as well as an informed consent form. In total, 36 individuals participated in the study. Table 1.2 presents a summary of co-researcher characteristics.

Table 1.2

Demographic Profile of Co-Researchers

	N	%		N	%
Racial Identity			*Functional Area*		
White or Caucasian	26	76%	Housing & Residence Life	15	44%
Hispanic, Latino/a, or Chicano/a	3	9%	Academic Advising	3	9%
Black or African American	2	6%	Campus Activities	2	6%
Native American or Indigenous	1	3%	College Unions	2	6%
Asian or Asian American	1	3%	Student Conduct	2	6%
Multiracial	1	3%	Admissions	1	3%
			Career Services	1	3%
Gender Identity			Case Management	1	3%
Woman	26	76%	Civic Learning & Engagement	1	3%
Man	6	18%	Enrollment Management	1	3%
Queer	2	6%	Fraternity & Sorority Life	1	3%
			International Student Services	1	3%
Sexual Orientation			LGBT+ Student Services	1	3%
Straight	23	68%	Multicultural Student Services	1	3%
Gay or Lesbian	5	15%	Title IX & Sexual Violence	1	3%

(Table continued on next page)

Table 1.2 (Continued)

Demographic Profile of Co-Researchers

		N	%			N	%
Sexual Orientation							
	Bisexual	5	15%				
	Queer	1	3%	*Institution Type*			
					Public 4-Year	23	68%
U.S. Region					Private 4-Year	8	24%
	Southeast	17	50%		Public 2-Year	3	9%
	Northeast	7	21%				
	Midwest	6	18%				
	West	4	12%				
	Southwest	3	9%				

Data Collection

Two forms of data collection served as the basis for analysis: virtual interviews and field texts.

Co-Researcher Interviews

Each co-researcher participated in a semi-structured interview (Merriam, 2009) that took place using Zoom software. Interviews were arranged via web-based scheduling software using predetermined co-researcher pseudonyms. On average, interviews lasted 30 minutes to one hour. The first part of the interview involved a reflective exercise to help bracket the topic of the interview and led to a broader discussion of participant experiences during the COVID-19 pandemic. The reflective activity used open-ended prompts similar to the format of a subject-object interviewing (Lahey et al., 2011), where co-researchers were provided with a list of words that may be associated with experiences of trauma (American Psychological Association, 2013), including: support; mood; trauma; fear; sadness; irritable; stress; guilt/shame; anxiety; alienation/isolation; avoidance; torn; angry; worry; recurring thoughts. Co-researchers were then given 10 minutes to reflect on these words and write down any initial thoughts, emotions, or memories that came to mind within the context of their experiences at home or at work since March 2020. We then engaged co-researchers in a conversation regarding words that stood out most and words that stood out least before moving onto the rest of the interview.

Field Texts

In order to document the detailed contexts in which each interview took place, researchers completed a brief reflective journal, or field text, after each interview (Merriam, 2009). Field texts included information documenting attitudes and dispositions of the researcher and interviewee that may be relevant to the later interpretation of transcripts, engagement in reflexivity, and lists of emergent ideas about the nature of trauma and stress in student affairs practitioners during the pandemic.

Data Analysis

Moustakas (1994) was used as a base-level guide for performing the steps of data analysis and interpretation. Given this resource is grounded in traditional phenomenological approaches, we remained cognizant of our intent in using a post-phenomenological framework by interrogating co-researcher interviews within the context of the local environments they described, as well as the broader national context. Additionally, co-researchers continually reflected on the dynamic and fluid nature of co-researcher experiences within the process of imaginative variation, as described below.

Data analysis involved engaging in phenomenological reduction, imaginative variation, and composite textural and structural descriptions. The goal of the phenomenological reduction was to explore commonalities regarding co-researcher descriptions of trauma during the pandemic. For each co-researcher interview, we identified statements that seemed to directly describe the experience of trauma and documented them in a spreadsheet. These statements were then grouped into invariant themes, which served as the basis for individual textural descriptions describing how each co-researcher experienced the phenomenon. A single composite textural description was then created using meta-themes that emerged across all individual textural descriptions.

The next step, imaginative variation, was used to describe commonalities across co-researcher experiences that describe how they came to experience trauma during the pandemic. Using the individual textural descriptions, we began the process of creating a list of ideas of how each co-researcher's experience led to their experience of the phenomenon described within the textural descriptions. These items were then grouped by similarity to create structural themes. Again, using these themes, we constructed individual structural descriptions for each co-researcher detailing how they came to experience the trauma during the pandemic. Finally, a single composite textural description was created highlighting common factors that led to the experience of the phenomenon across co-researcher experiences.

Limitations

This study is not without limitation, and findings should be interpreted in light of these constraints. First, co-researcher interviews occurred during a singular meeting taking place at a particular point in time and filtered through the fog of memory. The experience of trauma and chronic stress can often hinder narrative recall, as at the time of the trauma, the body is focused on survival (Bedard-Gilligan et al., 2017). Given this, many participants often described their early experiences during the pandemic as a "blur," which may have impacted the experiences they shared. Additionally, while we attempted to diversify the positionalities of our co-researchers, the majority of our sample still overly represented white cis-straight woman's experiences during the onset of the pandemic. Given the co-occurring incidents of racial violence during the summer of 2020, the additional narratives from Black and Asian professionals would have provided more nuance to the multiple points of potential traumatization for SAPs. Within this same vein, each interview's line of questioning specifically focused on the COVID-19 as a source of traumatization without directly asking about parallel issues of racial trauma (Human Rights Watch, 2020; Liu & Modir, 2020), financial trauma (Bonsaksen et al., 2020), and climate change disasters (Smith, A. B., 2021).

FINDINGS

Upon completion of our analysis, four key themes emerged within the composite description. These themes included: (1) Chronic stress, anger, and fear related to opaque and callous leadership, (2) Reconceptualizations of self and community care, and (3) Insidious neoliberal logics driving environmental stressors in student affairs, and (4) Social identity and positionality as drivers of stress and trauma. Below, we have provided a brief summary of each theme.

Theme 1: Chronic Stress, Anger, and Fear Related to Opaque and Callous Leadership

In March 2020, many higher education professionals thought they would leave their offices for a brief quarantine, not anticipating the months of isolation to follow. Yet, after it became clear that the world would be sheltering in place for the long-term, senior leaders scrambled to figure out what to do next. Unfortunately, these plans often centered on the short-term business priorities of their institutions over the staff, faculty, and students who make up the institution. During this time period, co-researchers consistently

10   R. J. LYNCH, C. GILBERT, L. CLARY, and B. GONZALEZ

recalled feelings of dehumanization as they were forced to choose between their well-being and their jobs, as well as a constant state of chaos as leaders were rarely transparent about the constantly changing directives being passed down to staff. Nicole, a live-in residential coordinator, describes managing constantly changing directives from senior leadership while also taking care of the students she served.

> I have like three or four other bosses in between me and [the leadership cabinet], and so a lot of what the summer held with the onset of COVID-19 was really just a lack of understanding of what exactly is going on. What's the university recommending? What systems is the President considering, and how is that gonna impact us on the ground? ... I had 16 student staff members hired and then was asked to reduce the staff at the last minute ... I was being asked to do a lot of the emotional support for our student staff ... I work with primarily students that are first generation, and I have a very high Latinx population that I work with, as well. Folks that just don't have the same financial backing, and so it's telling them like, "Hey, I totally know that you were banking on being an RA and getting this experience, and the benefits; but now I can't do that because I can't have you here."' And so we're putting them in less ideal situations ... and so that kind of impacted morale.

> And then we had the [wildfire] evacuation ... so literally like a week and a half before we were gonna welcome students back on campus ... we had a pretty big lightning storm one night that caused a bunch of fires in our area. So we ended up having to evacuate campus and part of the city ... so I was displaced. I was living about an hour away with my partner for about two and a half weeks. So in addition to that, the university decided that in addition to COVID measures, which was already facing a pretty significant reduction, so for this fall, we were only gonna welcome about 2000 students on campus, and we reduced it further to say, Okay, we are only taking students that literally have no other place to go, have a special circumstance, or don't have the equipment needed to be to do online learning, so they don't have the bandwidth and they're at their home, stuff like that, and so we have to communicate that within days and then reduce our staff further.... So my staff originally rested from sixteen to eight, and then now down to two, because I only had about 1000 students total that we were working with on campus, so that definitely was a pretty major impact.

> And then personally, I am at home, so I work from home pretty much all the time now, and because we don't have any office assistants in the housing office, I do about eight hours worth of shifts per week [in addition to regular duties].

Additionally, prior to the pandemic, issues of support from senior leadership were often cited as stressors (Barham & Winston, 2006; Lederman,

2022; Lynch & Glass, 2020) yet, these feelings were intensified as SAPs felt like they were being put in harm's way while senior leaders were able to remain isolated from the dangers of the coronavirus. Sarah, another live-in residential life professional, was visibly angry as she spoke of her experiences of tension between being essential personal and living with a risk factor for COVID complications:

> I am "high risk," [yet] because I'm essential personnel ... we were gonna have to provide meals to students who had been diagnosed with COVID, and I specifically asked what about people who are immunocompromised, because that is my high risk? And I was specifically told that I might need to consider changing my profession, in front of everyone, by our Executive Director. So I actually spoke with my doctor and my doctor was like, "No, no, no need to be on campus." And so I had to go to HR to fight about that. Since then I have been work-from-home, but it is one of those things where it's kind of a "touch and go" situation as to whether or not they are working with the staff in regards to their personal [medical] needs. It really has become a situation where I'm the only one that they have considered, whereas other individuals who are having medical issues, it's like, "No, you're still essential, so you have to do this."

An overwhelming majority of co-researchers spoke to similar stories of opaque and callous leadership that failed to understand the ground-level experiences of student affairs staff as decisions were being passed down. Regardless of institutional type, co-researchers painted a portrait of being on the front lines of student support and campus operations while senior leaders remained distant and cut-off.

Theme 2: Internalized Imbalance Between Self and Student Care

Even before the pandemic, the concept of self-care was often critiqued as a band-aid solution for systemic issues of over-worked and under-resourced professionals (Sambile, 2018; Strolin-Goltzman et al., 2020), yet many co-researchers reported the constant messaging they received from their institution to practice self-care without giving time and resources to do so. They also described the various ways in which they attempted to practice self-care during the pandemic, yet in many cases, their attempts felt more like survival than care. Sharon is an Assistant Director of Student Life at a small liberal arts college, spoke to the surface level, and often counterproductive, messaging that her institution's ad hoc Wellness Steering Committee would send as staff were burned through:

> Your institution sends out email reminders [about self care], and [I'm] like, "Taking a bubble bath does not make all your problems go away"... I'm so thankful that we have wellness coordinators and they kind of push back against the Steering Committee ... they were like, "This isn't working, you need to stop telling us to be shock absorbers. You need to stop telling them that...." Every unit has their own wellness champion now, which is really nice, and ours is just like, "I'm not gonna send you all these things because they're not helpful, I'm gonna tell your supervisor to let you take a day off or do whatever you need, if you need to come in. Like, do that, like you need to take that time [for yourself]." And so I've been very appreciative of that, but I mean, it just started a couple weeks ago ... I feel like it's so easy for upper level administration to be so disconnected and just say "here are some reminders [about self care]" .... We had a trivia the other night ... and my students invited [the college president] very last minute. He was like, "Yeah, I'll come with my family. That would be great." And it was incredible for him to see everything that's going into [the event], the amount of students that show up, and to be able to speak to that, and I just wish that more of the upper level administrators would be like, "Let me come visit you in your office or see what a day looks like in whatever office." Yeah, and I think it would change some of that toxic positivity.

Many co-researchers also spoke of being overworked and lacking healthy boundaries regarding student support. Maladaptive views of student support have previously been cited as contributing factors to secondary trauma and burnout among SAPs (Lynch & Glass, 2020), yet during the height of the pandemic, unclear communication and unreasonable expectations led many SAPs to fall deeper into their socialization to be of service, resulting in increased personal distress. While Eleanor was a Director of Career Services for her institution, and exemplified the ways internalized maladaptive views of student support prevented her from engaging in basic self-care practices like eating a meal:

> We put our students in front of ourselves ... we are in a helping profession, and we are motivated to help the people that we serve at the expense of pretty much everything for better or worse ... I think that you don't go into education from a selfish point of view. I don't think I know anybody that's an educator that I would call selfish. You're very aware of what's out there [regarding the difficult work], but the workload has been heavier and, I don't know, I think you're just kinda going day-to-day and you're not really thinking about the big picture impacts and ... I don't know, I've certainly gone through phases where I'm like, "Okay, do yoga at least once a day, in between a meeting or turn my camera off and do it during a meeting," but it's those little band-aids that I think I'm doing ... I'm not doing the big picture stuff that I would tell my students. I feel like at the end of the day, especially in education, it's just like another thing that you have to do ... I do have one practice, it's such a sad self-care practice, but I actually take a lunch break

now, which I never did before, but I have blocked a lunch break and I get up from my computer. When you're just sitting all day, it saps your energy ... I think people are aware of, but we haven't really changed anything about it.

Lee, a Director of Diversity and Inclusion at a small private liberal arts college, spoke of feelings of hopelessness in having such little agency in how they practice self-care while being pressured to maintain composure for the well-being of their students:

> A lot of the things that I would usually do for self-care have just not been an option, and so I struggled to figure out how to make up for that ... especially because I have these pre-existing mental health conditions.... Even when things are normal, I have to be careful about making sure that I'm not overdoing it, and I'm not pushing myself into a crisis that's avoidable. Right now, it just feels like I have so little control over what's happening around me. There aren't that many options to handle [my self-care], which is part of why I'm gonna try to go back to stay with my family for a little while ... I feel so much pressure to '[keep] it together' at work, even though I know that students can tell when [something is] up. They know that none of us really have it together right now, and I think that's okay, and we'd probably be doing them a disservice if we were pretending that everything is fine 'cause it's not.... But the feeling, the pressure of having to sort of hold it together when I'm really doing about as badly as I've ever been doing, that makes it harder to sort of draw boundaries around work in a way that is sustainable long-term..., This whole experience has made me less likely to wanna stay in higher ed long-term ... I just feeling like I'm running out of options. I don't know what else to do, short of taking medical leave from work or something really drastic, so.... Yeah, it's just really tough right now, I'm not sure what the right thing to do is.

While discussions of self-care are often parallel discussions of burnout, chronic stress and extreme burnout can become a traumatic experience in and of itself, overwhelming an individual's capacity to cope with the physical and emotional pressures that are placed upon them. Unfortunately, within student affairs, these feelings are often normalized early on, even within graduate programs (Lynch & Glass, 2020), putting SAPs at risk of traumatization from burnout by constantly putting their needs last.

Theme 3: Capitalist Neoliberal Logics Driving Environmental Stressors in Student Affairs

With the rise of neoliberalism in the U.S., public funding of postsecondary education has drastically fallen over the past decades, institutions have required student affairs divisions to do more with less (Leal, 2019;

Giroux, 2015). This has resulted in individuals taking on responsibilities that should be divided across multiple positions and departments being required to expand service offerings without the resources to do so effectively. In an era where senior administrators, policymakers, and the public view students and parents as "customers" to be served, the COVID-19 pandemic exploited student dissatisfaction with temporary remote learning, driving rapid re-openings and spikes in transmission (Hubler & Hartocollis, 2020). In addition, precarious budgeting and lack of foresight led to mass furloughs across the higher education sector (Hess, 2020; Hubler, 2020). These combined created a perfect storm of economic and workplace trauma, as some individuals saw their livelihoods upended, while others watched colleagues being laid off while also taking on the responsibility of those vacant positions. Juniper, a student leadership coordinator, spoke to the emotional toll she observed in her team due to overwork:

> It's a funny balance of recognizing that the university needs to stay open from an economic stance. You're purely thinking of the number of people in this area, of the amount of money that this area relies on…. But I see my colleagues across the university exhausted, and that there is a group on our campus that have been tasked with the CARES Act, all of the [students in quarantine], while also still being the support for any students in crisis. I have seen them exhausted and tired…. There's not enough time [to manage everything] … [leadership just] wants to make this normal, but it's not.

Jenny, a student union director, spoke of furloughs and economic precarity through job loss or reduction of force. Her experience speaks to the precarious financial situation that many found themselves in, as well as the lack of transparency or care that came from their institution as staff awaited potential layoff notices.

> For the last two weeks, I've been working part-time. My position was reduced to 50% as of two weeks ago, and the plan right now is to go back full-time the first of the year, so it'll be about nine weeks I think total. Which is not terrible, definitely a small hit financially, but I'm also able to get some unemployment even though I'm still working part-time. Just trying to figure that out with the state right now, and I think the biggest thing has been that since late April [2020], a complete or partial furlough has just been on the table floating around without any concrete decision about it [from leadership]. And so at that point, my supervisor and I wrote a proposal about why I should keep my job, and we never really heard anything back, so it was like a "no news is good news" sort of situation. I never heard like, "Yep, you're good." And so we were just kind of like planning for me to be working full-time, and from April [2020] until about August [2020], and then in the middle of August, my institution decided to go remote for the fall, which led to obviously a huge loss in income … so many people who had not

already been furloughed were taken down to part-time or their positions were terminated. My institution was already in a bad financial position, and obviously [COVID] has just exacerbated it, so this needed to happen for many positions anyway, and COVID kinda just pushed it along faster.

Ann, a live-off housing professional, added further context to the economic trauma of furloughs, speaking to a pervasive fear of judgment from peers in a profession that demands loyalty and sacrifice:

So my staff ... went through several times of being furloughed. They wouldn't always have a lot of notice, [leadership] would just be like, "'Okay, you're furlough this week, you're not working," or "somebody tested positive that works in the office, so none of you guys can work for the next two weeks." So constantly every day it was [just waiting to be furloughed] ... and when fall started with the kids in [virtual] school and working all these hours ... it's a little bit better now, but it's still an adventure. But yeah, having [kids in virtual school] on top of work, so not even knowing people's contexts of what is going on with their personal life and all the things that are trying to manage with that, and then having all the work stress on top of it, I guess it just felt very scared and overwhelmed ... and with the fear, I wondered if I should go look for another job? But the fear is, if I do that do I look like somebody who just "jumps ship" when it gets tough? If I don't get a job, then am I gonna be looked down upon for my reputation as somebody who wouldn't get promoted or be looked over for other opportunities because I was seen as a quitter because I decided to [job search]? .... So was there were larger career repercussions, and then I asked some other people, 'cause I am a part of a student affairs mom's group on Facebook, people who did get new jobs and then the job got canceled right before they started, so they lost it. So there's all of that stuff going on and not knowing if you can even trust your current institution ... but is it gonna be any better if you go somewhere else? So it was just all of that uncertainty and stuff.

In one way or another, each co-researcher experienced some impact to their workplace quality and personal wellness as a result of institutions putting business interests first. Unfortunately for many, these experiences reinforced the idea that they were just a cog in the higher education machine.

Theme 4: Social Identity and Positionality as Drivers of Stress and Trauma

Positionality may be thought of as "how differences in social position and power shape identities and access in society" (CTLT Indigenous Initiatives, p. 1). This concept was readily apparent throughout all co-researcher interviews, as the intersections of social class, race, gender, and (dis)ability came together to produce unique challenges for student affairs staff at the intersections of marginalized identities. Specifically, positionality impacted their ability to exercise agency within their work roles in order to maintain safety for themselves or their family. Additionally, positionality had a significant impact on the layered stressors that were experienced during the onset of the COVID-19 pandemic, including caregiving responsibilities and exposure to racially or politically motivated violence. Elle, a community college academic advisor at a rural campus, spoke of her experiences as a Latina professional living in a politically conservative southern rural community that had low adherence to pandemic health protocols:

> I think within this time period that we're discussing, the intersection of CO-VID-19, my own college leadership, and [The Trump Administration] has really put all of those emotions of alienation and anger together. Unfortunately, our leadership doesn't always demonstrate the most protection when it comes to COVID-19. Some are very relaxed, others are not, but of course, it comes from the top down in terms of examples for our students and for our staff. I also think it creates a whole lot of anxiety, and of course, the state of our elections as well, because I've actually seen people get violent at stores about the mask dispute. And it interestingly falls on the lines of race as well, so that's something that I'm very cognizant of in whatever space I inhabit and where the minoritized people are. And unfortunately the people causing the greatest disruptions and confrontations are folks who are not of color, and so it's a bit threatening going into particular spaces, noticing who wears a mask, who doesn't, and so that adds to the feeling of alienation and of course, anger because I just wish we could understand one another beyond what we see, even the snap judgments we make of people, those who wear masks and those who don't. The masks have just brought in a whole lot of disputes recently.... Personally, I think I have isolated myself emotionally because I don't know who to trust [at work] besides my fellow [people of color]. There's two other advisors who are [people of color], and I have no filter with them. I understand that they know where I'm coming from. Interestingly enough, I also have to navigate this liminal space where I also pass [as white], so [white] individuals tend to tell me more than they would probably tell someone who's darker skinned, which is interesting too. There's a whole lot to navigate there.

While Elle's story focused on her struggle with isolation and hypervigilance resulting from her positionality, Tia, a Black woman working as a live-in residence life staff member in the Midwest, illustrated the layered stressors of being a professional and personal caregiver. Much of her story centered around her role as a caregiver to her aging parents while maintaining an income to support herself. Tia recalled:

I think I'm still in my transition here. This is my fourth year in this job and is my last year. Anyway, so I feel very ... I keep using the word unsettled. I feel like there's this weird shift happening, I have to leave this job either now or by May or June. Since I'm still in school, I need to stay in [the state], 'cause I still have classes that are gonna be in person.... So when it comes to personal matters, there's a lot of anxiety around what my next steps are. Will I be in a job that will pay enough for me to pay tuition? .... And then also on top of that, my dad is starting to [have poor health].... My mom is starting to get more concerned of my dad's health. Mentally, he's very short and snappy, and she usually is [away for work], so she's been home since March, working from home. And with his age and her age, she's more aware of like, people get old and when they get old, things happen. You start to lose weight. Your fuse is shorter. Can he drive? Should he drive? So even just talking to her about that has been impactful around her thought of like, "maybe I am gonna retire early to be with your dad, 'cause I don't know if he could maintain this life by himself," which is concerning to me. I'm their only child together ... so I am in that weird support person or a caregiver role if they need me to be.

JoJo, a Student Development Coordinator at a suburban community college, identified as a straight white woman and a foster parent. With the onset of the pandemic, she and her husband found themselves caring for a newborn with nowhere else to go while also managing their work responsibilities:

I've definitely felt [support] from my supervisor and our team, which is awesome. Anxiety. You know the unknown. I don't like the unknown. And so knowing, Are we coming back [to work in-person]? Are we not coming back? We were going to start back [in-person] at the end of April. Then April turned into May, and May turn into June. So we're getting closer to the start of the semester, and I think anxiety was huge, just for our students in general too. They didn't know what was happening, and we couldn't always provide them the answers that they needed. [I felt] very torn, because ... my husband and I are foster parents, and so we [were placed with] a two-month-old and a four-year-old, and so it was really hard to wanna go back to work and leave my kids, especially the baby, because I'd never fostered a baby before. And so you know, you just feel like you want to be there and care for her, so I was very torn about coming back. And then being here [working from home] was a huge struggle for me. The sadness is huge. The students are sad. We get messages all the time, like "I miss being on campus. I miss being around faculty and staff. I miss that engagement," and I think that couples and with stress. Not only are we fortunate enough to know we have a job, but it does stress me out to think about a lot of my other co-workers or teammates and friends that I have in higher ed who are at different institutions, and how am I fortunate enough to have a job, but they lost theirs.

> How can you fix that? You can't really.... So there's that guilt and shame that comes in there as well.

While the stories of Elle, Tia, and Jojo focused on their specific struggles, many other co-researchers described the ways in which they felt powerless, voiceless, and stripped of agency because of their social circumstances and place with highly hierarchical organizations.

Aligning Themes and Research Questions

Using the themes described above, we summarize how this analysis served to answer the research questions posed at the beginning of this chapter. Our first question sought to better understand the lived experiences of trauma among college student affairs professionals during the onset of the COVID-19 pandemic. Despite the differences among circumstance or context, many SAPs reported extended periods of chronic stress without opportunities for rest, or spaces to process and make meaning of what was happening to them. SAPs also reported chronic exhaustion as the flimsy barriers between their personal and professional lives came crashing down. Finally, undergirded by chronic stress and exhaustion, SAPs reported ongoing feelings of fear, increased mistrust in their institutional leadership, and increased anger and frustration.

Our second line of inquiry sought to investigate how these professionals came to experience trauma and chronic stress during the onset of the COVID-19 pandemic. From a system point of view, many of the circumstances that lead to participant experiences of trauma and chronic stress originated from issues that had been building prior to the pandemic. Callous leadership, and neoliberal philosophies that overvalue funding and efficiency over the actual people within the organization, led already overburdened student affairs staff to take on even more responsibility. With the mindset of "students as customers," senior leadership seemed not to hesitate to demand student-facing staff to put aside their own well-being in the name of ensuring students were satisfied and still receiving the "college experiences." Additionally, as furloughs ran rampant through the higher education sector, many SAPs, who are often underpaid compared to their education and experience level, faced financial catastrophe, or faced taking on additional responsibilities from those laid off. Such conditions led to many of the feelings and experiences described in our first question.

Finally, through the lens of post-intentional phenomenology, we wanted to know how co-researchers' social and environmental contexts shaped their experiences of trauma and stress during the COVID-19 pandemic. As highlighted in our thematic analysis, social identity, place, and time had a significant impact on the circumstances that led to chronic stress and trauma exposure. For example, co-researchers working at smaller institutions were called on to do more, as there were fewer individuals to share the burden of keeping the institution afloat and providing support to students. This was felt no more acutely than for those within live-in residence life roles, where they were often called on as contact tracers and required to manage, and live within, designated quarantine residence halls. Additionally, for racially minoritized SAPs, particularly Black and Asian staff, they found themselves not only reacting to the health and financial ramifications of the pandemic but also threat to personal safety as white supremecists and police officers exacted violence against these communities. Finally, many co-researchers spoke to the ways in which they were able to lean into their surrounding community for support and rejuvenation. For those that had access to in-person communities, such as live-in partners or other family, they described much less maladjustment to the extended quarantine compared to professions who lived alone or far away from the core supports.

DISCUSSION

Our qualitative investigation uncovered several themes that extend our understanding of the ways in which trauma and stress manifested during the COVID-19 pandemic. As discussed, student affairs issues of burnout (Chessman, 2021; Connor, 2021; Kunk-Czaplicki, 2023; Vega & Coon, 2022) and secondary trauma (Lynch & Glass, 2019; Lynch & Glass, 2020) in student affairs practice is not a new phenomenon, even prior to the onset of the pandemic. Yet, issues directly related to, and tangential to, the pandemic further exacerbated existing stressors while introducing new complications. This study adds complexity to the existing literature on student affairs practitioner experiences during the COVID-19 pandemic by examining the lived experiences of trauma. For example, our work extends the findings of Kunk-Czaplicki and Wilson (2023) who acknowledged the role of trauma as a distinct and separate construct negatively impacting the well-being of student affairs practitioners during the pandemic. Additionally, this study helps to reframe burnout as a potentially traumatic experience by providing rich illustrations of how job demands and extreme burnout led to feelings and behaviors related to traumatic stress, including fear, anger, hopelessness, and exhaustion. These findings also served to illustrate findings from Chessman (2021) who linked SAP well-being to the quality of their work life. It was clear that most co-researchers were subjected to extended periods of poor work quality that negatively impacted their well-being. However, it should be noted that the connection between work life quality and overall well-being may also be a result of maladaptive socialization within the profession that subversively trains new professionals to put their job before their well-being. Finally, through the lens of post-intentional phenomenology, we aimed to counter traditional narratives of staff well-being as an individual issue, in turn situating this phenomenon in a social and organizational context that acts as a root cause of trauma and burnout.

Co-researcher narratives should serve as a catalyst for national and institutional leaders to re-imagine the roles and functions of student affairs positions as colleges and universities face future mass crises. Additionally, it is urgent that university leaders, human resource managers, and policymakers reassess and expand institutional support for student affairs professionals' mental health as institutions move into a post-pandemic era. These supports may include expansion of insurance options to make mental healthcare more affordable, as well as assessment of Employment Assistance Programs (EAPs) to ensure they are meeting the current needs of these professionals. As colleges begin to experience student support labor shortages in the near and distant future (Ellis, 2021), institutional leaders need only to look at the maltreatment and overwork of these professionals before, during, and after the COVID-19 pandemic to understand why shortages have occurred. Below, we have highlighted additional practical and scholarly implications grounded in the findings of this study.

Implications for Practice

The experiences shared within this phenomenological investigation serve as a foundation for several recommendations for policy and practice, with divisions of college student affairs and the profession at large. While this section could be used to explore recommendations for individual practitioners to improve self-care and well-being practice, the findings of this study clearly point to the social and environmental contexts that diminish professional well-being and focus on the individual responsibility of staff over the organization and profession's duty to ensure the care of their employees.

The most immediate recommendation for campus leaders, particularly those in senior positions, is to listen, without judgment, to the experiences of their staff. It is also incumbent upon senior leaders to make the first move to repair the relationship between staff and their organizations (Vivian & Hormann, 2013). This may take the form of offering a formal apology for the harm experienced by staff, whether the leader was present during the time of harm or not. Additionally, senior leaders should look towards the philosophies of restorative justice (Kidder, 2006) as a foundation for acknowledging the trauma their staff endured, as well as identifying a path forward that includes healing and career sustainability (Sallee, 2020).

Institutional leaders must also do better in recognizing and valuing the role of student affairs professionals in providing students with a safe and meaningful campus environment. The findings of this study depict the ways in which SAPs seemed to be viewed as disposable and undervalued by their institutions, as they were asked to manage student crises and expectations throughout the entirety of the pandemic without a break or opportunity for rest. Clearly defining and differentiating roles, as well as building protocols for those engaging with initial-triage or crisis management and long-term management, may be one step in avoiding traumatizing staff during future crises.

Finally, leaders within national organizations such as the American College Personnel Association (ACPA) or the National Association for Student Personnel Administrators (NASPA) should be leading the charge in re-envisioning ways in which the profession must shift, from graduate preparation to senior leadership training, with regard to the harm SAPs experience in the name of student support. There has yet to be any knowledge community, commissions, institute, or grant funding initiatives that center this issue, continuing decades of silence and disregard for a key issue that undergirds high attrition rates within the field (Bauer-Wolf, 2022).

Implications for Scholarship

Although this study aimed to provide depth and context to the lived experiences of the stress and trauma through which students affairs professionals lived through at the onset of the COVID-19 pandemic, there remains significant opportunity for further research on this topic. For example, this study focused on the reflections of SAPs during the first few months of the pandemic; however, future research may consider looking at how student affairs professionals processed and made meaning of their experiences as the pandemic transitions to an endemic status (Spencer, 2022). Such studies may also focus on how SAP experiences throughout the pandemic shifted their perspectives on the roles of SAPs on college campuses, as well as emergent leadership competencies relevant to a post-pandemic world. Furthermore, this study actively centered on the COVID-19 pandemic as the primary traumatic event for SAPs; yet, co-researchers often speak of co-occurring crises, including racial violence, political polarization, climate change, economic precarity, and extreme burnout as equally traumatizing circumstances. Future research should seek to better understand how the intersections of these co-crises create opportunities for complex traumatization within student affairs staff populations.

CONCLUSION

COVID-19 has presented numerous ongoing challenges for postsecondary institutions (Burke, 2020b)—among them, the well-being of staff members (Douglas-Gabriel & Flowers, 2020; Smith, 2020). Given the pivotal role that college student affairs professionals have played in supporting students in the midst of unprecedented stress and uncertainty (Copeland et al., 2021), it is crucial that institutional leaders attend to the needs of these front-line workers, including the provision of dedicated mental health resources. Additionally, higher education administrators at this pivotal juncture have the opportunity to re-envision the future of the student affairs profession and to build a more just, equitable, and humanized field. The traumatic impact of COVID-19 will likely be felt for many years to come (Silver, 2020); it is the responsibility of institutional leaders to attend to the conditions that may exacerbate this trauma for staff members, and, in doing so, bolster their mission of enhancing student learning and the public good.

REFERENCES

American Psychiatric Association. (2013). *Diagnostic and statistical manual of mental disorders* (5th ed.).

American Psychological Association. (2020). Trauma. *American Psychological Association Dictionary*. https://dictionary.apa.org/trauma

Barham, J. D., & Winston, R. B. (2006). Supervision of new professionals in student affairs: Assessing and addressing needs. *College Student Affairs Journal, 26*(1), 64–89.

Bauer-Wolf, J. (2022, July 22). *Over half of higher ed employees likely to seek another job, survey finds*. https://www.highereddive.com/news/over-half-of-higher-ed-employees-likely-to-seek-another-job-survey-finds/627926/

Bedard-Gilligan, M., Zoellner, L. A., & Feeny, N.C. (2017). Is trauma memory special? Trauma narrative fragmentation in PTSD: Effects of treatment and response. *Clinical Psychological Science, 5*(2), 212–225. http://doi.org/10.1177/2167702616676581

Benhamou, K., & Piedra, A. (2020). CBT-informed interventions for essential workers during the COVID-19 pandemic. *Journal of Contemporary Psychotherapy, 2020*, 1–9. https://doi.org/10.1007/s10879-020-09467-3

Bonsaksen, T., Heir, T., Schou-Bredal, I., Ekeberg, O., Skogstad, L., & Grimholt, T. K. (2020). Post-traumatic stress disorder and associated factors during the early stage of the COVID-19 pandemic in Norway. *International Journal of Environmental Research and Public Health, 17*(9210), 1–9. http://doi.org/10.3390/ijerph17249210

Brown, L. (1991). Not outside the range: One feminist perspective on trauma. *American Imago, 48*(1), 119–133.

Burke, L. (2020a, October 27). *Black workers and the university.* Inside Higher Ed. https://www.insidehighered.com/news/2020/10/27/black-workers-universities-often-are-left-out-conversations-about-race-and-higher

Burke, L. (2020b, March 9). *Colleges move online amid virus fears.* Inside Higher Ed. https://www.insidehighered.com/news/2020/03/09/colleges-move-classes-online-coronavirus-infects-more

Chessman, H. M. (2021). Student affairs professionals, well-being, and work quality. *Journal of Student Affairs research and Practice, 58*(2), 148–162. https://doi.org/10.1080/19496591.2020.1853556

Choo, H. Y., & Diaz, R. (2021, April 2). *Addressing anti-Asian racism in the university.* Inside Higher Ed. https://www.insidehighered.com/advice/2021/04/02/recommendations-stopping-anti-asian-racism-campuses-opinion

Clark, J. (2022). *Where is the support? Black men student affairs professionals' experience with secondary trauma* [Unpublished doctoral dissertation, University of Wisconosin]. La Crosse.

Connor, A. (2021). *Fizzing out: A correlational study of burnout and worklife perceptions among student affairs professionals in the mid-atlantic northeast region of the united states* [Doctoral dissertation, Abilene Christian University]. Digital Commons @ACU, Electronic Theses and Dissertations. Paper 331. https://digitalcommons.acu.edu/etd/331

Copeland, W. E., McGinnis, E., Bai, Y., Adams, Z., Nardone, H., Devadanam, V., Rettew, J., & Hudziak, J. (2021). Impact of COVID-19 pandemic on college student mental health and wellness. *Journal of the American Academy of Child and Adolescent Psychiatry, 60*(1), 134–141. https://doi.org/10.1016/j.jaac.2020.08.466

CTLT Indigenous Initiatives. (2023). *Positionality and intersectionality.* The University of British Columbia. https://indigenousinitiatives.ctlt.ubc.ca/classroom-climate/positionality-and-intersectionality/#:~:text=Positionality%20refers%20to%20the%20how,identities%20and%20access%20in%20society

Davis, T. E., Grills-Taquechel, A. E., & Ollendick, T. H. (2010). The psychological impact from Hurricane Katrina: Effects of displacement and trauma exposure on university students. *Behavioral Therapy, 41*(3), 340–349. https://dx.doi.org/10.1016%2Fj.beth.2009.09.004

Douglas-Gabriel, D., & Flowers, A. (2020, November 17). The lowest-paid workers in higher education are suffering the highest job losses. *The Washington Post.* https://www.washingtonpost.com/education/2020/11/17/higher-ed-job-loss/

Ellis, L. (2021). The great disillusionment: College workers are burning out just when they'll be needed most. *The Chronicle of Higher Education.* https://www.chronicle.com/article/the-great-disillusionment

Figley, C. R. (1999). Compassion fatigue: Toward a new understanding of the costs of caring. In B. H. Stamm (Ed.), *Secondary traumatic stress: Self-care issues for clinicians, researchers, and educators* (pp. 3–28). Sidran.

Flynn, C., & Heitzmann, D. (2008). Tragedy at Virginia Tech: Trauma and its aftermath. *The Counseling Psychologist, 36*(3), 478–489. https://doi.org/10.1177/0011000008314787

Galek, K., Flannelly, K., Greene P., & Kudler, T. (2011). Burnout, secondary traumatic stress, and social support. *Pastoral Psychology, 60*, 633–649.

Giroux, H. A. (2015). Democracy in crisis, the specter of authoritarianism, and the future of higher education. *Journal of Critical Scholarship on Higher Education and Student Affairs, 1*(7). https://ecommons.luc.edu/jcshesa/vol1/iss1/7

Hess, A. J. (2020, July 2). *At least 50,904 college workers have been laid off or furloughed because of Covid-19*. C-NBC. https://www.cnbc.com/2020/07/02/218-colleges-have-laid-off-or-furloughed-employees-due-to-covid-19.html

Hubler, S. (2020, October 26). Colleges slash budgets in the pandemic, with 'nothing off-limits.' *The New York Times*. https://www.nytimes.com/2020/10/26/us/colleges-coronavirus-budget-cuts.html

Hubler, S., & Hartocollis, A. (September 11, 2020). How colleges became the new covid hot spots. *The New York Times*. https://www.nytimes.com/2020/09/11/us/college-campus-outbreak-covid.html

Human Rights Watch. (2020). *COVID-19 fueling anti-Asian racism and xenophobia worldwide*. https://www.hrw.org/news/2020/05/12/covid-19-fueling-anti-asian-racism-and-xenophobia-worldwide

Jones, L. K., & Cureton. J. L. (2014). Trauma redefined in the DSM-5: Rationale and implications for counseling practice. *The Professional Counselor, 4*(3), 257–271. https://doi.org/10.15241/lkj.4.3.257

Kidder, D.L. (2007). Restorative justice: not "rights", but the right way to heal relationships at work. *International Journal of Conflict Management, 18*(1), 4–22. http://doi.org/10.1108/10444060710759291

Knight, C. (2013). Indirect trauma: Implications for self-care, supervision, the organization, and the academic institution. *The Clinical Supervisor, 32*(2), 224–243. https://doi.org/10.1080/07325223.2013.850139

Kunk-Czaplicki, J. A., & Wilson, M. E. (2023). An investigation of work factors and trauma exposure on burnout in housing and residence life professionals. *Journal of College & University Student Housing, 48*(3).

Lahey, L., Souvaine, E., Kegan, R., Goodman, R., & Felix, S. (2011). *A guide to the subjectobject interview: Its administration and interpretation*. Minds at Work.

Leal, D. R. (2019). *The colonizing condition of neoliberalism in higher education: What is it, why it matters, and what we can do*. ASHE Grads Blog. https://ashegrads.wordpress.com/2019/05/31/the-colonizing-condition-of-neoliberalism-in-higher-education-what-it-is-why-it-matters-and-what-we-can-do/

Lederman, D. (2022, May 4). *Turnover, burnout and demoralization in higher ed*. Inside Higher Ed. https://www.insidehighered.com/news/2022/05/04/turnover-burnout-and-demoralization-higher-ed

Liu, S. R., & Modir, S. (2020). The outbreak that was always here: Racial trauma in the context of COVID-19 and implications for mental health providers. *Trauma Psychology: Theory, Research, Practice, & Policy, 12*(5), 43–442. http://dx.doi.org/10.1037/tra0000784

Lynch, R. J. (2017). *Breaking the silence: A phenomenological exploration of secondary traumatic stress in US college student affairs professionals* [Doctoral dissertation, Old Dominion University]. ProQuest.

Lynch, R. J. (2020). *COVID-19 trauma among higher education professional at the onset of the 20-21 academic year* [Unpublished manuscript]. Appalachian State University.

Lynch, R.J. (2022). Prevalence and predictive factors of secondary traumatic stress in college student affairs professionals. *Journal of Student Affairs Research & Practice, 60*(3), 293–306. http://doi.org/10.1080/19496591.2022.2080555

Lynch, R. J., & Glass, C. R. (2019). The cost of caring: An arts-based phenomenological analysis of secondary traumatic stress in college student affairs. *The Review of Higher Education, 43*(4), 1041–1068. https://doi.org/10.1353/rhe.2020.0030

Lynch, R. J., & Glass, C. (2020). The cost of caring: An arts-based phenomenological analysis of secondary traumatic stress in college student affairs. *Review of Higher Education, 43*(4), 1041–1068. http://doi.org/ 10.1353/rhe.2020.0030

May, C., & Wisco, B. (2016). Defining trauma: How level of exposure and proximity affect risk for posttraumatic stress disorder. *Psychological Trauma: Theory, Research, Practice, and Policy, 8*(2), 233–240. https://psycnet.apa.org/doi/10.1037/tra0000077

Merriam, S. (2009). *Qualitative research: A guide to design and implementation.* Jossey-Bass.

Moustakas, C. (1994). *Phenomenological research methods.* SAGE.

Newell, J. N., & MacNeil, G. (2010). Professional burnout, vicarious trauma, secondary traumatic stress, and compassion fatigue: A review of theoretical terms, risk factors, and preventative methods for clinicians and researchers. *Best Practices in Mental Health, 6*(2), 57–68.

Philimon, W. (2020, July 7). Black Americans report hate crimes, violence in wake of George Floyd protests and Black Lives Matter gains. *USA Today.* https://www.usatoday.com/story/news/nation/2020/07/07/black-americans-report-hate-crimes-amid-black-lives-matter-gains/3259241001/

Reynolds, A. L. (2010). Counseling and helping skills. In J. H. J. Schuh & S. R. Harper (Eds.), *Student services: A handbook for the profession* (pp. 399–412). Jossey-Bass.

Sallee, M. (2020). *Creating sustainable careers in student affairs: What ideal worker norms get wrong and how to make it right.* Stylus.

Sambile, A.F. (2018). Energy exchange: The urgency to move from self-care to community-care in student affairs. *The Vermont Connection, 39*(1), 32–39. https://scholarworks.uvm.edu/tvc/vol39/iss1/7

Silver, R. C. (2020). Surviving the trauma of COVID-19. *Science, 369*(6499), 11. https://doi.org/10.1126/science.abd5396

Smith, A. B. (2020). *2020 U.S. billion-dollar weather and climate disasters.* Climate.gov. https://www.climate.gov/disasters2020

Smith, W. (2020, July 31). *The irony of essential work: COVID-19's impact on campus workers.* The Labor and Working Class History Association. https://www.lawcha.org/2020/07/31/irony-of-essential-work-covid-19s-impact-on-campus-workers/

Soule, K. E., & Freeman, M. (2019). So you want to do post-intentional phenomenological research? *The Qualitative Report, 24*(4), 857–872.

Spencer, S. E. W. (2022, August 17). *Is COVID-19 reaching the endemic stage? UMass Chan virologist Jeremy Luban weighs in*. UMass Chan Medical School Communications. https://www.umassmed.edu/news/news-archives/2022/08/is-covid-19-reaching-the-endemic-stage-umass-chan-virologist-jeremy-luban-weighs-in/

Stevens, M. (2009). From the past imperfect: Towards a critical trauma theory. *Letters: The Semiannual Newsletter of the Robert Penn Warren Center for the Humanities, 17*(2), 1–5.

Stoves, D. R. (2014). *Compelled to act: The negotiation of compassion fatigue among student affairs professionals* [Doctoral dissertation, Texas A&M University]. Corpus Christi. ProQuest.

Strolin-Goltzman, J., Breslend, N., Hemenway Deaver, A., Wood, V., Woodside-Jiron, H., & Krompf, A. (2020). Moving beyond self-care: Exploring the protective influence of interprofessional collaboration, leadership, and competency on secondary traumatic stress. *Traumatology*. Advance online publication. https://doi.org/10.1037/trm0000244

Szymanski, D. M., & Balsam, K. F. (2011). Insidious trauma: Examining the relationship between heterosexism and lesbians' PTSD symptoms. *Traumatology, 17*(2), 4–13. https://doi.org/10.1177/1534765609358464

Turk, J., Soler, M.C., Chessman, H., & Gonzalez, A. (2020). *College and university presidents respond to COVID-19: 2020 fall term survey, part II*. American Council on Education. https://www.acenet.edu/Research-Insights/Pages/Senior-Leaders/College-and-University-Presidents-Respond-to-COVID-19-2020-Fall-Term-Part-Two.aspx

Vagle, M. D. (2014). *Crafting phenomenological research*. Left Coast Press.

van Dernoot Lipsky, L. (with C. Burk). (2009). *Trauma stewardship: An everyday guide to caring for self while caring for others*. Berrett-Koehler.

Vega, M., & Coon, S. R. (2022). Chapter 9: The burnout warning. In A. A. Bergerson & S. R. Coon (Eds) *Understanding Individual Experiences of COVID-19 to Inform Policy and Practice in Higher Education*. Routledge.

Vivian, P., & Hormman, S. (2013). *Organizational trauma and healing*. CreateSpace.

Wells, J. B. (2015). *CAS professional standards for higher education* (9th ed). Council for the Advancement of Standards in Higher Education.

Council for the Advancement of Standards in Higher Education.

Williamson, V., Murphy, D., & Greenberg, N. (2020). COVID-19 and experiences of moral injury in front-line key workers. *Occupational Medicine, 70*(5), 317–219. https://doi.org/10.1093/occmed/kqaa052

Yehuda, R., Schmeidler, J., Elkin, A., Wilson, S., Siever, L., Binder-Brynes, K., Wainberg, M., & Aferior, D. (1998). Phenomenology and psychobiology of the intergenerational response to trauma. In Y. Danieli (Ed.), *International handbook of multigenerational legacies of trauma* (pp. 639–655). Springer.

CHAPTER 2

ASIAN INTERNATIONAL PHD STUDENTS' PERCEIVED CHALLENGES, STRESS, COPING STRATEGIES, AND RESILIENCE DURING AND BEYOND THE COVID-19 PANDEMIC

Jun Ai
University of Tennessee, Knoxville

Ankita Bhattashali
University of Kansas

Ming-Tso Chien
Fulbright Taiwan

Hyesun Cho
University of Kansas

Yi Zhang
University of Tennessee, Knoxville

ABSTRACT

The COVID-19 pandemic has brought unprecedented challenges and stressors to members of educational systems in the United States. The intersectional

Research on College Stress and Coping: Implications From the COVID-19 Pandemic and Beyond, pp. 27–52
Copyright © 2024 by Information Age Publishing
www.infoagepub.com
All rights of reproduction in any form reserved.

identities of Asian international PhD students (AIPS) may exacerbate the challenges and stress they experience, especially when anti-Asian racism has worsened since the unfolding of the pandemic. AIPS is a unique group among the diverse Asian communities in the United States. In this study, we focused on AIPS in the multidisciplinary field of early care and education, in which they are receiving doctoral-level training to become leading professionals who serve to better the care and education of young children.

Limited literature has explored the experiences and wellness of AIPS studying in the United States. Even scarcer is the investigation of the challenges and stress AIPS experienced during the COVID-19 pandemic. We analyzed the biographical narratives of 36 AIPS using a lens of intersectionality to explore their perceived challenges, stress, coping strategies, and resilience during the pandemic and beyond. Our findings suggested that AIPS experienced significant challenges and stress (e.g., language barriers, difficulty of being a doctoral student, experience of racism) during and beyond the pandemic in their personal and professional lives. Nevertheless, AIPS perceived themselves as highly resilient and shared various coping methods to navigate challenges and stress. Implications for higher education institutions to better support AIPS and counteract institutional inequities in the United States are discussed.

INTRODUCTION

Asian international PhD students (AIPS) in the United States are critical yet often invisible contributors to higher education. AIPS are susceptible to various forms of oppression and discrimination because of their intersectionality of race, ethnicity, national origin, language, membership in the U.S. academia, and more (Simon et al., 2022). For example, AIPS are seen as aliens and perpetual foreigners in the United States (Wing, 2007). Meanwhile, they are subjected to the model minority myth alongside Asian Americans. The model minority myth perpetuates a stereotypical narrative that characterizes Asian American as a polite, compliant group who have achieved a high level of success through some combination of innate talent and pull-yourselves-up-by-your-bootstraps immigrant striving. The model minority myth erases the differences among individuals, ignores the diversity of Asian and Asian American cultures, and blankets racism against Asian Americans (Wing, 2007). Although AIPS tend to undertake a formidable and strenuous journey to become doctors and leaders in their fields, they can be left at the bottom of the power hierarchy of academia due to unfair distribution of resources, limited leadership opportunities, and other systemic barriers for international students (Hyun, 2005). Multiple forms of discrimination and systemic barriers AIPS face in U.S. higher education can exacerbate their struggles with disadvantageous identities (Kim & Cooc, 2020). The rising anti-Asian discrimination during the COVID-19 pandemic (Jeung et al., 2021) further aggravates the struggles AIPS may face in and outside the classrooms.

Prior research (e.g., Heng, 2018) reported Asian international students' experiences in the U.S. pre-COVID-19 era; the majority of studies suggested Asian international students were facing linguistic, academic, and acculturalization challenges. However, few of those studies focused on doctoral students and little is known if those findings hold true during the COVID pandemic. The American Educational Research Association (AERA; Levine et al., 2021) investigated doctoral students' experiences during COVID-19; findings suggested that the COVID-19 pandemic brought unprecedented stress and challenges to doctoral students in both their personal and professional lives. However, Levine and colleagues (2021) shed little light on Asian international doctoral students due to the scope of the research. In short, the current literature lacks investigation of the experiences and wellness of AIPS in the United States, especially during the ongoing COVID-19 pandemic.

In the present study, we focused on exploring the perceived challenges, stress, coping strategies, and resilience of AIPS during and beyond the COVID-19 pandemic. Specifically, we were interested in learning from AIPS, whose scholarship interests are pertinent to the interdisciplinary field of early care and education. We aimed to amplify the voices of AIPS who are often underrepresented in educational research. In the multidisciplinary field of early care and education, AIPS engage in impactful scholarship to tackle social problems and usually serve as educators for future teachers or health service providers. They are not only indispensable contributors to the U.S. education system; but also future leaders in academia or significant institutes to better young children's lives worldwide. Therefore, we also aimed to provide recommendations to higher education institutions (HEI) to better support AIPS's thriving in the U.S. academia and beyond.

Literature Review

In the following, we review the knowledge base on stress, challenges, coping strategies, and resilience of AIPS studying in the United States. Given the scarcity of research solely focused on AIPS, we review the literature that studied participants who shared identities with AIPS. Specifically, the literature review included empirical research focused on Asian American students, Asian international students, and graduate students.

Challenges and Stress

AIPS face various challenges when they acculturate in the United States and engage in doctoral studies. Those acculturative stressors include language barriers, educational difficulties, loneliness, discrimination, and practical problems associated with changing environments (Smith & Khawaja, 2011). For example, international students can face challenges in understanding language and cultural nuances in their interactions with professors or domestic peers (Macgregor & Folinazzo, 2018).

All aspects of using a foreign language can burden Asian international students. For instance, unproficiency in listening and speaking prevents Asian international students from actively participating in classroom interaction and social networking and makes it difficult to comprehend class content. Asian international students may also find writing particularly challenging which impacts their performance in course assignments and important academic milestones (Lin & Scherz, 2014). Language barriers and cultural differences are also associated with international students' experiences of social isolation and may result in mental health issues (Lin & Scherz, 2014). Researchers found that Asian international students had limited social opportunities with their peers who are native speakers and residents, and often struggled with developing friendships, feeling left out, and not belonging (Sherry et al. 2010). Moreover, Bonazzo and Wong (2007) reported that Japanese female international students studying in predominantly white universities had experienced overt discrimination that Asians commonly reported in the United States. Hwang et al. (2014) argue that, compared to American students, compound challenges and adjustment issues put Asian international students in a vulnerable state and more susceptible to mental health problems.

Not only do AIPS experience those everyday challenges and stress that regular Asian international students share, but they also must cope with other layers of difficulties when studying in doctoral programs. Researchers exploring challenges and stress facing PhD students suggest that there is a mental health crisis in academia (Pervez et al., 2020). The challenges and stress doctoral students face include rigorous academic standards, demanding workload, the pressure to publish in high-impact journals, a lack of work-life balance, the experience of imposter syndromes, financial pressure, and the uncertainty of career pathways (Bazrafkan et al., 2016).

It is common for doctoral students to struggle with mental health issues such as loneliness, depression, and anxiety (Sverdlik et al., 2022). The COVID-19 pandemic worsened life's uncertainty and isolation, thus significantly making doctoral students more vulnerable to stress (Levine et al., 2021). Levine and colleagues (2021) conducted a study of 58 early career scholars and doctoral students and found seven themes of impacts brought by the pandemic. The pandemic (1) disrupted and delayed research, (2) demanded sudden shift and adjustment in teaching practice, (3) worsened the difficulties in balancing life and work, (4) magnified the issues of racism and resulted in a dual pandemic, (5) brought more uncertainty to employment, (6) revealed institutional (in)capacity to respond and support scholars and doctoral students, and (7) witnessed an unprecedented loss of social connections (Levine et al., 2021).

AIPS are not only subject to the above challenges but also needed to manage the unique stressors such as restrictions for travel, impact on international academic work, concerns about visas, and in general, xenophobia caused by ignorance (Sustarsic & Zhang, 2021). However, as some scholars (Glass, 2017; Heng, 2018) have suggested researchers and practitioners working with international students should look beyond the one-sided narrative of struggling international students. It is invaluable to understand how AIPS effectively cope with challenges and stressors and demonstrate resilience because those successful stories not only encourage fellow AIPS but also shed light on how to better support Asian international students in general.

Coping Strategies and Resilience

Research suggests a number of ways in which Asian international students use coping strategies to respond to the challenges and stressors associated with studying in the United States. Coping refers to cognitive and behavioral efforts to master, tolerate, or reduce external and internal demands and conflicts among them. Individuals' level of appraisal determine their level of stress and the unique coping strategies (Lazarus & Folkman, 1984). For example, Xiong and Zhou (2018) found that, when encountering challenges, East Asian international graduate students proactively sought support and assistance from their personal connections or institutional resources. In addition to the external resources, their participants also adopted some internal strategies, such as adjusting their own behaviors and mindset to meet specific challenges. A typical behavioral strategy was allocating more time to study or work. This idea of studying harder is also reflected in another study that explores the best practices in teaching international students in higher education (Macgregor & Folinazzo, 2018). According to survey responses, studying harder and improving English were ranked by the international students as the first and fourth most important factors contributing to enhancing their study experience while joining activities and social life as well as communicating with domestic students ranked second and third, respectively.

Some of the abovementioned coping strategies were also used by early career scholars and doctoral students facing the impacts of the pandemic (Levine et al., 2021). Specific to the pandemic's impact on research, participants reported adjusting their own mindset, such as remaining optimistic, to face the sudden and drastic changes in their dissertation research. In terms of the pandemic's impact on employment prospects, some participants changed their behaviors to cope, such as extending their program of study to avoid entering the job market at a bleak time. Even though some voices from doctoral students can be heard in this timely piece of research, the experiences, and coping strategies from AIPS were not explicitly explored and discussed because the study only reported findings related to participants of color and did not identify Asians in the sample. Therefore, our goal is to target the perspectives of this segment of doctoral students in the U.S. to foreground the nuances of COVID-19's implications for stress in education.

Effective coping strategies are connected to high levels of resilience. Masten (2018) defines resilience as individuals' ability to withstand or to recover from adversities. A review (Herrman et al., 2011) of the concept of resilience found that even though its definitions have evolved over time, resilience is essentially understood as "positive adaptation, or the ability to maintain or regain mental health" after one has experienced adverse circumstances" (p. 258). The findings from Heng's (2018) study on Chinese international students revealed that even with the overall growth in their personal and academic lives, the experiences of these Chinese students remain varied and multidimensional. Specifically, as these students evolved for the duration of the study, they manifested resilience when continuously learning to face and cope with the challenges emerging under new circumstances. Our study aimed to follow this perspective of countering the dominant narrative that solely focuses on international students' stress and highlights the multidimensionality of AIPS's experiences and their coping strategies and resilience.

Our Positionality and the Aims of This Chapter

We wrote from a perspective that foregrounds the need to give voices to the oppressed. From the lens of the intersectionality model, we explored how AIPS's interlocked identities perceive and experience challenges and stressors, particularly those pertaining to discrimination and oppression (Simon et al., 2022). As AIPS ourselves, each of us holds multiple intersectional identities, namely race, nationality, gender, immigration status, emerging bilingual, and studying or used to study in doctoral programs in the United States as an international student. As the complexity of our identities and social locations overlap, they also differ in some respects. Although we are all Asians, we are from different countries (i.e., Chinese mainland, Taiwan, India, and South Korea) and represent different ethnicities and cultures. Our difference is also in the duration of staying in the United States, the level of English proficiency, and the characteristics of our doctoral programs and institutions. However, there are many commonalities regarding our perceptions and experiences of challenges and stress during our doctoral studies.

The COVID-19 pandemic undoubtedly aggravated those challenges and stress. For all of us, the rising anti-Asian sentiment, racism, and violence during the COVID-19 pandemic were especially difficult to manage. For some of us, it was traumatizing. Our commitment to confronting the persistent and intensified oppression facing AIPS derives from our personal experiences of educational inequities as international students in the United States and our concerns as educators/advocates—particularly our frustration with the rising anti-Asian racism during the pandemic. In fact, the catalyst for the authors to initiate this study was witnessing the Atlanta spa shooting on March 16, 2021, where eight people were killed, six of whom were Asian women.

To unravel the complexities of AIPS's identities and their lived experiences during and beyond the COVID-19 pandemic, we weaved together theories of multiple dimensions of identities (Jones & McEwen, 2000), intersectionality (Crenshaw, 2017), the transactional model of stress and coping (Lazarus & Folkman, 1984), as well as resilience (Masten, 2018). According to Jones and McEwen (2000), the multiple dimensions of identities model emphasizes that we must consider all relevant personal (e.g., gender, age, race, sexual orientation) and social factors (e.g., class, profession, nationality) when we learn about who we are. The concept of intersectionality (Crenshaw, 2017) focuses on the intersecting oppression an individual experiences when different facets of their identities interact with the system.

As AIPS enter the U.S. academia and progress through scholarship development, their multiple identities interact with one another and with systems of privileges and disadvantages. AIPS cope with challenges and stress and manifest resilience when their adaptive capacities, often distributed in networks of interconnected systems, are engaged to restore equilibrium, or transform the systems so they can continue with their life and development (Masten, 2018). Five research questions (RQ) guided our inquiry. RQ1: How do AIPS perceive and experience challenges and stress when studying in the United States? RQ2: How does the ongoing COVID-19 pandemic impact AIPS's experiences of challenges and stress? RQ3: How do AIPS cope with challenges and stress during and beyond COVID-19? RQ4: How do AIPS perceive themselves as resilient? RQ5: How do the intersectional identities of AIPS relate to their perceptions and experiences of challenges, stress, and manifestation of resilience? We recognized these qualitative research questions inter-relate (e.g., RQ5 is connected to the other RQs) and they serve to guide data analysis and meaning making instead of dictating a neat nomothetic explanation of the phenomena.

METHODS

Participants

We recruited AIPS who were studying in the field of early care and education (ECE) because of the scope of the funding secured by the first author. After receiving Institutional Review Boards approval, the author team distributed participant recruitment materials via professional organizations (e.g., AERA Graduate Student Council, Society for Research in Child Development Asian Caucus) and personal contacts. A total of 36 AIPS (age in year, $M = 30.2$, $SD = 4.06$) participated in the interview. Participants identified themselves as coming from Chinese Mainland, India, Pakistan, Taiwan, Malaysia, South Korea, Japan, studying across 13 subdisciplinary areas in social sciences pertinent to ECE. Those participants were from 25 U.S. universities. The identified subdisciplines include early intervention/ early childhood special education ($n = 7$), educational psychology ($n = 5$), special education ($n = 5$), school psychology ($n = 4$), early childhood education ($n = 3$), developmental psychology ($n = 3$), interdisciplinary studies ($n = 3$), clinical psychology ($n = 2$), speech language pathology ($n = 1$), early childhood policy ($n = 1$), bilingual education ($n = 1$), cognition and neuroscience ($n = 1$), and cultural studies ($n = 1$). Table 2.1 presents the participants' other demographic information.

Table 2.1

Participant Demographics and Characteristics (N = 36)

	% (n)		% (n)
Gender		Nationality Origin	
Female	83.33 (30)	Chinese mainland	66.67 (24)
Male	13.89 (5)	India	8.33 (3)
Nonbinary	2.78 (1)	Pakistan	2.78 (1)
Year in the PhD program		South Korea	5.56 (2)
1st	11.11 (4)	Malaysia	2.78 (1)
2nd	11.11 (4)	Japan	2.78 (1)
3rd	13.89 (5)	Taiwan/China	11.11 (4)
4th	25.00 (9)	Universities in U.S. regions (25 uni.)	
5th	16.67 (6)	West	24.00 (6)
6th	13.89 (5)	Midwest	24.00 (6)
Graduated	8.33 (3)	South	36.00 (9)
		Northeast	12.00 (3)
		Not disclosed	4.00 (1)

Note. Uni. = universities

Data Collection/Co-Construction

We conducted biographical narrative interviews (Duff & Bell, 2002) to explore the perceived and experienced challenges, stress, coping strategies, and resilience of AIPS in relation to their intersectional identities during and beyond the COVID-19 pandemic. The biographical narrative method was chosen to allow participants to reflect upon their lived experiences and reach new meanings and understandings about their lives (Duff & Bell, 2002). In narrative inquiry, the data need not be gathered as it needs to be co-constructed along the dynamic between the participants and the researchers (Duff & Bell, 2022). Understanding AIPS's experience holistically requires a method capable of achieving empirical depth; thus, biographical narrative was employed because of its capacity to "penetrate cultural barriers, give voice to human experience, and understand human intention and action" (Larson, 1997, p. 455). We interviewed each participant once via a one-on-one Zoom meeting for 60 to 90 minutes. Upon completing the research, each participant received a $60 gift card. The open-ended interview questions were designed to solicit personal narratives from AIPS, focusing on their general experiences in U.S. academia and how the pandemic impacted their experiences. In addition, questions were designed to understand their intersectional identities, as well as their experience and perception of challenges, stress, coping strategies, and resilience. Table 2.2 presents interview questions.

Table 2.2

Interview Questions

- Tell me a little bit about yourself and your background.
- What made you decide to pursue a doctoral degree in your field of study in the United States?
- How is your experience studying in the United States?
- How did the experience affect you?
- What is your plan after graduation?
- What is the biggest challenge since you started your doctoral program?
- Did COVID-19 cause any challenges for you? If yes, how?
- Have you experienced discrimination based on some aspects of your identity (e.g., race, gender, language, nationality)?
- If yes, how did you deal with such situations?
- How did the COVID-19 pandemic impact your PhD study? How did you navigate those challenges caused by the pandemic?
- How did the anti-Asian racism during the pandemic impact you?

(Table continued on next page)

Table 2.2 (Continued)

Interview Questions

- Could you share with me a story in which you overcame a difficult situation during your doctoral study or your work?
- Could you tell me about your thoughts on "being resilient?"
- Would you describe yourself as resilient? Why?
- What is your career goal? What supports and resources do you think are important for you to achieve your career goal?
- If you are to start your doctoral program again, what advice would you give to yourself?
- What advice would you like to give to future Asian international doctoral students?

Data Analysis

We employed the Rapid and Rigorous Qualitative Data Analysis (RADaR; Watkins, 2017) technique—a quick and comprehensive qualitative analysis strategy that can be used for analyzing qualitative data gathered from any types of qualitative methods—to improve efficiency for analyzing a large amount of interview data. We conducted two cycles of coding to analyze the interview data and generate themes to address the research questions. First, we utilized interview memos and In-Vivo coding to generate In-Vivo codes. Both structural and topical codes (Saldaña, 2021) were used to guide the first cycle of coding. Second, we generated higher-level themes based on the codes that were counted repeated across participants or were uniquely noteworthy. Furthermore, we employed *emotional* codes (Saldaña, 2021) to highlight the stressful emotions AIPS expressed in their narratives.

Trustworthiness

To ensure the trustworthiness of our data collection, analysis, and interpretation, we strived to meet Guba and Lincoln's (1994) five criteria of trustworthiness: credibility, dependability, confirmability, transferability, and authenticity. During data collection, we took several steps to promote the trustworthiness of this research. First, the first author developed the interview protocol based on an intensive study on how to create questions for biographical narrative interviews. The protocol was then revised based on the second and fourth authors' feedback. We paid particular attention to how we phrased the interview questions to ensure their open-endedness; we also composed potential follow-up questions to prompt further reflections from the participants. Second, the first and second authors, who were also the interviewers, met three times to view the protocol, rehearse the interview, and finalize the protocol. Additionally, the first and second authors used English and their home languages during the interviews based on the participants' preferences.

During data analysis, we also sought to maximize trustworthiness. The first three and fifth authors transcribed the interview recordings using the same process and format. After conducting the first three interviews, the first author transcribed the interview recordings, completed the first cycle coding, and produced a codebook for the second and third authors. Three coders met multiple times throughout the data analysis phase to review coding results, refine the code book, address disagreements and concerns, and discuss coding memos and emerging themes. All codes and themes were generated in English. Noteworthy quotes were highlighted in the transcripts and translated to English if English was not what was used in the interview. Moreover, a second coder reviewed one-third of the coding results to ensure the codes and themes make sense and to discover valuable data that were missed in coding and thematization. Finally, while the findings from this study are not generalizable, they are transferable because triangulation was realized across multiple participants. This means that the findings from this study "can be extrapolated beyond the immediate confines of the site, both theoretically and practically" (Charmaz, 2005).

Last, we conducted member checks with participants throughout and after the interview to further improve the trustworthiness of the data accuracy and interpretation. During the interview, we constantly verbally confirmed with the participants if we understood them correctly by paraphrasing their narratives and asking clarification questions. After we completed the data analysis, we requested participants' review of (1) a summary of the themes generated from their narratives to check interpretive validity and (2) a summary of our interpretation of the themes across participants to check descriptive validity.

FINDINGS

Guided by research questions, participants' narratives were compared to generate themes and make sense of each commonality and uniqueness among participants' perceptions and experiences. Three main themes emerged from data analysis. The first theme "AIPS's intersectionality and experiences of compound challenges and stress" answers RQ1 (How do AIPS perceive and experience challenges and stress when studying in the United States?) and RQ5 (How do the intersectional identities of AIPS relate to their perceptions and experiences of challenges, stress, and manifestation of resilience?) The second theme "COVID-19 pandemic and anti-Asian racism exacerbated stress" addresses RQ2 (How does the ongoing COVID-19 pandemic impact AIPS's experiences of challenges and stress?) and RQ5. The third theme "effective coping strategies manifests AIPS's high level of resilience" answers RQ3 (How do AIPS cope with challenges and stress during and beyond COVID-19?), RQ4 (How do AIPS perceive themselves as resilient?), and RQ5. We inserted participants' quotes in double quotation marks ("") and used a number sign following a number within square brackets ([# number]) to signal the participant ID. Given the relatively large size of our sample ($N = 36$), we decided not to create a pseudo name for each quoted participant. This decision was made for clarity and not to dehumanize participants.

AIPS's Intersectionality and Experiences of Compound Challenges and Stress

Most participants perceived their overall experiences studying in the U.S. as positive because of the learning and growth in academic pursuits and personal lives. However, in those participants' narratives, the generally positive experience was accompanied by various challenges associated with managing a doctoral program while transitioning and adjusting to a new sociocultural environment. As described in the literature review, challenges faced by AIPS were related to their perceptions and experiences of stress, which was consistent with our findings. In narrating challenges experienced during PhD studies, all participants named stressful emotions (e.g., stressful, anxious, depressing, desperate, worried, concerned, inferior, invisible) they experienced and how such stress impacted their mental health. In the following, we focused on the most salient challenges and stress that emerged from participants' narratives. Specifically, (1) the most mentioned challenge—language barriers; (2) difficulties related to being a doctoral student; (3) inequities in professional development; and (4) perceptions and experiences of discrimination and racism. We deepened our understanding of participants' perceived and lived challenges and stress through the lens of intersectionality, which created a space to discuss the complexity of identities and how individuals experience oppression and privilege.

"Language was the Biggest Challenge"

Many participants ($n = 33$, 91.67%) identified language barriers as the biggest challenge during graduate studies. Language was a challenge, particularly in the first few semesters when they had just moved from their home country to the United States. However, three participants did not perceive language as a challenge during their doctoral study because two of them spoke English as their first language, and the other had been in the United States since age 18. Shared perceptions among participants who perceived language was challenging included "it was hard to catch up with study because of language differences" [#7], and "I could not keep up with the pace of lecture and group discussion" [#1]. Besides class participation, the perceived lack of English proficiency also affected other major activities in the doctoral study, such as teaching or clinical practices and participation in professional networking (e.g., attending a conference). In addition, the perceived lack of English proficiency provoked various negative emotions in participants. Those negative emotions included lack of confidence or self-doubt, self-conscious about accent, stress when teaching, worried if others understood them, uncomfortable in professional networking interactions. As participant [#33] stated, "I'm just not feeling very confident and comfortable whenever I have to use English."

Participants also pinpointed how certain aspects of using language (i.e., listening, speaking, reading, and writing) created different levels of challenges for their professional and personal experiences. For instance, listening and spoken language were barriers for participants to freely participate in-class participation or social situations. However, time spent in an English-dominant environment helped participants overcome difficulties in listening, speaking, and reading. On the other hand, writing, particularly academic writing, remained challenging. Participants shared that "English academic writing was definitely a major challenge" [#4]; "I struggled a lot with writing" [#25]; and "although I have made lots of progress, there is always lots of space to improve in my writing" [#6]. Many other participants echoed similar concerns and stated that academic writing remained as a language-related challenge throughout their doctoral studies.

"Being a Doctoral Student is Already Very Hard"

Participants greatly emphasized the difficulties of being a doctoral student. Many stated that time management and balancing life and work were most challenging because the PhD program was demanding in nature with its heavy course load and various requirements and responsibilities. Dealing with the difficulties of doctoral studies in a foreign country aggravates the challenges. As participant [#24] shared, "There are always lots to do. Sometimes, I had to just work on research for two or three days at a stretch, and then I would fall behind in my coursework. Then you also need to publish papers. That balance has been the hardest." Adding to the inherent difficulties of a PhD program, taking care of daily affairs in a strange environment along with studies was really hard for some participants. For instance, participant [#32] who majored in school psychology and interned as a counselor, shared, "I need to find roommates/housemates when moving frequently, and deal with tax and health insurance systems. Juggling all those while doing research and clinical practice was just overwhelming."

Related to constructing an identity as a doctoral student, several participants stated that they had to cope with imposter syndrome. The experience of imposter syndrome—feeling like you are an imposter for not having the qualities or skills of the opportunity you have been given—is common among doctoral students (Pervez et al., 2021). Impostor syndrome can be worsened for AIPS when provoked by their multiple identities or perceptions of selves. As participant [#26] put it, "As an international student, you have to deal with many different issues. And at the same time, you have to fight your anxiety about your abilities. As a grad student, you constantly think about your capability and are unsure if you are good enough. You are in academia; you will be in academia after graduation and will keep having these thoughts about yourself. So, a lot of stress and insecurity."

Being an international student studying in a PhD program also heightens peer pressure. As participant [#8] shared, "I realized the limitations I have when comparing myself with other American students in our specialization. They have already published a lot, had work experience, and still worked really hard. Such comparison was very stressful." Several participants (e.g., [#26], [#31], [#10]) shared those negative feelings associated with imposter syndrome and peer pressure (e.g., self-doubt, feeling incompetent, or feeling like a fraud) had significant impacts on their mental well-being. Other challenges related to becoming and being an academic included academic writing, publishing, collaboration, mentorship, networking, graduation, and job opportunities. According to the literature (Mackie & Bates, 2019), those challenges were commonly faced by PhD students. However, for AIPS, their compound identities put them in a more vulnerable position and exacerbate the significance of these challenges, which may result in severe stress and mental health issues. For example, participants [#2] and [#16] described how their immigration status, race, nationality, gender, language, and lack of experience working in U.S. schools all come together to make them less "competitive" and "desirable" than their domestic peers.

Inequitable Access to Professional Development Opportunities and Resources

Participants shared their experiences of not being able to access professional development opportunities and resources that they perceived were essential to their success as emerging academics. They attributed the experiences of such inequitable treatments to their intersectional identities, including immigration status, lack of English proficiency, and lack of working experiences in U.S. contexts. For example, several participants mentioned that many scholarship and grant opportunities were not accessible to international students. Participants believed it was understandable that some public funding agencies only support U.S. citizens or permanent residents. They accepted the limits as long as the funding agencies communicated the eligibility criteria clearly. However, participants felt treated unfairly when the funding policies were not transparent. For example, participant [#2] shared that it took her three years to learn that a college-level scholarship would only be given to domestic applicants, even though an international student applicant might appear more competitive on paper. She believed, "The issue was the college was never transparent about this."

Another major issue raised by participants was that their program or lab only provided or encouraged certain types of professional development opportunities for them because of their language disadvantages and unfamiliarity with American cultures. For example, professional development opportunities such as providing training to community partners or conducting research activities in schools were usually assigned to domestic students. In contrast to those leadership building opportunities, the participants were assigned to those "technical and laborious jobs" [#7]. The participants with such an experience rationalized that their advisors who made such a decision perceived them as incompetent in English proficiency and leadership. As participant [#7] said, "because of our English, our supervisor decided we should be the ones who stay in the lab to do video coding instead of doing those jobs that involved in-person communication and interaction with community patterners ... because they needed someone capable and could represent the lab." While sharing those similar experiences, participants expressed the frustration, anger, and helplessness of being perceived as incompetent by their supervisors.

Ambiguous Experiences of Discrimination and Racism

Through an intersectionality lens, we explored the oppression and privilege AIPS may experience because of the multiple layers of their identities. Our findings revealed that most of our participants ($n = 21, 58.33\%$) believed they had not personally experienced overt or blatant discrimination or racism. Participants attributed the lack of such experience to three main reasons: (1) living on campus where people are "educated and nicer" (e.g., [#2], [#24]); (2) working at a lab or program or department that cared about diversity (e.g., [#19], [#27]), and (3) not sensitive enough to detect or lack the language to identify an incident of discrimination (e.g., [#1], [#6]). The third reason is worth attention because, although some participants initially said they did not personally experience discrimination, as they started to reflect on their experiences, they were able to recall the discomfort or unfairness they felt in certain situations. The participants were hesitant to name an uncomfortable situation as an incidence of discrimination because they thought themselves to be "insensitive" or said, "it took me a while to realize that was wrong" [#7]. As participant [#16], whose specialization was multicultural education, explained, "Before we moved to the United States, we probably had never experienced racism. Race was not an issue in China because most of us were the majority ... I think all international students should learn about racism in the United States. Otherwise, they may not even know how to describe it when they face discrimination. It is just the fabric of this country." Finally, while those participants suggested that they did not experience racial discrimination or personal attacks, they also shared stories of their close friends who had experienced racial attacks, which affected the participants' emotional wellness and were perceived as stressful.

Alarmingly, several participants explicitly identified their experiences of discrimination, racism, prejudice, or microaggression. Those experiences ranged from linguistic racism (i.e., the use of language resources for dissemination), tokenism (i.e., only make a symbolic effort to include underrepresented groups), and verbal racism sentiment, to microaggression (Sue et al., 2007; i.e., brief and commonplace daily verbal, behavioral, or environmental indignities that communicate negative racial slights towards people of color) related to one's skin color, professional competence, gender, and disability.

For example, a Chinese participant [#6] shared an incident when she and her lab mate, who was also a Chinese international doctoral student, were chatting in the lab, speaking Mandarin. One of their lab mates walked by, looked at them, and commented, "I wish the university requires everybody to speak English." That was an incident of linguistic racism when a native English speaker and American implied English was superior to the participants' home language. Another participant [#13] passionately expressed frustration and anger because she was treated as a diversity token. She shared that her department head once invited her to be a collaborator on a grant proposal because the head explicitly believed, "It would make our proposal competitive with your diversity work." The participant was promised a share of funding to support her research in the proposal. However, after the grant was awarded, the department head hesitated to allocate the fund to the participant, who had to "fight for it" by raising the issue to persons at higher positions multiple times. Several other participants also experienced tokenism and shared that they felt unvalued because they were only seen because of their minoritized identities instead of their competence. Some participants also shared their emotional burdens when they were selected to be spokespersons for diversity, equity, and inclusion-related issues. Participant [#32] said she was experiencing stress with an expectation of being the spokesperson against racial violence. She said, "Usually, my program just makes the minorities to be the one, educating everyone else … it became another source of stress … I'm already facing more difficulties than others, but I still need to spend more time educating other people."

COVID-19 Pandemic and Anti-Asian Racism Exacerbated Stress

When asked if the COVID-19 pandemic had caused challenges and stress, all participants responded "yes." Specifically, the COVID-19-related preventative measures, such as the shutdown of business, travel restrictions, social distancing, and quarantining, had interrupted participants' progress in doctoral programs and worsened their experiences of social isolation in a foreign country. Several participants' human subject-involved research projects had to be halted, resulting in the delay of important milestones (e.g., comprehensive exams, dissertation defense, entering the job market, and graduation). Although some participants were able to change their dissertation topics or find alternative ways to conduct their research, the revision of the original plan and delayed program progress caused significant mental stress to participants. Two participants mentioned the loss of funding had brought serious anxiety to them. The restriction of in-person interaction also affected those participants whose program involved practicum or clinical practices (e.g., participants studying school psychology or counseling psychology provide in-person counseling services).

Some of them (e.g., [#32]) felt "worried" but "lucky" because they were placed at an agency that adapted to the situation efficiently and was able to promptly change all in-person services from in-person to telehealth. Unfortunately, other participants felt "horrible" and "miserable" because their practicum had to be entirely suspended, which resulted in delayed graduation. For participants who were teaching assistants, teaching practices were also negatively affected by the pandemic. The sudden shift from face-to-face to online teaching demanded participants to abruptly change their schedule when other responsibilities were already pressing.

While the interruption of program progress was the main concern raised by many participants, the pandemic also negatively impacted other aspects of participants' studies and resulted in dissatisfactory learning experiences. For example, participant [#31] commented, "Besides those apparent impacts on my research and teaching, I just really missed those learning opportunities I could only gain from in-person interaction…. For example,

I enjoyed just observing how my advisor interacts with their students or how my cohort friends conduct themselves in meetings or presentations. I was able to learn a lot by just observing."

Participant [#24] echoed the lost values one could gain from in-person learning and shared, "I attended my first semester in my home country because of the travel ban. Attending classes online and away from the United States was chaotic due to time zone differences and cultural differences.... Everything was online, even the orientation. So, there was basically no college experience." Finally, several participants brought up how the pandemic made their advisor "even busier" and "less available," therefore indirectly impacted their doctoral studies by limiting the essential support they need. In terms of the experience of worsened social isolation, the most mentioned challenge for the participants was not being able to travel back to their home countries because of international travel restrictions. Participants shared that going back home regularly was an important opportunity to "recharge." Participant [#6] even described going home as a "salvation of the very stressful PhD program."

One of the main motivations of this study was to understand how the rising anti-Asian racism and violence during the COVID-19 pandemic affected the wellness of AIPS. Overall, our participants, especially Eastern Asians, expressed general negative and stressful emotions as the anti-Asian sentiment and violence became an accentuated issue. Feelings such as "worried," "scared," "unsafe," and "not belong" were shared emotions in participants' narratives. Many participants mentioned specific cases of Asians being attacked and killed, from the murder of 84-year-old Vicha Ratanapakdee in San Francisco to the Atlanta spa shooting. Negative feelings such as "heartbreaking," paranoia," "angry," "shocked," "feel the need to do something," and "enough is enough" were repeated and shared by our participants and deeply resonated with the researchers.

Several participants shared that, at the beginning of the pandemic, they had personally experienced ridicule because they were the first to wear masks to prevent COVID. They feared being attacked for wearing masks when it had not become a well-accepted preventative measure. In terms of personal experience of overt anti-Asian attacks, most participants stated they had not experienced such. They believed it was due to their immediate environment (e.g., on-campus, college town). Four participants mentioned encountering microaggression. For example, participant [#21] was a teaching assistant for an online class. The participant chose to show his name in both English and Chinese on Zoom. While waiting for the class to begin, one of the students commented, "Oh, we have a Chinese virus here." The participant said he was "a little shocked" but did not respond immediately because he "never experienced such verbal attack and literally did not know how to call that person out and speak up for himself (myself)." Several participants also shared their close friends' experiences of overt racial violence (e.g., "they got spit on while walking on campus" [#31], "someone drove right into them at the parking lot, they thought they were gonna be killed" [#20]). Participants' tone was frustrating while narrating their friends' stories; some of them explicitly stated their friends' experiences negatively affected their emotions.

To sum up this section, for many participants, those COVID-related challenges and stress were "too much," "very stressful," and "horrifying," and caused some to seek mental health services. Interestingly, a few participants did not perceive the pandemic had caused significant challenges. For example, participant [#18] said that her research was not affected because it was a secondary data analysis project and did not involve in-person interaction. Another participant shared that they enjoyed online learning more because it allowed them access to recorded lectures to listen to them multiple times. It also helped to release social anxiety caused by speaking English in person.

Effective Coping Strategies Manifests AIPS's High Level of Resilience

To cope with the abovementioned challenges and stress, participants adopted an array of strategies to overcome negative emotions, tackle demanding tasks, respond to a crisis, and mentally restore themselves. The majority of participants perceived themselves as highly resilient. Coping strategies to overcome doctoral study-related hardship can be grouped into three main categories. The first category involved changing studying behaviors and adjusting cognition and mentality. For example, many participants described how they "worked extra hard" and "spent more time" to "catch up with study" or "figure (difficult) things out." They emphasized the importance of "never give up," "keep coming back to it (challenges)," and eventually learned to "normalize or become accustomed to difficulties" and "not to internalize failure." For example, participant [#34] stated, "You have to endure the pain and discomfort and grow out of it."

The second category of coping strategies involved seeking and receiving external support and resources when overcoming difficulties. For example, many participants mentioned how their advisors, mentors, peers, families, and friends had played significant roles in helping them find solutions to problems or deal with stress. Participants also sought professional support and resources, including writing coaches or mental health counselors.

The third category of coping strategies involved establishing a personal system to recharge, restore, and bounce back from difficult situations. Participants identified a range of methods they found effective in helping them reduce stress and self-care, including workouts (e.g., strength training,

Yoga, running, walking), regular contact with families and friends, seeking mental health services, playing video games, watching television, meditation, and religious practice. Generally, finding time to do non-academic tasks or to rest and play was important for participants to overcome difficulties and maintain a sense of life and work balance.

The participants mentioned some specific cognitive and behavioral strategies to cope with the biggest challenge—language barriers. Participant [#24] described they had to spend at least triple the time reading or writing than their cohort peers who use English as their first language. Participant [#2] realized that they needed to "try to output (i.e., speak, write) instead of only input (i.e., listen, read)" to improve language skills. She said, "I just had to step out of my comfort zone to speak up in the class." Notably, academic writing has been reported by researchers (Gupta et al., 2022) as one of the main new skills that graduate students found challenging to acquire and master, even though it was in a person's first language. Several participants shared their observations that academic writing was also difficult for their peers who use English as their first language. As participant [#4] acknowledged, "academic writing is a general challenge for all doctoral students, not simply international students." Such a realization helped participants to normalize the writing challenge and avoid attributing it to their own lack of language proficiency.

Interestingly, in coping with negative emotions such as lack of confidence and the feelings of imposter syndrome, several participants mentioned that external validations were critical for them to "regain confidence," or "build confidence" and "become more and more resilient facing challenges." Those external validations mainly included explicit praise from professors or peers, publications or awards, and successfully reaching significant milestones. More importantly, when reflecting if they think of themselves as resilient, many participants immediately said, "I am very resilient."

Internal core identities, such as a person's character or life and career goals, were linked to participants' ability to cope with challenges and stress and perceived high levels of resilience. When we asked participants what their career goals were, we found that most of them were to become a professor or an academic working in the industry. Some personal characteristics, such as being highly motivated, passionate, ambitious, hard-working, and having grit, also contributed to their resilience and ability to cope with difficult situations. Finally, to cope with the impact of rising anti-Asian racism, several participants chose to "just not go outside," or "I stopped looking at social media because it was not good for my mental health," while some were actively engaged in community services and activities related to the "Stop Asian Hate" movement. Participant [#4], who led efforts to raise awareness of anti-Asian racism and call for change, shared, "Just because I have not encountered this personally doesn't mean others have not. I think it's important to do my best to disseminate information about Stop Asian Hate, so I have actively done this to let people know that we are not an easy target."

DISCUSSION

As described in the above, each of the three main findings addressed at least two of the five research questions; all three findings answered RQ5, which inquires the impact of AIPS's intersectionality on their experiences and perception of challenges, stress, and manifestation of resilience. Studying in a PhD program is a difficult and challenging endeavor. Our results suggested that the intersectional identities of AIPS further exacerbated the challenges and stress they perceived and experienced. Particularly, through the lens of intersectionality (Crenshaw, 2017), we found that different facets of those interlocked identities were associated with specific challenges and stressful emotions. For example, being an emerging bilingual using English as a foreign language is linked to experiencing difficulties in catching up with study, imposter syndrome, linguistic racism, and inequitable access to leadership opportunities in their doctoral studies. The immigration status of international students is connected to their experience of structural inequity that prevents them from accessing professional resources (e.g., funding, grant, and certain jobs). Being Asian, particularly East Asians, was significantly affected by the anti-Asian racism that intensified during the COVID-19 pandemic.

We conclude that all the acculturative stressors (e.g., loneliness, culture difference, discrimination) and challenges related to being a doctoral student coalesced into massive burdens on AIPS's shoulders. The COVID-19 pandemic and the ongoing and rising anti-Asian racism augmented the oppressions AIPS face. Nevertheless, AIPS demonstrated high levels of resilience, accumulated cultural and career capital, sustained aspirations to pursue professional and leadership excellence, and called for enhanced support and resources from higher education institutions (HEIs). Finally, our findings also revealed a spectrum of emotional intensity when AIPS narrated lived experiences of stress and challenges related to studying in the U.S. and during and beyond the COVID-19 pandemic. Our findings bridged the literature gaps on coping strategies and resilience of a specific racial group of graduate students and fulfilled our goal for amplifying the voices of our focused marginalized group—AIPS.

Implications for Higher Education

AIPS in ECE engage in impactful research to tackle social problems and usually serve as educators for future teachers or health service providers.

They are not only indispensable contributors to the U.S. education system but also future leaders in academia or significant institutes to better young children's lives worldwide. However, there is a scarce discussion on how to provide tailored support and resources to help alleviate AIPS's stress, optimize their experience in the U.S. HEIs, and support the achievement of their career goals. We amplified the voices of AIPS by making meaning of 36 participants' biographical narratives.

At the end of the interview, we asked participants what supports and resources from their department or doctoral program they thought were essential to achieve their career goals. Several suggestions emerged from the narratives. Foremost, faculty and programs must understand the needs and challenges AIPS face from a lens of multiple dimensions of identities and intersectionality; and provide tailored support and resources accordingly. When an AIPS faces common challenges that all doctoral students may encounter, it is important to realize that they also need to cope with other layers of stress associated with being an international student and being an Asian. Additional awareness and resources need to be allocated for AIPS to overcome language barriers and cultural differences. For example, several participants suggested that they wished they could have more constructive feedback to help them improve in academic writing. Participants also shared how simple encouragement and affirmation from their professors or advisors helped them to overcome cultural differences and become more vocal and confident in class. HEIs could also facilitate networking among AIPS or between current and graduated AIPS and help them form a community. Participants shared that it was difficult for them to find a faculty or an advanced doctoral student who shared their identities and had similar backgrounds and experiences. Therefore, it is hard to find a mentor or peer who understands their difficult situation.

Second, HEIs must strive to provide an inclusive environment and cultivate a sense of belonging for AIPS by removing structural barriers that create unnecessary burdens for AIPS and prevent AIPS from accessing equitable resources. For example, many universities require international students to enroll in a certain number of classes to maintain their F1 visa status, even though they no longer need to take any classes or do not have the financial means to pay for those extra classes. Another issue participants raised was that HEI personnel lack the knowledge to handle immigration-related issues (e.g., external hiring of graduate assistants). Additionally, supervisors and advisors should strive to counteract implicit biases and dismantle racism by truly perceiving AIPS as equally capable individuals compared to domestic doctoral students; and provide more leadership building opportunities for AIPS. Finally, HEIs need to diversify its faculty and doctoral program by hiring racially minoritized and/or international faculty so that marginalized students such as AIPS could have role models to learn from and receive support from minority faculty who have shared experiences in U.S. HEIs. The above suggestions apply not only to AIPS, but also to international doctoral students from other marginalized racial groups.

Limitation and Future Research

We acknowledge the following limitations of this study and discuss potential directions for future research. First, due to the restriction of funding agency, we were only able to recruit AIPS whose study/work was pertinent to the field of ECE. We anticipate that AIPS studying/working in fields such as STEM may perceive or experience challenges and stress differently compared to AIPS in education or social sciences. For example, although all AIPS may experience language as the biggest challenge, AIPS in ECE might experience stress brought by language barriers at higher levels because studying in ECE fields require more interpersonal activities and skills compared to AIPS studying in STEM. Future research should include AIPS studying in all disciplines to obtain a full picture of their perception and experience of challenges and stress.

Second, we have a limited number of participants; the findings of this study should not be simply generalized to all AIPS in ECE or all AIPS. However, the investigation and findings of this qualitative study is transferrable and could be applicable to populations similar to AIPS. Future researchers may utilize the results of this qualitative study, develop a survey to understand challenges and coping strategies from a lens of intersectionality, and reach a broader group of participants.

Third, the main purpose of this chapter is to amplify voices of AIPS so that HEIs could hear it and provide better and tailored supports and resources. As described in the Methods section, this qualitative research is a part of a larger study in which we also aimed to provide recommendations to current and incoming AIPS to be better prepared for challenges and be informed with resources. Our research team and other researchers should devote continuous efforts to develop deliverables for AIPS to thrive in U.S. academia.

Fourth, the participants of this study were students and had not realized their career goals. It would be interesting and inspirational to follow up with those participants and hear successful (or unsuccessful) stories as they progress in their doctoral programs, navigate the job markets, and secure jobs after graduation.

Conclusion

We aimed to amplify the voices of AIPS who have intersectional identities and are often underrepresented in educational research. When we proceeded with the study, we continuously heard from our participants how meaningful it is for them to have a space to share their stories and voice their concerns. As scholars and current or past AIPS, having the opportunities to converse and co-create meanings with our participants was, in one of our participants' words, therapeutic and empowering.

REFERENCE

Bazrafkan, L., Shokrpour, N., Yousefi, A., & Yamani, N. (2016). Management of stress and anxiety among PhD students during thesis writing: A qualitative study. *The Health Care Manager*, *35*(3), 231–240. https://doi.org/10.1097/HCM.0000000000000120

Bonazzo, C., & Wong, Y. J. (2007). Japanese international female students' experience of discrimination, prejudice, and stereotypes. *College Student Journal*, *41*(3), 631–639.

Charmaz, K. (2014). *Constructing grounded theory*. SAGE.

Crenshaw, K. W. (2017). *On intersectionality: Essential writings*. The New Press.

Duff, P. A., & Bell, J. S. (2002), Narrative research in TESOL: Narrative inquiry: More than just telling stories. *TESOL Quarterly*, *36*(2), 207–213.

Glass, C. R. (2017). Resilience for a world in flux. *Journal of International Students*, *7*(2), I–III. https://doi.org/10.32674/jis.v7i2.316

Guba, E., & Lincoln, Y. (1994). *Competing paradigms in qualitative research*. In N. Denzin & Y. Lincoln (Eds.), *Handbook of qualitative research* (pp. 105–117). SAGE.

Gupta, S., Jaiswal, A., Paramasivam, A., & Kotecha, J. (2022). Academic writing challenges and supports: Perspectives of international doctoral students and their supervisors. In *Frontiers in Education* (Vol. 7, p. 891534). Frontiers Media SA.

Heng, T. T. (2018). Exploring the complex and non-linear evolution of Chinese international students' experiences in U.S. colleges. *Higher Education Research & Development*, *37*(6), 1141–1155. https://doi.org/10.1080/07294360.2018.1474184

Herrman, H., Stewart, D. E., & Diaz-Granados, N. (2011). What is resilience? The Canadian *Journal of Psychiatry*, *56*(5), 258–265.

Hwang, B. J., Bennett, R., & Beauchemin, J. (2014). International students' utilization of counseling services. *College Student Journal*, *48*(3), 347–354.

Hyun, J. (2005). *Breaking the bamboo ceiling: Career strategies for Asian Americans*. HarperCollins.

Jeung, R., Yellow Horse, A. J., & Cayanan, C. (2021). *Stop AAPI hate national report*. Stop AAPI Hate. https://stopaapihate.org/wp-content/uploads/2021/05/Stop-AAPI-Hate-Report-National-210506.pdf

Jones, S. R., & Mcewen, M. K. (2000). A conceptual model of multiple dimensions of identity. *Journal of College Student Development*, 405–414.

Kim, G. M., & Cooc, N. (2021). Asian Americans and Pacific Islanders in academe: Race and gender through the tenure pipeline from 1993–2017. *Race Ethnicity and Education*, *24*(3), 338–356.
https://doi.org/10.1080/13613324.2020.1753675

Larson, C. L. (1997). Representing the subject: Problems in personal narrative inquiry. *International Journal of Qualitative Studies in Education*, *10*(4), 455–470.

Lazarus, R. S., & Folkman, S. (1984). *Stress, appraisal, and coping*. Springer.

Levine, F., Nasir, N. S., Rios-Aguilar, C., Gildersleeve, R., Rosich, K., Bang, M., Bell, N., & Holsapple, M. (2021). *Voices from the field: The impact of COVID-19 on early career scholars and doctoral students*. American Educational Research Association. https://doi.org/10.3102/aera20211

Lin, S.-Y., & Scherz, S. D. (2014). Challenges facing Asian international graduate students in the U.S.: Pedagogical considerations in higher education. *Journal of International Students*, *4*(1), 16–33. https://doi.org/10.32674/jis.v4i1.494

Macgregor, A., & Folinazzo, G. (2018). Best practices in teaching international students in higher education: Issues and strategies. *TESOL Journal*, *9*(2), 299–329. https://doi.org/10.1002/tesj.324

Mackie, S. A., & Bates, G. W. (2019). Contribution of the doctoral education environment to PhD candidates' mental health problems: A scoping review. *Higher Education Research & Development*, *38*(3), 565–578.
https://doi.org/10.1080/07294360.2018.1556620

Masten, A. S. (2018). Resilience theory and research on children and families: Past, present, and promise. *Journal of Family Theory and Review, 10*(1), 12–31.
https://doi.org/10.1111/jftr.12255

Pervez, A., Brady, L. L., Mullane, K., Lo, K. D., Bennett, A. A., & Nelson, T. A. (2021). An empirical investigation of mental illness, impostor syndrome, and social support in management doctoral programs. *Journal of Management Education*, *45*(1), 126–158. https://doi.org/10.1177/1052562920953195

Saldaña, J. (2021). The coding manual for qualitative researchers. *The Coding Manual for Qualitative Researchers*, 1–440.

Sherry, M., Thomas, P., & Chui, W. H. (2010). International students: A vulnerable student population. *Higher Education*, *60*(1), 33–46.

Simon, J. D., Boyd, R., & Subica, A. M. (2022). Refocusing intersectionality in social work education: Creating a brave space to discuss oppression and privilege. *Journal of Social Work Education*, *58*(1), 34–45.
https://doi.org/10.1080/10437797.2021.1883492

Smith, R. A., & Khawaja, N. G. (2011). A review of the acculturation experiences of international students. *International Journal of Intercultural Relations*, *35*(6), 699–713. https://doi.org/10.1016/j.ijintrel.2011.08.004

Sue, D. W., Capodilupo, C. M., Torino, G. C., Bucceri, J. M., Holder, A., Nadal, K. L., & Esquilin, M. (2007). Racial microaggressions in everyday life: implications for clinical practice. *American Psychologist, 62*(4), 271.

Sustarsic, M., & Zhang, J. (2021). Navigating through uncertainty in the era of COVID-19: Experiences of international graduate students in the United States. *Journal of International Students*, *12*(1), 61–80. https://doi.org/10.32674/jis.v12i1.3305

Sverdlik, A., Hall, N. C., & Vallerand, R. J. (2022). Doctoral students and COVID-19: Exploring challenges, academic progress, and wellbeing. *Educational Psychology*, 1–16. https://doi.org/10.1080/01443410.2022.2091749

Watkins, D. C. (2017). Rapid and rigorous qualitative data analysis: The "RADaR" technique for applied research. *International Journal of Qualitative Methods*, *16*(1). https://doi.org/10.1177/1609406917712131

Wing, J. Y. (2007). Beyond Black and White: The model minority myth and the invisibility of Asian American students. *The Urban Review*, *39*(4). https://link.springer.com/content/pdf/10.1007/s11256-007-0058-6.pdf

Xiong, Y., & Zhou, Y. (2018). Understanding East Asian graduate students' sociocultural and psychological adjustment in a U.S. Midwestern university. *Journal of International Students*, *8*(2), 769–794. https://doi.org/10.32674/jis.v8i2.103

CHAPTER 3

A DESCRIPTIVE PHENOMENOLOGICAL STUDY OF THE FACTORS INFLUENCING MULTINATIONAL FEMALE GRADUATE STUDENTS' ACADEMIC PRODUCTIVITY DURING THE COVID-19 PANDEMIC

A Feminist Perspective

Nuchelle L. Chance
Fort Hays State University

Tricia M. Farwell
Middle Tennessee State University

ABSTRACT

The current chapter explores the factors influencing multinational female graduate students' academic productivity (AP) during the COVID-19 pandemic. Using descriptive phenomenology, the results show that a mix of internal and external changes brought about by the pandemic impacted

---

Research on College Stress and Coping: Implications From the COVID-19 Pandemic and Beyond, pp. 53–77
Copyright © 2024 by Information Age Publishing
www.infoagepub.com
All rights of reproduction in any form reserved.

their motivation, attention, and focus toward completing their degree. Those interviewed explained that internal motivations included an increased focus on needing to conduct research that interacted with the external benefit of experiencing decreased expectations from their mentors and universities. However, for some, mental pressures and external responsibilities resulted in less attention being paid to their work while needing to maintain "on-ground" expectations. The chapter concludes by suggesting ways universities and mentors can provide greater support to aid multinational female graduate students in their educational journey.

Keywords: academic expectations, academic motivations, academic productivity, academic stress, COVID-19, dissertation, doctoral students, graduate students, higher education, phenomenology

EXPLORING FACTORS THAT INFLUENCE THE ACADEMIC PRODUCTIVITY OF MULTINATIONAL FEMALE GRADUATE STUDENTS DURING THE COVID-19 PANDEMIC

Scholars and professionals agree that the COVID-19 pandemic shook the foundations of higher education (Goldberg, 2021; Gurukkal, 2020). More importantly, it has exposed and exacerbated disparities and inequities faced by different constituencies, such as lack of support and feelings of isolation in female graduate students. Graduate students have numerous expectations and challenges, including committing significant time and energy to their coursework, meeting research and scholarship deadlines, and responding to feedback from faculty, advisors, and supervisors. Institutionally, graduate students must accept rules, policies, and procedures set by their programs of study and meet university deadlines. In addition, if the graduate student holds a faculty or staff role, such as a graduate teaching assistant, that creates additional levels of responsibility and significant added stress (Ryan, 2014). This pressure generally comes without additional institutional support, as graduate student workers have been alluded to as the "forgotten tribe" (McCready & Vecsey, 2013; Ryan, 2015). Furthermore, the added pressures of navigating the transitions that the COVID-19 pandemic presented have created adversity, leading students to readjust and prioritize their roles and responsibilities (Chance et al., 2022).

Both undergraduate and graduate students reported that their mental health had declined drastically since the onset of the pandemic (Ogilvie et al., 2020; Wang et al., 2020). This was in part due to uncertainty around their academics (Hotez et al., 2022); in part due to their personal and familial responsibilities (Avorgbedor & Vilme, 2021; Nicholson et al., 2023); and in part due to the sociopolitical shifts in the world revolving around the immigration and customs laws (Enriquez et al., 2023), social justice and Black Lives Matters (BLM) protests (Boitet et al., 2022; Dong et al., 2022), and governmental election outcomes [i.e., 2020 United States Presidential election] (Rizvi et al., 2022; Roche & Jacobson, 2019) which leads to continuous stress and anxiety.

The pandemic was predicted to negatively impact female scholars more disparately than their male counterparts due to work-life imbalances (Kramer, 2020; Myers et al., 2020; Power, 2020). This implies that, by virtue of being a woman alone, these academic professionals were more likely to struggle with time management of their scholarship with their personal and familial responsibilities due to traditional gender roles and expectations. Accordingly, a significant body of literature from the COVID-19 pandemic underscores the need for colleges and universities to establish more equitable policies and practices and supportive environments for academic women scholars (Dönmez, 2022; Goldberg, 2021; Malisch et al., 2020; Oleschuk, 2020). Nonetheless, it is reasonable to expect female graduate students will face opposition similar to that predicted for female academic professionals.

Graduate students are a "vulnerable population" due to the pressures of academic performance, publishing, and learning the professorate, often in an underpaid and under-resourced environment (Chance et al., 2022; Jenei et al., 2020; Wang et al., 2020). Therefore, ongoing assessment and evaluation of the changes in their academic productivity due to the pandemic will be beneficial for career trajectory planning. Graduate students are essential to the continued vitality of the academy. They are the next generation of scholars, researchers, and educators who can bring a wealth of diversity, equity, and inclusion to higher learning. As such, it is important to examine circumstances affecting the scholarship of multinational graduate students during crises, such as the COVID-19 pandemic.

The COVID-19 pandemic presented overwhelming challenges for graduate students globally, leading to learning loss and exacerbated gender inequalities in graduate education. These challenges included disruptions to academic progress, research delays, hindered access to technology, facilities, and equipment, financial hardships due to losses of teaching assistantships, research assistantships, and adjunct teaching contracts, limited professional development opportunities, and physical and mental health challenges associated with increased isolation, loneliness, stress, and anxiety (Donohue et al., 2021; Jenei et al., 2020; Goldstone & Zhang, 2021; Sustarsic & Zhang, 2021; Swanson et al., 2022). For instance, female master and doctoral students reported significantly higher levels of academic burnout than male students during the COVID-19 pandemic. These disparities were largely attributed to dissatisfaction with their university's pandemic response and perceived lack of support.

Feminist theory is ideally situated to guide our inquiry into the gender inequalities that the COVID-19 pandemic has exacerbated. This framework aims to understand and challenge gender inequalities and power relations in society (Leavy & Harris, 2018). It can also help us critique the dominant norms and assumptions that underlie academic culture and practices that may marginalize or exclude women's voices and contributions (Acker & Armenti, 2004; Macfarlane & Burg, 2019; Morley & Crossouard, 2016). Furthermore, feminist theory can help us envision alternative research methods that challenge power relations, such as the balance of power in research relationships.

In addition to a feminist theoretical framework, we examine this phenomenon through a cross-cultural lens. This allows us to compare different cultures to understand human behavior. From a cross-cultural understanding, the pandemic similarly influenced multinational female graduate students (Chance et al., 2022), as evidenced by the challenges and opportunities the participants described experiencing while navigating the pandemic, which were also reported by graduate students from countries all over the world (Donohue et al., 2021; Jenei et al., 2020).

Therefore, guided by feminist theory, we took a qualitative cross-cultural approach to explore the factors influencing multinational female graduate students' academic productivity (AP) during the COVID-19 pandemic. This framework allows us to highlight these diverse students' unique and complex realities during an unprecedented global crisis. This study's outcomes will contribute to our understanding of the cross-cultural gender inequalities that the COVID-19 pandemic has exacerbated.

REVIEW OF THE LITERATURE

Graduate school is a time of considerable change, both academically and professionally. Students face pressure associated with teaching classes while also conducting research and meeting the expectations of faculty, departments, and universities. In addition, they may need to balance their studies with family responsibilities, personal relationships, and self-care. These compounding expectations can lead to stress and burnout (Allen, 2020; Hyun et al., 2006; Oswalt & Riddock, 2007; Kernan et al., 2011).

Various factors contribute to graduate student burnout, a major one being lack of sleep. For example, Hunter and Devine (2016) conducted a cross-cultural study with doctoral students from the United States, Canada, Australia, and New Zealand, finding that exhaustion is predictive of students' intentions to leave academia. In the United States, burnout among doctoral students was manifested as emotional exhaustion, whereas in Canada, Australia, and New Zealand, it primarily presented as cynicism. Additionally, a review of burnout in graduate medical students found that poor sleep patterns were associated with exhaustion, burnout, lowered professional efficacy, and depression (Wolf & Rosenstock, 2017). Unsurprisingly, stress increases exhaustion, disillusionment, and lack of productivity (Allen et al., 2020).

Though shifting demands can increase stress, self-care is a meaningful way to help graduate students cope and prevent burnout. Batterson (2004) argued from a feminist perspective that women's coping strategies are limited by their need to balance their personal and professional lives. She suggested that female doctoral students develop empowering coping strategies to thrive in a patriarchal society. These strategies include increased social support, assertive communication, cognitive reframing, physical activity, spirituality, humor, and alternating study locations. Mind-body stress-reduction techniques also effectively reduce stress for graduate students (Cohen & Miller, 2009; Stilwell et al., 2017). Finally, regarding professional development, Quigley et al. (2021) found that access and adequate training with technological tools helps reduce stress and prepare graduate students for career readiness when the tool itself is not a source of stress.

The Dual Roles of Attention, Mental Focus, and Motivation in Graduate Student Success Versus Failure

Attention, mental focus, and motivation are necessary for graduate students to meet coursework and research requirements; however, their reduction can result in falling behind. With the onset of the COVID-19 pandemic, students' focus on education has been limited as personal and professional responsibilities began to transition. Furthermore, the compounding stress of academic uncertainty, the social climate, and the risk of infection significantly hindered students' ability to focus and pay attention, therefore diminishing motivation to complete schoolwork (Hotez et al., 2022).

Diverse identity characteristics can create unique academic challenges for students. For example, female graduate students may find it difficult to balance their academic responsibilities with their personal and familial responsibilities (Maher et al., 2004). Women with intersectional, racially, and ethnically diverse identities may face even more challenges, such as adapting to cultural norms, discrimination, language barriers, and meeting the expectations of family members back home. These challenges can be stressful and can negatively affect their ability to pay attention and succeed in their studies. A study of international female graduate students found that cultural and gender-specific challenges caused stress that negatively

58 N. L. CHANCE and T. M. FARWELL

affected their ability to pay attention, thus discouraging some participants from completing their studies (Fatima, 2001).

Graduate Student Motivations: A Tug-of-War Between Stamina and Fatigue

Motivation is the drive or action toward achieving a goal (Tranquillo & Stecker, 2016). By default, graduate students are highly motivated as they chose to pursue an advanced degree, knowing the challenges and expectations. Graduate student motivations can be intrinsic—internal and for personal enjoyment, subjective well-being, curiosity, and autonomy—such as a desire to learn and make a difference in the world, or extrinsic—external factors, such as rewards or praise—like prestigious job titles and higher salaries (White, 1959).

Doctoral students are motivated primarily by intrinsic factors, such as the desire to learn and grow, rather than extrinsic factors, such as salary or professional advancement (Lynch et al., 2018). The intrinsic motivating factors necessary for continuing professional are *autonomy, competence,* and *relatedness*. Similarly, Tranquillo and Stecker (2016) argue the value of intrinsic motivation to promote competence in continuing professional development. Conversely, Arceño (2018) found that graduate students of advanced education programs were extrinsically motivated by salary augmentation and professional affluence. However, it is more likely that graduate students are similarly motivated by both intrinsic and extrinsic factors to varying degrees. For instance, Fatima (2001) found that international female graduate students in the United Kingdom were motivated by a desire to (1) improve their and their families' lives, (2) make a difference in the world, and (3) to challenge traditional gender roles and stereotypes. With this group, intrinsic motivation was strongest, and ethnicity was a factor such that Asian students were more intrinsically motivated while White students were extrinsically motivated.

Graduate student motivations change over time. For example, students seeking medical degrees found that their expectations and motivations changed at the start of their graduate program. Furthering their academic progress made them more aware of the workload and challenges experienced in medical graduate studies (Magalhães-Alves et al., 2017). Additionally, failure for these students led to increased frustration at their choice of a degree program and their future opportunities.

The COVID-19 pandemic has significantly impacted the mental health of graduate students, particularly marginalized groups. For example, research shows that female graduate students reported feeling more stressed, anxious, depressed, isolated, and lonely while having more difficulty accessing mental health care than their male peers did. However, graduate students of color reported even higher rates of those ailments than their White peers (Wasil et al., 2021). Furthermore, the science of motivation tells us that with diminished happiness and, thus, mental health comes a diminished motivation to achieve (Schneider & Preckel, 2017). Therefore, examining how the pandemic has influenced graduate students' motivations to support these learners is crucial.

Graduate Student Productivity

Directly influenced by motivation, graduate student productivity encompasses coursework, satisfactory progress towards thesis/dissertation defenses, presentations at conferences and publications, and sometimes student teaching and lab work. In addition, for graduate students entering the academy, there may be added pressure to present and publish, making them more appealing to hiring institutions. Loma Linda University, for example, created supplemental support for their graduate students in the sciences field to assist them with writing (Gardner et al., 2018).

Publication can be a motivating factor for graduate students, but there are challenges. For example, a study of journalism and mass communication journals from 1997–2006 found that graduate students published between 15%–24% of the articles, and approximately half of the lead authors were graduate students, indicating they were "quite active." However, the rate of graduate student publications did not show signs of a significant increase over the study period (Carpenter, 2008, p. 232). Additionally, international students seek out faculty with similar ancestry as mentors, which can limit research collaboration opportunities and impact on their productivity (Borjas et al., 2016). Finally, the economic status of the graduate student's home country may also impact their postgraduate productivity (Obuku et al., 2018).

Recognizing the importance of publication for doctoral candidates, some universities have taken steps to increase the support provided to help students overcome fears and barriers to publication. The additional support gave graduate students increased confidence in their writing abilities, leading to increased productivity and publication (Gardner et al., 2018).

Research Question

Since graduate students are often future faculty members, scholars must investigate what supports and barriers graduate students encounter when pursuing their studies, especially potentially underrepresented students.

Moreover, the COVID-19 pandemic put additional stressors on students and faculty alike. Nevertheless, both groups have an element of success tied to their academic productivity, impacting their ability to continue their education, find jobs and lead a positive life in academia. Therefore, the research question guiding this study is:

1. How do multinational female graduate students describe their academic productivity since the onset of the COVID-19 pandemic?

METHODOLOGY

We conducted a qualitative study exploring the lived experiences of multinational female graduate students as they navigated the transitions of higher education during the COVID-19 pandemic. Using a descriptive phenomenological approach, we aimed to identify and describe factors influencing this group's academic productivity (AP) (Giorgi, 2009, 2012). This five-step method is appropriate for describing and comprehending the meaning, structure, and essence of a participant's experience of a phenomenon. Furthermore, descriptive phenomenology lends itself to cross-cultural experiences (DeRobertis, 2017; DeRobertis & Bland, 2020), feminist experiences (Kruks, 2014), and educational psychology (Farrell, 2020; Stolz, 2020).

Researcher Positionality Statement

As women researchers, scholars, and academics similarly navigating the pandemic, we are invested in contributing to this research, especially considering the claim that women would be less productive and struggle academically and professionally. We know the strains put on students, faculty, staff, and other stakeholders during these unprecedented times and we want to use our insider status (Xu, 2017) to genuinely understand and explain the experiences of multinational female graduate students during the COVID-19 pandemic.

Data Gathering Procedures

Data was gathered through an online survey of 31 multinational female graduate students enrolled in either a master's or doctoral program globally. The survey was hosted on Qualtrics, a web-based data and experience

A Descriptive Phenomenological Study 61

management program. This method was the most beneficial because society was in the midst of a stay-at-home order, and students and academics were already experiencing Zoom fatigue (Bullock et al., 2022; Tucker et al., 2021). The survey consisted of demographic and content-specific open-ended questions inquiring about the participants' academic experiences since the onset of the pandemic. Exploratory items from the questionnaire included: *"How has the pandemic and the stay-at-home orders specifically impacted your scholarly activity?"*, *"How have, if at all, expectations for academic/scholarly productivity from your institution/employer shifted as a result of the pandemic?"* and *"What supports, e.g., technology, professional development, etc., did your institution/employer(s) put into place as a result of the pandemic?"*. There were also unstructured follow-up prompts that allowed participants to elaborate on information they felt was applicable that we did not explicitly inquire about.

Once IRB approval was obtained, we received permission from the I Should Be Writing (ISBW) Facebook group administrator to recruit participants. The administrators established the group to give women and nonbinary academics support on their academic writing journeys. Based on the membership guidelines, participants were verified to be women and committed to scholarly writing. We directly messaged the group's administrator requesting permission to recruit and explained the study's purpose, critical components, and participant expectations.

After receiving approval, data collection began. First, participants accessed the survey via a link shared in weekly recruitment posts. When accessing the survey, participants provided informed consent and self-selected pseudonyms to retain anonymity. Next, the participants completed a brief demographic portion and then finished with the semi-structured content-specific questions. We enabled the save your progress feature so participants could take breaks and return to complete the surveys later. Finally, at submission, they were thanked and debriefed. This data-gathering approach was appropriate for the study because it allowed us to collect a large amount of data from a diverse group of participants in a relatively short time. Additionally, the online survey format was convenient for participants and allowed them to provide honest and thoughtful responses.

Research Participants

The ISBW Facebook group membership criteria mirrored our research criteria for this study, making it the perfect place for participant recruitment. Data from this study comes from 31 multinational female graduate students, all members of the ISBW Facebook group. According to our data analysis, all our participants identified explicitly as women/female; therefore, we respectfully use the terms *women* and *female* when referring to our participants collectively throughout this paper. The participants' demographic information is presented in Table 3.1.

Table 3.1

Participants Demographic Information

Demographic	Participants Demographic Data
Ages	24–45
Racial Ethnicity	25 White
	6 BIPOC*
Area of Resudence	42% Domestic (USA)
	58% International [3 = Australia; 1 = Bulgaria; 4 = Canada; 1 = France; 2 = Norway; 1 = Scotland; 2 = South Africa; 3 = UK]
Highest Degree‡ (Completed)	5 Bachelor's degrees
	26 Master's degrees
Relationship Status	8 Single
	21 Partnered
	2 Other
Employee Status	7 Part-Time
	12 Full-Time
	12 Other/Non-Disclosed
Student Status	13 Part-Time
	18 Full-Time

* *Black, Indigenous, and Persons of Color*

‡ *These degrees are at different levels depending on the participant's country of residence. All participants were graduate students working on a master's or doctoral degree at the time of the study*

Data Analysis Procedures

To identify and describe the lived experiences of multinational female graduate students, an analysis technique that is both inductive and deductive and helped us to identify themes was necessary. Descriptive phenomenology calls for objective data analysis. We analyzed participants' responses using Dedoose qualitative data coding and analysis software. We employed Giorgi's five-step descriptive phenomenological data analysis method, as it is a practical approach in social and human sciences (Giorgi & Giorgi, 2003). This method of data analysis is a five-step process that involves interpreting, organizing, and describing the data (Giorgi, 2009, 2012).

In Step 1, we read the participant responses to get a basic understanding of what being a female graduate student during the onset of the pandemic entailed. In Step 2, we started the process of phenomenological reduction as we re-read the participants' responses and began delineating meaning units from the salient data. In Step 3, phenomenological reduction continued as we moved from the general to the abstract by identifying similar expressions of the phenomenon of study between participants. It is in step three that the essence of the phenomenon begins to emerge as the participants' lived meanings are emphasized (meaning units). Step 4 allowed us to transform the participants' statements (meaning units) into constituent parts without changing the meaning content. Finally, Step 5 involved synthesizing the participants' insights into a descriptive structure of the collective experience of being a multinational female graduate student traversing higher education during the pandemic as articulated in the discussion.

Trustworthiness and Dependability

Verification in qualitative research refers to ensuring trustworthiness (Creswell, 2013) and dependability (Lincoln & Guba, 1985) of the study and its findings. We engaged in bracketing/bridling by journaling and sharing thoughts with the collective research group to put aside bias and preconceived notions while conducting the analysis throughout the research process. We also triangulated the data with different sources to provide corroborating evidence on the emerging units and structures. To enhance dependability, we often referred to the original data sets after structures were identified to see if they were aligning.

Strengths and Limitations

One strength of this research is the use of self-administered online questionnaire for data collection. By participants being able to access the measure virtually and anonymously, as well as create a pseudonym, this minimized interviewer bias and increased participant confidence and honesty. A secondary strength of the design was the participants' option to save and return to the questionnaire to complete it if they were interrupted. This advantage of flexibility is highly beneficial for professional women and students alike. Finally, using social media for recruiting and an online medium for data collection allowed us to recruit an internationally diverse sample of participants representative of nine different countries.

To protect the reliability and trustworthiness of the study, limitations will also be addressed being that all scientific inquiry has limitations (Creswell, 2013). First, the study was limited by its exclusion criteria (sex and graduate student status). However, the importance of the research might not have been as important without niche specificity. Though no specific guidelines indicate the appropriate sample size for descriptive phenomenology, Creswell and Miller (2000) suggest between 5–25. Our sample of 31 has likely reached saturation levels; however, there is no definitive baseline set thus far. The current study was limited by the recruiting pool. The ISBW Facebook group is global, but we did not recruit outside of that social space for this phase of the project. Therefore, the data may not reflect the experiences of all female graduate students matriculating through the pandemic.

FINDINGS

In examining the lived experiences of multinational female graduate students, specifically, the conditions surrounding their academic productivity (AP) during the COVID-19 pandemic, themes related to motivation emerged. Thus, as the literature suggests, graduate students are internally and externally motivated or driven; however, psychological factors and life experiences while in a pandemic moderate that.

Internal Drivers of Academic Productivity

The participants in this study identified internal drivers that had both positive and negative effects on their AP. In many cases, the participants had increased attention, focus, and motivation on their AP; however, there were more cases speaking to decreases due to challenges presented by the pandemic.

Increased Attention, Focus, or Motivation

The participants heavily described increased attention, focus, or motivation as a factor influencing their AP. For example, several participants identified increased AP during the pandemic. Though these participants benefited from increased AP due to increased driving factors, not all the contexts were the same.

Some participants took full advantage of the stay-at-home order as Abe was staying "busy" as "it feels like [her] work weeks never end" and Toffee-Maky "has more time and fewer distractions" to get work done. Likewise, Peyton states, "The time I would have spent commuting to and from work and staying after work to complete activities was able to be spent focusing

A Descriptive Phenomenological Study   65

on my own schoolwork." Similarly, M found "focused time to write" due to the "lack of extra service work that comes with being off-campus." Echoing the sentiments of her peers, Gabi Mandl states, "Surprisingly, I have become much more productive because I have much less non-research responsibilities ... so I have a lot more time to work on my thesis and produce data for publications." As a doctoral student specifically, Beckella shared some of the challenges of working on her dissertation and balancing other scholarly opportunities.

> Now that things are relatively normalized, I'm productive ... I've also had three incredible opportunities land in my lap in the last few weeks, and I'm able to do those (two of which require extensive writing) because of the time the pandemic has given me. I've found that I have a lot more time to write and that I'm more productive now ...

Some of the participants had much more time to write and focus on their research due to the pandemic, and many of them were able to capitalize on that.

Decreased Attention, Focus, or Motivation

Alternatively, the participants likewise described having their attention, focus, and motivation reduced/canceled altogether by the pandemic. Nell stated, "It killed it. Was hoping to edit a whole chapter in spring and did not have a chance to do anything," along with Evie, who feels the same, saying, "It stopped completely, and I have to work hard just to try and meet deadlines even with taking the leave-break." Andrea describes having "no motivation whatsoever to work [or] study." She further stated that "being locked inside does not help [her] productivity."

Suze had similarly been "much less productive and fallen behind on three projects, including [her] comprehensive exam." She went on to say, "The work I am doing feels like it is lower quality, and I lack the motivation to make daily progress." KS shared she simply does "not get as much work done for sure." She elaborated on that to say, "sometimes [she] feels guilty as [she] has no 'reason' not to work, i.e. [she] has no kids, etc., but still does not manage to get much done."

Beyond just lacking the internal drives to advance scholarly productivity, the pandemic has directly limited some participants' ability to participate in certain scholarly activities. Catherine McCatty could not "collect in-person data, reducing [her] mentorship and publishing abilities." Bextrad discussed reduced AP, academic conferences, and delays in data collection as a doctoral-level graduate student:

I missed two conferences and did one online, but it was very much cobbled together at the last minute. I can't really design a study for September as I don't know what teaching is going to look like. I am also a Ph.D. student (I have allocated time in my schedule for that), but my research definitely took a back seat during the lockdown.

Florence, too, found it more difficult to be productive when working from home than in her office.

All of my work is computational, so the actual work is not a problem; it is just difficult to get into a working mindset ... I am finding it incredibly hard to sit down and write during this. I've completed all the work for a paper, and I just can't seem to get it written no matter how hard I try. My brain can't get the story out.

Other participants' challenges with motivation and drive for AP during the pandemic came from personal demands and expectations they had to attend to after the stay-at-home order began. For example, Claire shared how her AP was not going very well and expressed that "colleagues with kids are coping by controlling what they can, their work and they work a lot, as I probably would too if I were them ... so, it's hard to see because they are raising forward while I am drowning." TSVM, also a parent, shared that her AP "decreased because of the unpredictability of when my child would need me during the day." Due to the uncertainty and challenges associated with the pandemic, motivation, and ability to focus on academic productivity diminished, and in some cases, participants took academic hiatuses.

Academic Hiatus

After completing their coursework, most doctoral-level graduate students are expected to complete a dissertation as the final step in their formal degree requirements. The COVID-19 pandemic has negatively impacted the scholarly activity of some doctoral-level graduate students causing them to have to take an academic hiatus.

Evie had to take leave from her PhD studies due to the pandemic. Although she had support for her supervisor, she shared in her reflection that it was just not enough:

My Ph.D. supervisors have been great, but I wasn't able to maintain progress in line with expected timelines during the pandemic. I'm struggling to get back on track and [my university] basically only has taking a leave of absence as the solution.

Nell indicated that the pandemic caused her to have to take an "unofficial hiatus" as she was unable to work on her dissertation.

> An unofficial hiatus, similar to mid-PhD when I had to take several months off to care for my father when he was terminally ill. In both cases, this was unofficially approved by my advisor/department but not formally requested through the university.

External Drivers of Academic Productivity

The participants in this study also identified external drivers that influenced their AP during the pandemic. For this group, external drivers presented as *decreased* or *maintained* expectations from external bodies such as academic institutions, faculty, supervisors, and advisors.

Decreased Expectations

The participants described decreased expectations of their AP related to external bodies, such as from their institutions, department chairs, program directors, editors, publishers, employers, academic supervisor/advisors, or dissertation chairs. For instance, expectations for Bextrad have become so lax at her workplace regarding AP that "it almost seems to have been forgotten!" TSVM and Nell had a similar experience with understanding supervisors. TSVM stated, "When the lockdown started, our supervisor explicitly ensured us that our personal lives and safety come first and it is fine if this leads to a little slower research productivity," much like Nell's advisor who was "understanding of the halt in productivity ... final task-related expectations are the same, but the timeline was greatly extended wherever possible." To make the necessary adjustments due to the changes brought on by the pandemic, Dog-Mum states they were informed that "for next academic session [they] have been told to focus on either [writing] a grant application or writing a REFable paper, not both; to give space for moving to blended learning."

Maintained Expectations

Participants broadly described the external maintained expectations on their AP during the pandemic. This maintenance of expectations came from their institutions, colleagues, academic supervisors/advisors, and dissertation chairs. Though this can be perceived as harsh while navigating the pandemic and their academics, some see this as a positive push.

M took a practical approach comparing the expectations between faculty and graduate students, ever aware of the unknown, likely longevity of this global pandemic:

> There has been an extra year on the tenure clock for faculty but nothing for grad students; mostly, we are being encouraged to maintain our earlier timelines. I suppose that seems uncaring to some people, but grad school can be such a morass for so many people that I think the department is right to encourage people to maintain their momentum and progress towards a degree.

Darwino, much like M, reported not having reduced academic expectations with the pandemic either, stating, "I still think I need to work more; maybe I feel more so now, especially since the job market is an absolute disaster." Nightskey is facing increased challenges with her data collection as her institution "did not shift their expectations at all" although, "as a public-school teacher, [she] is finding it more difficult to obtain site permission from public schools for research permissions." Even with the struggle of navigating work/life balance during a stay-at-home order, Catherine McCatty is "expected to meet milestones still," and Claire stated, "The expectation has been to continue to do as much as I can ... I am still paying tuition ... I am still expected to check in regularly on progress."

For others, expectations have remained the same with slight variations. ToffeeMaky shared that her expectations are the same, and "France fortunately finally shifted online, so it's easier for [her] to meet their demands." In contrast, Florence described having "slightly more relaxed" timing expectations; however, "the content and level of research are the same." TSVM does not feel any added pressure from her supervisor or research team, as they are all "extremely understanding." She explained, "Because all of [her] colleagues are male and most of them do not have children, [she] is usually less productive than them—before and during the pandemic ... this hasn't changed much."

Having demanding or supportive advisors and supervisors seems to be associated with consistency in maintained scholarly productivity expectations. Amyrlin shared that for her, not much has changed regarding expectations, further elaborating:

> I was co-authoring an article with my advisor and a couple other members of her research team when this started. We slowed down for a few weeks but we got it submitted only a month later than planned. Otherwise, there really hasn't been any change.

Academic expectations for KS have not shifted either as she recalled "still having the same deadlines etc. ... [but her] supervisors have always

A Descriptive Phenomenological Study   69

been very chill about what [she] sent in, though, so they haven't been too harsh on [her] sending less work to them." Andrea had tougher experiences in those scholarly expectations "have not shifted for [her]. [Her] advisor, especially during the beginning of the pandemic and state's lockdown, was still demanding even though there was no way to go into work and acquire data."

DISCUSSION

This study contributes to a greater understanding of the challenges that multinational female graduate students faced at the onset of the COVID-19 pandemic. While the pandemic may have been a unique situation, it exposed or provided an opportunity to discuss the challenges and stressors that students, especially multinational female students, face when pursuing a graduate degree. In looking at the findings, this study builds upon the body of literature by engaging with multinational female graduate students. As with some pre-pandemic studies, there were points where graduate students felt burnout and exhaustion (Hunter & Devine, 2016; Wolf & Rosenstock, 2017); however, the pandemic may have added to these feelings. Furthermore, there are several issues that, when combined with pandemic stressors, could negatively influence students broadly.

The findings suggest that the pandemic had a mixed influence on multinational female graduate students' AP and their mental well-being. While some found the work-from-home (WFH) opportunity allowed for focused research and class time, others found the situation detrimental to their productivity. For those with increased AP, the common themes were that they had more time to focus and write. Developing these intrinsic motivations to write is essential to AP, as finding time to write is often a concern of academics, as evidenced by numerous writing groups that academics can participate in. Those who found the situation a detriment to their AP often reported that their productivity stopped completely due to a lack of motivation and/or other obligations taking precedence. The lack of motivation may not be surprising as stress has strongly been found to have an inverse relationship with motivations for academic productivity during the pandemic (Ogilvie et al., 2020; Rahe & Jansen, 2021). Additionally, the lack of opportunities for extrinsic motivational factors to impact their progress may have contributed to the lack of AP.

Cross-Cultural and Feminist Perspectives

No significant cross-cultural differences emerged in the factors influencing female graduate students' AP or motivations implying that the pandemic had a similar effect on students from all countries. The conditions surrounding female graduate student experiences may be more universal than previously thought (Ogilvie et al., 2020). This may be because challenges and stressors are particularly academic and enhanced by the pandemic (Andrade et al., 2023), not cultural differences. Alternatively, we understand that gender inequality contributes to female graduate students' AP and motivational challenges. Feminist theory helps us to understand how gender roles and expectations shape women's educational experiences and how sexism and discrimination impact women's academic productivity and motivation, especially in a global pandemic (Leavy & Harris, 2018).

Faculty Expectations and Interactions

Faculty expectations and interactions impacted productivity as well. As faculty shifted to online instruction, students felt lower expectations from their mentors, thus hindering their motivation to produce high-quality work. While faculty may have lowered expectations due to online course revisions, students reported that mentors understood the pandemic would slow progress. Support from research advisors is critical to graduate student success (Blanchard & Haccoun, 2019). This suggests lowered expectations slowed progress, but it is too early to say what the impact of the return to the "new normal" will be on students who may be behind due to faculty leniency. Students who experienced faculty that maintained expectations felt a disconnect because they noticed that faculty were given consideration for reduced productivity, such as an extension of the tenure clock, yet students were not. This hints at an academic hierarchy where graduate students are seen as workhorses. Interestingly, a common complaint from students who reported maintained expectations was that they were left to find their own way to overcome challenges such as loss of lab time, decreased access to technology, and decreased access to library resources. It is important to remember that not all students have the same access to technology and software working from home as they did on campus prior to the global shutdown.

Factors for Success

There is no easy answer to help graduate students maintain AP during a pandemic or other stressful situation. However, the lived experiences of female graduate students point to some specific items universities and mentors can take to ensure student success. These steps include: (1) keeping the lines of communication clear regarding motivations and expectations, (2)

A Descriptive Phenomenological Study   71

encouraging and bringing graduate students into faculty research projects in meaningful and insightful ways while keeping the authorship expectations clear, (3) providing multiple levels of support for graduate students such as scheduled mentoring sessions or weekly webinars, and being transparent in university communications, and (4) creating a more inclusive and supportive environment for culturally diverse and underrepresented groups.

Considering that graduate students are the next generation of faculty and administrators, it is essential that universities find a better way to identify, acknowledge, and assist them through their education. The experiences they have as graduate students will inform their scholarly activities, their mentoring, and their interactions in the classroom. Faculty who are understanding but have high expectations for their students can help those students achieve their goals in supportive and challenging environments.

Conclusion

Our study found that internal and external factors influenced female graduate students' AP. However, many students demonstrated resilience as they strived to find the right balance between adjusting to the world of the pandemic while desiring pre-pandemic academia. To better support students, institutions, and advisors should continue encouraging graduate students to prioritize their mental health, communicate expectations, encourage accountability, promote a growth mindset, and increase resources for their empowerment and academic success. This initiative cannot exist in a vacuum—federal governments and governing bodies must allocate funding for schools that must be shared with the students through human capital, learning materials, and extracurricular resources for socioemotional well-being. Students of the new Millenium have overcome numerous crises, including the terrorist attacks on 9/11, Hurricane Katrina, the 2008 economic recession, and other cultural shifts. Nevertheless, with adequate support, students can persevere through crises and minimize stress (Fernando & Hebert, 2011; Pascoe et al., 2020).

ACKNOWLEDGEMENTS

We have no known conflicts of interest to disclose. We want to acknowledge and thank the other members of the COVID G.A.P. (Gendered Academic Productivity) research team for their support in this ongoing, global collaborative project; listed in alphabetical order: Anoud Abusalim, Sara Bender, Stefani Boutelier, Kristina S. Brown, Hala Guta, Deanna L. Hensley, Joanne

Hessmiller, Agata Lambrechts, Pipiet Larasatie, Iwona Leonowicz-Bukała, Alpha A. Martínez-Suárez, Shikha Prashad, and Olga Vega. Detailed information on the collaborative team and subgroups' focus areas can be found at https://www.covidgap.co.uk/. We also thank Cathy Mazak, academic writing coach and administrator of the I Should Be Writing Facebook group (decommissioned), for allowing us to communicate, collaborate, and assemble to launch the first phase of this international, multi-institutional, interdisciplinary research initiative.

REFERENCES

Acker, S., & Armenti, C. (2004). Sleepless in academia. *Gender and Education*, *16*(1), 3–24. https://doi.org/10.1080/0954025032000170309

Allen, H. K., Barrall, A. L., Vincent, K. B., & Arria, A. M. (2020). Stress and burnout among graduate students: Moderation by sleep duration and quality. *International Journal of Behavioral Medicine*, *28*(1), 21–28. https://doi.org/10.1007/s12529-020-09867-8

Andrade, D., Ribeiro, I. J. S., & Máté, O. (2023). Academic burnout among master and doctoral students during the COVID-19 pandemic. *Scientific Reports*, *13*(1), 4745. https://doi.org/10.1038/s41598-023-31852-w

Arceño, R. (2018). Motivations and expectations of graduate students of the College of Advanced Education (CAEd). *International Journal of Social Sciences*, *4*(1), 239–256. https://dx.doi.org/10.20319/pijss.2018.41.239256

Avorgbedor, F., & Vilme, H. (2021). The dual role of students pursuing a higher degree and providing care to their children and family members during the COVID-19 pandemic. *European Journal of Education Studies, 8*(12), 161–173. https://doi.org/10.46827/ejes.v8i12.4018

Batterson, S. E. (2004). *Graduate women's survival in academia: Identifying specific sources of stress and valuable coping strategies for females in doctoral clinical psychology programs* (3133428). [Doctoral Dissertation, Alliant International University]. ProQuest Dissertations Publishing.

Blanchard, C., & Haccoun, R. R. (2019). Investigating the impact of advisor support on the perceptions of graduate students. *Teaching in Higher Education*, 25(8), 1010–1027. https://doi.org/10.1080/13562517.2019.1632825

Boitet, L. M., Estep, C., Schwiebert, L. M., Upshaw, K., Wolfner, C., Hutson Chatham, A., Garner, S., Stowe, A., & Lanzi, R. G. (2022). Racism and racial injustice during COVID-19: Impact on university student mental health. *MedRxiv*, 2022–08. https://doi.org/10.1101/2022.08.30.22279409

Borjas, G. J., Doran, K. B., & Shen, Y. (2016). Ethnic complementarities after the opening of China: How Chinese graduate students affected the productivity of their advisors. *The Journal of Human Resources*, *53*(1), 1–31. https://doi.org/10.3368/jhr.53.1.0516-7949R

Bullock, A., Colvin, A. D., & Jackson, M. S. (2022). Zoom fatigue in the age of COVID-19. *Journal of Social Work in the Global Community, 7*(1), 1–9. https://doi.org/10.5590/JSWGC.2022.07.1.01

A Descriptive Phenomenological Study   73

Carpenter, S., (2008). A study of graduate student authorship in journalism and mass communication journals: 1997–2006. *Journalism and Mass Communication Educator*. *63*(3), 224–240. https://doi.org/10.1177%2F107769580806300303

Chance, N., Farwell, T. M., & Hessmiller, J. (2022). Exploring scholarly productivity, supports, and challenges of multinational, female graduate students during a global pandemic. *Journal of Comparative & International Higher Education, 14*(3A), 69–87. https://doi.org/10.32674/jcihe.v14i3%20(Part%201).4168

Cohen, J. S., & Miller, L. J. (2009). Interpersonal mindfulness training for well-being: A pilot study with psychology graduate students. *Teachers College Record, 111*(12), 2760–2774. https://doi.org/10.1177/016146810911101202

Creswell, J. W. (2013). *Qualitative inquiry & research design: Choosing among five approaches* (3rd ed.). SAGE.

Creswell, J. W., & Miller, D. L. (2000). Determining validity in qualitative inquiry. *Theory into Practice, 39*(3), 124–130. https://doi.org/10.1207/s15430421tip3903_2

DeRobertis, E., & Bland, A. M. (2020). From personal threat to cross-cultural learning: An eidetic investigation. *Journal of Phenomenological Psychology, 51*(1), 1–15. https://doi.org/10.1163/15691624-12341368

DeRobertis, E. M. (2017). *The phenomenology of learning and becoming.* Palgrave McMillan.

Dong, F., Hwang, Y., & Hodgson, N. A. (2022). Relationships between racial discrimination, social isolation, and mental health among international Asian graduate students during the COVID-19 pandemic. *Journal of American College Health,* 1–8. https://doi.org/10.1080/07448481.2022.2052076

Dönmez, P. E. (2022). The COVID-19 pandemic, academia, gender, and beyond: A review. *Publications, 10*(3), 1–13. https://doi.org/10.3390/publications10030030

Donohue, W. J., Lee, A. S. J., Simpson, S., & Vacek, K. (2021). Impacts of the COVID-19 pandemic on doctoral students' thesis/dissertation progress. *International Journal of Doctoral Studies, 16,* 533–552. https://doi.org/10.28945/4818

Enriquez, L. E., Morales, A. E., Rodriguez, V. E., Chavarria, K., & Ro, A. (2023). Mental health and COVID-19 pandemic stressors among Latina/o/x college students with varying self and parental immigration status. *Journal of Racial and Ethnic Health Disparities 10,* 282–295.
https://doi.org/10.1007/s40615-021-01218-x

Farrell, E. (2020). Researching lived experience in education: Misunderstood or missed opportunity? *International Journal of Qualitative Methods, 19,* 1–8.
https://doi.org/10.1177/1609406920942066

Fatima, N. (2001, April). *International female graduate students' perceptions of their adjustment experiences and coping strategies at an urban research university* [Paper presentation]. The American Educational Research Association Annual Meeting, Seattle, WA.

Fernando, D. M., & Hebert, B. B. (2011). Resiliency and recovery: Lessons from the Asian tsunami and Hurricane Katrina. *Journal of Multicultural Counseling and Development, 39*(1), 2–13.
https://doi.org/10.1002/j.2161-1912.2011.tb00135.x

Gardner, S. A., Salto, L. M., Riggs, M. L., Casiano, C. A., & De Leon, M. (2018). Supporting the writing productivity of biomedical graduate students: An integrated, structured writing intervention. *CBE Life Sciences Education. 17*(3), 1-10. https://doi.org/10.1187/cbe.16-12-0350

Giorgi, A. P., (2009). *The descriptive phenomenological method in psychology: A modified Husserlian approach.* Duquesne University Press.

Giorgi, A. P., (2012). The descriptive phenomenological psychological method. *Journal of Phenomenological Psychology, 43*(1) 3–12. https://doi.org/10.1163/156916212X632934

Giorgi, A. P., & Giorgi, B. M. (2003). The descriptive phenomenological psychological method. In P. M. Camic, J. E. Rhodes, & L. Yardley (Eds.), *Qualitative research in psychology: Expanding perspectives in methodology and design* (pp. 243–273). American Psychological Association. https://doi.org/10.1037/10595-013

Goldberg, S. B. (2021, June 9). *Education in a pandemic: The disparate impacts of COVID-19 on America's students.* U.S. Department of Education, Office for Civil Rights. https://www2.ed.gov/about/offices/list/ocr/docs/20210608-impacts-of-covid19.pdf

Goldstone, R., & Zhang, J. (2021). Postgraduate research students' experiences of the COVID-19 pandemic and student-led policy solutions. *Educational Review, 74*(3), 422–443. https://doi.org/10.1080/00131911.2021.1974348

Gurukkal, R. (2020). Will COVID-19 turn higher education into another mode? *Higher Education for the Future, 7*(2), 89–96. https://doi.org/10.1177/2347631120931606

Hotez, E., Gragnani, C. M., Fernandes, P., Rosenau, K. A., Wang, K., Chopra, A., Chow, K., Chung, A., Khorasani, L., & Kuo, A. A. (2022). A mixed methods investigation of college student mental health during the first year of the COVID-19 pandemic. *Journal of American College Health,* 1–8. https://doi.org/10.1080/07448481.2022.2089842

Hunter, K. H., & Devine, K. (2016). Doctoral students' emotional exhaustion and intentions to leave academia. In*ternational Journal of Doctoral Studies, 11*(2), 35–61. http://ijds.org/Volume11/IJDSv11p035-061Hunter2198.pdf

Hyun, J. K., Quinn, B. C., Madon, T., Lustig, S. (2006). Graduate student mental health: Needs assessment and utilization of counseling services. *Journal of College Student Development, 47*(3), 247–266. https://doi.org/10.1353/csd.2006.0030

Jenei, K., Cassidy-Matthews, C., Virk, P., Lulie, B., & Closson, K. (2020). Challenges and opportunities for graduate students in public health during the COVID-19 pandemic. *Canadian Journal of Public Health, 111*, 408–409. https://doi.org/10.17269/s41997-020-00349-8

Kernan, W., Bogart, J., & Wheat, M. E. (2011). Health-related barriers to learning among graduate students. *Health Education, 111*(5), 425–445. https://doi.org/10.1108/09654281111161248

Kramer, J., (2020, August 12). Women in science may suffer lasting career damage from COVID-19. *Scientific American.* https://www.scientificamerican.com/article/women-in-science-may-suffer-lasting-career-damage-from-covid-19/

Kruks, S. (2014). *Women's 'lived experience': Feminism and phenomenology from Simone de Beauvoir to the present.* SAGE. https://doi.org/10.4135/9781473909502

A Descriptive Phenomenological Study   75

Leavy, P., & Harris, A. (2018). *Contemporary feminist research from theory to practice.* Guilford.

Lincoln, Y. S., & Guba, E. G. (1985). *Naturalistic inquiry.* SAGE.

Lynch, M. F., Salikhova, N. R., & Salikhova, A. (2018). Internal motivation among doctoral students: Contributions from the student and from the student's environment. *International Journal of Doctoral Studies, 13*, 255–272. https://doi.org/10.28945/4091

Macfarlane, B., & Burg, D. (2019). Women professors and the academic housework trap. *Journal of Higher Education Policy and Management, 41*(3), 262–274. https://doi.org/10.1080/1360080X.2019.1589682

Magalhães-Alves, C., Barbosa, J. Ribiero, L., & Ferreira, M. A. (2017), Graduates in the medicine course: Motivations, socialization and academic recognition. *Scientific Journal of the Portuguese Medical Association, 30*(4), 285–292. https://doi.org/10.20344/amp.8400

Maher, M. A., Ford, M. E., & Thompson, C. M. (2004). Degree progress of women doctoral students: Factors that constrain, facilitate, and differentiate. *The Review of Higher Education, 27*(3), 385–408. https://doi.org/10.1353/rhe.2004.0003

Malisch, J. L., Harris, B. N., Sherrer, S. M., Lewis, K. A., Shepherd, S. L., McCarthy, P. C., Spott, J. L., Karam, E. P., Moustaid-Moussa, N., McCrory Calarco, J., Ramalingam, L., Talley, A. E., Cañas-Carrell, J. E., Ardon-Dryer, K., Weiser, D. A., Bernal, X. E., & Deitloff, J. (2020). In the wake of COVID-19, academia needs new solutions to ensure gender equity. *Proceedings of the National Academy of Sciences, 117*(27), 15378–15381. https://doi.org/10.1073/pnas.2010636117

McCready, R., & Vecsey, S. (2013). Supporting the postgraduate demonstrator: Embedding development opportunities into the day job. *Practice and Evidence of the Scholarship of Teaching and Learning in Higher Education, 8*(2), 104–111. https://pestlhe.org/index.php/pestlhe/article/view/79

Morley, L., & Crossouard, B. (2016). Gender in the neoliberalised global academy: the affective economy of women and leadership in South Asia. *British Journal of Sociology of Education, 37*(1), 149–168. https://doi.org/10.1080/01425692.2015.1100529

Myers, K. R., Tham, W. Y., Yin, Y., Cohodes, N., Thursby, J. G., Thursby, M. C., Schiffer, P., Walsh, J. T., Lakhani, K. R., & Wang, D. (2020). Unequal effects of the COVID-19 pandemic on scientists. *Nature Human Behaviour, 4*(9), 880–883. https://doi.org/10.1038/s41562-020-0921-y

Nicholson, M., Bennett, J. M., Modesto, O., & Gould, R. (2023). Understanding university students during COVID-19: A longitudinal mixed-methods analysis of their experiences of online learning, mental health, academic engagement, and academic self-efficacy. *Psychopathology*, 1–17. https://doi.org/10.1159/000528441

Obuku, E. A., Lavis, J. N., Kinengyere, A., Ssenono, R., Ocan, M., Mafigiri, D. K., Ssengooba, F., Karamagi, C., & Sweankambo, N. K. (2018). A systemic review on academic research productivity of postgraduate students in low- and middle-income countries. *Health research and Policy Systems, 16*(86), 1–8. https://doi.org/10.1186/s12961-018-0360-7

Ogilvie, C., Brooks, T. R., Ellis, C., Gowen, G., Knight, K., Perez, R. J., Rodriguez, S. L., Schweppe, N., Smith, L. L., & Smith, R. A. (2020, December). *NSF rapid: Graduate student experiences of support and stress during the COVID-19 pandemic*. National Science Foundation. https://www.montana.edu/covid19_rapid/updated%20NSF_RAPID_GraduateStudentExperiences_Covid19_White_Paper.pdf

Oleschuk, M. (2020). Gender equity considerations for tenure and promotion during COVID-19. *Canadian Review of Sociology, 57*(3), 502–515. https://doi.org/10.1111/cars.12295

Oswalt, S. B., & Riddock, C. C. (2007). What to do about being overwhelmed: graduate students, stress and university services. *Journal of College Student Affairs, 27*(1), 24–44. https://eric.ed.gov/?id=EJ899402

Pascoe, M. C., Hetrick, S. E., & Parker, A. G. (2020). The impact of stress on students in secondary school and higher education. *International Journal of Adolescence and Youth, 25*(1), 104–112. https://doi.org/10.1080/02673843.2019.1596823

Power, K. (2020). The COVID-19 pandemic has increased the care burden of women and families. *Sustainability: Science, Practice and Policy, 16*(1), 67–73. https://doi.org/10.1080/15487733.2020.1776561

Quigley, J. L., Schmuldt, L., Todd, S., & Bender, S. (2021). Do something different as an intervention for perceived stress reduction in graduate counseling students. *Journal of Technology in human services, 40*(1), 1–24. https://doi.org/10.1080/15228835.2021.1904324

Rahe, M., & Jansen, P. (2021). Understanding the relationship between perceived stress and academic motivation in college students during the coronavirus pandemic. *International Journal of Educational Research Open, 100109*, 1–21. https://doi.org/10.1016/j.ijedro.2021.100109

Rizvi, S. L., Finkelstein, J., Wacha-Montes, A., Yeager, A. L., Ruork, A. K., Yin, Q., Kellerman, J., Kim, J. S., Stern, M., Oshin, L. A., & Kleiman, E. M. (2022). Randomized clinical trial of a brief, scalable intervention for mental health sequelae in college students during the COVID-19 pandemic. *Behaviour research and Therapy, 149*(2022), 1–10. https://doi.org/10.1016/j.brat.2021.104015

Roche, M. J., & Jacobson, N. C. (2019). Elections have consequences for student mental health: An accidental daily diary study. *Psychological Reports, 122*(2), 451–464. https://doi.org/10.1177/0033294118767365

Ryan, B. J. (2014). Graduate teaching assistants; critical colleagues or casual components in the undergraduate laboratory learning? An exploration of the role of the postgraduate teacher in the sciences. *European Journal of Science and Mathematics Education, 2*(2), 98–105. https://doi.org/10.21427/D7T045

Ryan, B. (2015). Postgraduates: How can national policy centralise this forgotten tribe and celebrate their skills in tackling the challenges of higher education. *All Ireland Journal of Higher Education, 7*(2). http://ojs.aishe.org/index.php/aishe-j/article/view/208

Schneider, M., & Preckel, F. (2017). Variables associated with achievement in higher education: A systematic review of meta-analyses. *Psychological Bulletin, 143*(6), 565–600. http://dx.doi.org/10.1037/bul0000098

A Descriptive Phenomenological Study   77

Stilwell, S. B., Vermeesch, A. L., & Scott, J. G. (2017). Interventions to reduce perceived stress among graduate students: A systematic review with implications for evidence-based practice. *Worldviews on Evidence-Based Nursing*, *14*(6), 507–513. https://doi.org/10.1111/wvn.12250

Stolz, S. (2020). Phenomenology and phenomenography in educational research: a critique. *Educational Philosophy and Theory*, *52*(10), 1077–1096. https://doi.org/10.1080/00131857.2020.1724088

Sustarsic, M., & Zhang, J. (2021). Navigating through uncertainty in the era of COVID-19: Experiences of international graduate students in the United States. *Journal of International Students*, *12*(1), 61–80. https://doi.org/10.32674/jis.v12i1.3305

Swanson, H. L., Pierre-Louis, C., Monjaras-Gaytan, L. Y., Zinter, K. E., McGarity-Palmer, R., & Clark Withington, M. H. (2022). Graduate student workload: Pandemic challenges and recommendations for accommodations. *Journal of Community Psychology*, *50*(5), 2225–2242. https://doi.org/10.1002/jcop.22769

Tranquillo, J., & Stecker, M. (2016). Using intrinsic and extrinsic motivation in continuing professional education. *Surgical Neurology International*, *7*(Suppl 7), S197–S199. https://doi.org/10.4103%2F2152-7806.179231

Tucker, S., Layson-Wolf, C., Coop, A., Lebovitz, L., & Anagnostou, G. (2021). Combating 'Zoom-fatigue': A comprehensive approach to academic program adaptation and supporting digital wellness during COVID-19. In T. Bastiaens (Ed.), *Proceedings of EdMedia + Innovate Learning* (pp. 727–731). Association for the Advancement of Computing in Education (AACE). https://www.learntechlib.org/primary/p/219734/

Wang, X., Hegde, S., Son, C., Keller, B., Smith, A., & Sasangohar, F. (2020). Investigating mental health of US college students during the COVID-19 pandemic: Cross-sectional survey study. *Journal of Medical Internet Research*, *22*(9), e22817. https://doi.org/10.2196/22817

Wasil, A. R., Taylor, M. E., Franzen, R. E., Steinberg, J. S., & DeRubeis, R. J. (2021). Promoting graduate student mental health during COVID-19: Acceptability, feasibility, and perceived utility of an online single-session intervention. *Frontiers in Psychology*, *12*. https://doi.org/10.3389/fpsyg.2021.569785

White, R. W. (1959). Motivation reconsidered: The concept of competence. *Psychological Review*, *66*(5), 297–333. https://doi.org/10.1037/h0040934

Wolf, M. R., & Rosenstock, J. B. (2017). Inadequate sleep and exercise associated with burnout and depression among medical students. *Academic Psychiatry*, *41*(2), 174–179. https://doi.org/10.1007/s40596-016-0526-y

Xu, X. (2017, Fall). Researchers' positioning: insider or outsider? *The Morning Watch: Educational and Social Analysis*, *44*(1–2), 1–6. https://journals.library.mun.ca/ojs/index.php/mwatch/article/view/1748/1356

CHAPTER 4

FIRST GENERATION COLLEGE STUDENTS' HEALTH AND WELL-BEING, ACADEMIC ENGAGEMENT, AND SENSE OF SELF DURING THE COVID-19 GLOBAL PANDEMIC

Megan K. Rauch Griffard
University of Nevada, Las Vegas

Rex A. Long
Texas State University

Cassandra R. Davis
University of North Carolina at Chapel Hill

ABSTRACT

As the U.S. transitions from a pandemic to an endemic status for the novel coronavirus (COVID-19), it is important that institutions prepare for the long-term impacts that the pandemic, lockdowns, and long periods of isolation have had on individuals. In higher education, one such group that has been particularly affected by the pandemic is first-generation college students (FGCS). Prior research has found that FGCS face considerably greater obstacles in navigating and persisting in higher education compared with

---

Research on College Stress and Coping: Implications From the COVID-19 Pandemic and Beyond, pp. 79–108
Copyright © 2024 by Information Age Publishing
www.infoagepub.com
All rights of reproduction in any form reserved.

their non-FGCS peers. This study investigated how the pandemic influenced FGCS' (1) health and well-being and (2) academic engagement and success, and (3) sense of self. We employed an explanatory sequential mixed methods research design to make deeper meaning of the problems that FGCS faced during school closures. We found that the transition to remote learning severely disrupted students' living arrangements, economic security, and overall well-being. Despite these obstacles, most participants' sense of self and determination to complete their education remained stable. Because the instruments employed in our study specifically targeted FGCS experiences and data was collected across multiple universities, our work adds new understanding to how the pandemic impacted FGCS.

HOW THE COVID-19 PANDEMIC INFLUENCED FIRST GENERATION COLLEGE STUDENTS' HEALTH, WELL-BEING, AND SENSE OF SELF

This study investigated how first-generation college students' (FGCS) physical and mental health and academic experiences and performance were impacted by the university closures due to the COVID-19 pandemic. We also investigated what support they received from their universities during school closures and whether their sense of self was changed as a result of the challenges they experienced during the pandemic. Starting in March 2020, the COVID-19 pandemic caused most U.S. colleges and universities to physically close for prolonged periods of time. Nationwide shutdowns and social distancing policies lead to various disruptions in the lives of their students. However, a variety of socioeconomic and contextual factors likely amplified difficulties for FGCS during this time. The study contributes to the growing need for policymakers and educational leaders to understand the impacts of the COVID-19 pandemic on student experiences, especially for students from marginalized and underrepresented groups, such as FGCS.

Prior research suggests that FGCS already experience numerous challenges to success in college. Results show that they experience more difficult transitions to college, have lower rates of persistence, and are less likely to graduate within six years—or graduate at all (Lohfink & Pauleson, 2005; Pascarella et al., 2004; Postsecondary National Policy Institute [PNPI], 2021; Redford & Hoyer, 2017; Terenzini et al., 1996; Toutkoushian, 2021). Compared with continuing-generation college students (CGCS), FGCS also have fewer role models in the family, less family support, and less familiarity with the higher education environment (PNPI, 2021). FGCS often come from families with lower household incomes, are more likely members of marginalized racial/ethnic groups and frequently report encountering racial discrimination on campus (Bettencourt et al., 2022; Forbus et al., 2011).

First Generation College Students' Health and Well-Being   81

Early research on the pandemic has shown that FGCS may have been disproportionately affected by hardships related to COVID-19 compared with CGCS. These hardships include loss of income, increased stress, and lowered well-being (Bono et al., 2020; Fruehwirth et al., 2021; Soria et al., 2020). FGCS who moved home with their families also reported new or resumed personal responsibilities, such as taking care of siblings or other family members (Soria et al., 2020). Some FGCS also suffered from depression or isolation as a result of the pandemic (Soria et al., 2020; Fruewirth et al., 2021). Rates of infection, serious illness, and deaths were also higher among low-income communities and communities of color (Gracia et al., 2020). FGCS often struggled with remote learning. In a sample of 121 students, Gonzalez-Ramirez et al. (2021) identified several barriers to remote learning including Wi-Fi quality (60%), hardware (36%), video software (43%), other software (15%), finding a quiet space (71%), and finances (45%). These challenges were reported to be higher among FGCS.

Despite these obstacles, FGCS often demonstrate considerable resilience to the challenges they face during their undergraduate careers (Verdín et al., 2018). Our study investigates how FGCS encountered additional barriers during remote learning and the extent these obstacles impacted their determination to graduate college. We identify the areas where students felt the greatest impacts of the pandemic and how they responded. We then show how these challenges have affected students' long-term visions for their futures and their self-perceptions.

CONCEPTUAL FRAMEWORK

The conceptual framework for this study is shaped by two related psychological theories that explain how individuals perceive themselves and the world around them, as well as how obstacles can problematize these perceptions. The first theory guiding the study was the sense of self theory. The theory was popularized in psychotherapy in the first half of the 20th century. Spiegel (1959) described the sense of self as an individual's awareness and ability to differentiate the body and consciousness from the outside world. Prebble and colleagues (2013) developed a framework for the sense of self, arguing that it is composed of two dimensions, the subjective self and the content of self. The subjective self is the "conscious, phenomenological experience of selfhood" (Prebble et al., p. 816). The content of self is the "mental representation of all things we perceive and know about ourselves" (p. 817). Individuals can have either a weak or strong sense of self, with the former having sudden and dramatic shifts in values and choices in short periods of time and the latter showing more stability (Flury & Ickes, 2007). In our study, we expected that many FGCS will report having a strong sense of self, even in spite of the difficulties arising from the pandemic for two reasons. First, Lichtenberg (1975) posited that an individual's sense of self is typically fully formed by adolescence. Second, as Verdín and colleagues (2018) found, FGCS often demonstrate considerable resilience and determination to overcome obstacles they encounter during their undergraduate careers. For these reasons, we hypothesized that the difficulties they experienced during distance learning, many of which may be related to their FGCS status (e.g., financial impacts, access to quiet study spaces, etc.), would not fundamentally alter how FGCS perceived themselves. In fact, we expected that many students would report feeling stronger and more resilient for having navigated these challenges.

The study is also framed by a social-cognitive approach to human agency. Defined by Bandura (2002), social cognitive theory posits that an individual's thinking and behavior are shaped by the environment and context in which the individual is situated. Accordingly, changes in environment and context would lead to corresponding changes in thinking and behavior. The study examined changes in FGCS' environments due to university closures. We anticipated that these environmental changes would lead to changes in thinking and behavior, particularly around FGCS' health and academics.

Specifically, we expected that students' overall health, well-being and academic experiences would likely be diminished. A survey conducted by the Student Experience in the Research University (SERU) across nine universities found that FGCS were more likely to experience financial hardships, lack of access to safe and stable housing, and a lack of access to the technology and environment suitable for learning (Soria et al., 2020). In a related paper, Soria and colleagues from SERU (2022) found that FGCS were more likely to report experiencing depression and anxiety than the national average. Similarly, Davis et al. (2021) found that FGCS felt more overwhelmed, lonely, and stressed during the pandemic compared to how they felt before. FGCS in the study also reported having additional family responsibilities and financial obligations during the pandemic. Researchers at UCLA also found that FGCS and underrepresented minorities were more likely to be responsible for helping siblings with remote learning, as well as increased economic and food insecurity (Barber et al., 2021). Additionally, Umeda and colleagues (2023) found that among FGCS who were experiencing food insecurity due to the pandemic, overall health and student GPA declined.

In addition to the negative outcomes associated with their status as FCGS, we anticipated that study participants would also be impacted by the general mental health, physical health, and academic difficulties that were ubiquitous to many individuals during the pandemic. From a mental health perspective, early research into the pandemic showed that stress, depression,

First Generation College Students' Health and Well-Being   83

and anxiety increased among adults in the United States (Ettman et al., 2020; North, 2020; Vahratian et al., 2021). From a physical health perspective, contracting COVID-19, especially without vaccination, could lead to long-term physical and cognitive impairment or death (Centers for Disease Control and Prevention, 2020 and 2021; Taquet et al., 2021). In addition, research has shown that the pandemic contributed to an increase in other unhealthy behaviors, such as a sedentary lifestyle and increased alcohol and drug use (MacMillan et al., 2021). Moreover, because students have reported negative experiences with remote learning (Gonzalez-Ramirez et al., 2020), we expected that students would be less enthusiastic and engaged academically during university closures. Aristovnik and colleagues (2020) also found that mental health and academic experiences during school closures may be interrelated. The authors explained, "While studying isolated at home, students may face a lack of self-discipline or an inappropriate learning environment, which evokes a feeling of work overload and thus a higher level of stress" (p. 9).

The findings of our study would provide additional insights into the experiences of FGCS during school closures due to the pandemic. The goal of this chapter is to leverage the findings of the study to inform decision-making and planning to support FGCS when future disruptions to in-person school occur.

Research Questions

Coupling the persistent and systematic difficulties that FGCS likely encounter in non-pandemic times with the challenges presented by the pandemic, we asked the following research questions:

1. How did university closures and the transition to distance learning impact FGCS' health and well-being?
2. How did university closures and the transition to distance learning impact FGCS' academic engagement and ability to succeed in college?
3. How did the disruptions to their living and learning environments and other challenges FCG students encountered related to the pandemic influence their senses of self?

METHODS

The research team employed an explanatory sequential mixed methods research design to conduct the study. In this type of research design,

Participants

Eligible participants for the study were undergraduate students who identified as FGCS. Participants were recruited to participate in the study from five U.S. universities. Recruitment began in summer 2020, shortly following the initial transition to distance learning due to the nationwide shutdown of the pandemic. At the time of data collection, participants had completed the second half of the spring 2020 semester remotely. University campuses had plans to reopen in a limited capacity in the fall, with new social distancing measures in place and a large number of courses offered online.

The five universities with participants in the study varied in location, size, and institution type (public or private). Sampled sites fall across four states. Two are located in the northeast and two are located in the southeast. Three colleges represented campuses larger than 15,000 undergraduates compared to two representing less than 10,000. Overall, three identify as public, one identifies as a Historically Black College and University (HBCU), and one as a private liberal arts school. The universities also varied in the proportion of their undergraduate population that identified as FGCS. According to publicly available enrollment data, at two of the large public universities, more than 30% of undergraduates were FGC. One-fifth of undergraduates were FGCS at a third large public university. One-third of undergraduates at the HBCU were first generation. Nine percent of undergraduates at the private liberal arts college were FGC.

The final quantitative sample consisted of 658 students across the five universities who completed an online survey. Most survey respondents attended the three large public universities (83.77%). The remaining students attended the HBCU (12.59%) or the private school (3.64%). The majority of respondents were white (45.60%), followed by Hispanic/ Latinx (22.01%), Asian (11.62%), and Black or African American (8.80%). The majority of respondents also identified as female (70.93%), followed by males (23.70%). Other gender identities (e.g., transgender, genderqueer, questioning, and gender non-conforming) or preferring not to answer comprised the remaining sample (5.37%). Nearly all students (90.44%) attended a school in the state where they live. Students were spread fairly evenly across all their first (26.52%), second (18.20%), third (29.98%), and fourth (23.05%) years of higher education. The

First Generation College Students' Health and Well-Being 85

additional respondents (2.25%) reported being enrolled in some other type of year of higher education.

As part of the survey, students could indicate whether they would be interested in participating in a follow-up interview to share more in-depth about their experiences as FGCS during school closures. A total of 48 students participated in interviews, which took place over Zoom and over the phone. These interviews compose a qualitative sample.

Data Collection and Methods

Following the explanatory sequential research design, we first deployed a survey to collect quantitative data, which then informed the direction of qualitative data collection. The purpose of the qualitative strand of the study is to inform, better explain, and provide deeper, richer interpretations than the quantitative results alone (Creswell & Plano Clark, 2018). Both the qualitative and quantitative stages of the study were designed to address all research questions. With the quantitative data, we sought to understand how large the impact of the pandemic was on FGCS' health, well-being, academic engagement, and sense of self on a large sample of FGCS. With the qualitative sample, we sought to explore more specifically the ways in which these factors were impacted by FGCS in their own words. The survey allowed for a broad understanding of experiences, while in-depth semi-structured interviews granted the opportunity to obtain a more granular understanding of FGCS experiences. Accordingly, this approach allowed us to leverage qualitative data to provide more in-depth understandings of the experiences of FGCS that were observed in the quantitative data.

Quantitative Data Collection

The research team developed the survey using three key concepts from the literature and conceptual framework. First, the instruments were based on prior research on FCG students' experiences and the barriers they often face to having a successful college experience, such as a lack of preparedness for the academic rigor and hidden curriculum of higher education, limited family and financial support, and fewer feelings of connectedness and belonging to college life than non-FGCS. Second, the instruments were also informed by early research about how the pandemic caused increased stress for many individuals and disrupted schooling for learners across the world. Third, the instruments were guided by the conceptual framework,

86 M. K. RAUCH GRIFFARD, R. A. LONG, and C. R. DAVIS

as we considered how the obstacles FGCS faced during the pandemic may have impacted their sense of self.

Quantitative Measures

Quantitative data was derived from online surveys administered across the five universities across four U.S. states in the spring of 2020. Due to the urgency of collecting the data while students' experiences during the pandemic were still fresh and ongoing, the surveys were developed by the research team. In alignment with the research questions for the study, the survey was intended to capture FGCS' experiences during distance learning, especially as it related to their health, well-being, academic engagement, and overall sense of self. We partnered with university officials to identify eligible students and disseminate the survey invitation via campus listservs to FGCS, who could then opt whether to complete the survey. In total, 658 students completed the survey. Because each university was responsible for disseminating the survey to their FGCS via internal channels of communication, we could not have information about how the listservs were compiled, whether all FGCS receive the emails, and how many students on a particular university's listserv actually read the emails from the listserv regularly. Therefore, we are not able to calculate the survey response rate.

Question topics included students' ratings of the quality of their health and well-being (RQ1), including their relationships with others (RQ1); learning experiences and opportunities, their ability to study and feel engaged with schoolwork, and their connectedness to campus (RQ2); and how these factors influence their senses of self (RQ3). The survey consisted primarily of multiple choice and yes/no question types. For multiple-choice questions, respondents were asked to rate their experiences related to university closures due to the pandemic on 5-point Likert scales, with five as the highest rating and one as the lowest. The precise wording for these scales varied according to the question asked, with some asking for a rating from excellent to poor and others asking for a rating from very negative to very positive. For the binary response question types, respondents were asked whether a particular survey item did or did not apply to them before and during the pandemic. Demographic information, including the name of their school, year in school, majors and minors, race and ethnicity, and gender, were also collected. The estimated time it took respondents to complete the survey was between 10 and 20 minutes.

Quantitative Data Analysis

Quantitative data were analyzed using the features of Qualtrics, an online survey software, as well as Stata and Microsoft Excel. Descriptive statistics were then compiled related to each research question.

Qualitative Instruments

Two separate datasets—open-ended survey responses and in-depth interview data compose the qualitative data for the study. The survey presented students with several optional open-ended questions in which they could share specific recommendations for their campus officials about how to improve their distance learning experience and provide better overall support for FGCS.

Qualitative Data Collection

At the end of the quantitative survey, respondents could also indicate whether they were interested in being contacted for an in-depth follow-up interview. With the research questions in mind, the interview guide was organized to gain insight into the areas of general pandemic experiences, specific impacts to health, changes in living and/or work situation following campus shutdowns, the experiences and challenges of transitioning to remote learning, and the aspects of life and education in which students felt they were or were not supported by their institution. The interview guide was designed to be semi-structured; this approach allows for standardization in analysis, while giving space for organic, on-the-spot follow-up questions as students share their personal experiences.

In total, 45 FGCS participated in interviews. Interested participants were contacted by a member of the research team to set up a time for the interview. Each interview lasted approximately 60 minutes. The follow-up interviews took place via online video conferencing or over the phone, depending on logistical constraints and participant preference. The interview protocol (see Appendix A) followed a semi-structured format, which enabled interviewers and participants to further probe statements, remarks, and topics of interest (Brinkmann, 2020). The decision to employ a semi-structured format was made because it could best inform the quantitative findings from the survey. As Smith (1995) explained, semi-structured interviews allow participants to reveal more personal and detailed information than can be obtained from survey data.

During interviews and in the open-ended survey questions, participants were asked to share how the pandemic had impacted them personally, academically, what support their schools provided to help students adjust school closures, and what recommendations they would offer their schools to improve support in the event of disasters and pandemics. More specifically, participants were asked to share details about their living situations, job and finances, relationships and social lives, and health and well-being. Academic impacts discussed included engagement and enthusiasm during distance learning, a sense of belonging within the university, confidence in their ability to persist and graduate, and barriers to success. Regarding supports received and recommendations for improving supports, participants were asked to share across a wide array of topics, including academic accountability, empathy—or lack thereof—from faculty and administration, health, and guidance about preventing COVID-19, campus reopening and enforcing social distancing policies, and the availability of needed resources, such as reliable internet and access to food.

Qualitative Data Analysis

Interviews were recorded and transcribed using an automated transcription service. The transcripts were then de-identified and reviewed for accuracy, with a member of the research team correcting transcriptions errors produced by the automation. Cleaned interview transcripts and open-ended survey responses were then uploaded into NVivo Qualitative Software for analysis (QSR International Pty Ltd., 2020). The analysis followed a rigorous, iterative approach rooted in the tenets of content analysis. First, two members of the research team established a baseline *a priori* coding framework based on the study's organizing research questions, literature review, and interview protocol. As an example, based on the literature and the interview protocol, the team knew that students would provide responses to health and well-being, and so "Health" was generated as a parent code before the team began formal analysis. Researchers coded three of the in-depth interviews independently, using the base code book—generated by expectations informed from the literature and protocols—to identify child and sub-child codes. Researchers coded closely to the text during this process, relying heavily on student descriptions of their experiences to inform the generation of code labels (e.g., the "sleep disruption" sub-child was generated based on students describing changes to sleeping patterns).

The researchers then met to compare codes. This process gave room for discussion and agreement around code labels, including relevant inclusion and exclusion criteria, leading to the construction of a revised code book.

First Generation College Students' Health and Well-Being 89

Here, for example, the researchers agreed that "Mental Health," "Physical Health," and "Aids to Health" were relevant child codes to "Health" based on student responses. Researchers met regularly as more interviews were coded, checking agreement with criteria or determining when criteria should be modified—which would lead to re-coding of relevant interview excerpts and revising the code book. After coding, the codebook was reviewed to ensure alignment with the research aims of the study. This process produced deductive framing around expected overarching topics—health, supports, changes to learning environment—while providing space to inductively generate the content of themes within these topics (e.g., mental health impacts as a result of the pandemic). Quotes were then identified to represent common themes across interviews.

Convergence

In the final stage of analysis, the researchers then integrated the quantitative and qualitative data. As Creswell and Plano Clark (2018) explained in their seminal text on mixed methods research, mixing the two strands is integral to the research design and validates the findings. For this study, qualitative data was used to substantiate quantitative findings, as well as provide more depth of understanding. This was possible because the research team designed the qualitative protocol to correlate with the questions asked, and emergent findings of, the survey instrument. This integration also allowed the research team to make larger inferences about FCG students' health and well-being, stressors, and sense of self during school closures due to the pandemic. We present these findings using a joint display, which is a table that depicts the qualitative and quantitative findings side-by-side to capture similarities and differences.

RESULTS

We first present the summary statistics for our quantitative and qualitative samples. Next, we present our findings in the order of the four research questions, as they informed *a priori* categories by which data were iteratively analyzed. These questions asked how the pandemic influenced FGCS' (1) health and well-being and (2) academic engagement and success, and (3) how the pandemic impacted participants' senses of self. For each research question, we first present the quantitative results from the online survey, followed by the qualitative findings. Overall, the findings reveal that the transition to remote learning severely disrupted students' living arrangements, economic security, and overall well-being. Despite these obstacles,

90   M. K. RAUCH GRIFFARD, R. A. LONG, and C. R. DAVIS

most participants' sense of self and determination to complete their education remained stable.

1. How Did University Closures and the Transition to Distance Learning Impact FGCS' Health and Well-Being?

Both the quantitative and qualitative survey findings on FGCS' health and well-being showed that study participants experienced a decline in both their physical and mental health during university closures. On average, survey participants reported that they were in good health overall, with 70.52% indicating that they were in excellent, very good, or good health. However, participants did report more instances of physical discomfort during the pandemic, as shown in Table 4.1. Table 4.1 compares how students' reported physical discomforts, such as their energy levels, various aches and pains, and nutritional health, before and during the pandemic. For most items, a larger proportion of respondents indicated experiencing the given physical discomfort during the pandemic compared with before the pandemic. Notably, on another survey question that asked respondents to compare whether they had felt really healthy before the pandemic and during the pandemic, 69.83% of respondents reported feeling really healthy pre-pandemic compared to only 30.17% during the pandemic. This large decrease suggests that students' perceived physical health suffered during the university closures.

Table 4.1

FGCS' Reported Physical Discomforts

	% Before the Pandemic	% During the Pandemic
Felt really sick overall	45.07	54.93
Woke up feeling tired	35.23	64.77
Tired easily or felt like I didn't have energy	30.17	69.83
Had watery or itchy eyes	36.97	63.03
Had skin problems	45.45	54.55
Had a cough	46.81	53.19
Had a fever or chills	52.17	47.83
Was dizzy	44.78	52.22

(Table continued on next page)

Table 4.1 (Continued)

FGCS' Reported Physical Discomforts

	% Before the Pandemic	% During the Pandemic
Was wheezing or had trouble breathing	51.22	48.78
Had chest pain	46.34	53.66
Had a headache	46.20	53.80
Had soreness in muscles or joints	35.80	64.20
Had a stomach ache	42.17	57.83
Had bothersome pain	42.37	57.63
Vomited or felt like vomiting	31.58	68.42
Had trouble urinating	55.56	44.44
Had poor appetite	36.36	63.64
Had diarrhea	35.71	64.29
Had constipation	43.86	56.14
Was pain free	65.00	35.00
Felt really healthy	69.83	30.17
Lost weight without trying	47.56	52.44

Some of the physical discomfort's students reported experiencing, such as low energy, tiredness, and decreased appetite, may also be related to the increase in emotional discomforts they reported experiencing during the pandemic. For example, when asked to compare their emotional discomforts before and during the pandemic, 20% more respondents said they had trouble sleeping (see Table 4.2). Similarly, only 20.65% of respondents reported waking up refreshed during the pandemic, a 58.70% decrease from before the pandemic. On another dimension of emotional health, fewer respondents reported feeling loved during the pandemic, which suggests that students' relationships with others suffered from the pandemic, as shown in Table 4.2. When asked how the pandemic impacted their relationships, 38.22% of survey respondents reported negative impacts on family relationships and 61.78% reported negative impacts on friendships, compared with respondents who reported positive impacts, 26.94% for family and 14.22% for friends.

Table 4.2

FGCS' Reported Emotional Discomforts

	% Before the Pandemic	% During the Pandemic
Had trouble sleeping	40.00	60.00
Felt depressed	41.06	58.94
Had trouble relaxing	38.59	61.41
Was nervous	39.11	60.89
Was moody	35.87	64.13
Was irritable or grouchy	32.90	67.10
Cried a lot	33.79	66.21
Was afraid of things	38.93	61.07
Woke up refreshed	79.35	20.65
Felt like I did right	65.75	34.25
Felt loved	52.36	47.00
Vomited on purpose	55.00	45.00
Binged	38.00	62.00

As the interview data revealed, there were several reasons why students felt less physically and mentally fit during the pandemic. For example, one survey respondent shared that they had "settled into smoking weed" as a way to cope during the pandemic. Several participants described erratic sleep patterns, such as staying up and sleeping much later. One participant noted that he would wake up five minutes before his online classes would start, which he said made his time management for the rest of the day less efficient. Some participants described being caught in a slippery slope of not having the energy or desire to exercise, eating poorly, gaining weight, and then not feeling energized enough to exercise or eat healthier because they had gained weight. For example, a participant that was underweight pre-pandemic shared how additional weight loss became a cause for concern:

> I lost ten pounds … I was so, like, lazy and lethargic during quarantine, I would just not leave my bed very often. … I didn't notice that I lost ten pounds. Like, I didn't notice it—oh, until my doctors were like, "yeah, that's not okay."

First Generation College Students' Health and Well-Being 93

For another participant, weight gain and stress were also tied to loss of income, as the participant's job was as a bicycle food delivery person. The participant explained:

> I gained weight, and I don't have as much stamina or energy like I used to have.... My other daily stresses are getting to me because now I don't have an outlet to exhaust myself.

While the circumstances of this participant's job were unique in the sample, the loss of routine around health and fitness described was common across many participant's experiences. The response also highlights how many FGCS also maintained employment in addition to attending school full time, and many had lost their jobs and income due to pandemic-related shutdowns. Not working was a common reason why participants reported feeling more stressed, both due to the financial loss and the loss of routine.

For a small subset of participants, however, the pandemic introduced new routines to support health. One participant, for example, shared that she and her partner had begun taking long walks daily. This participant, aged 34, was a nontraditional college student as well as FGCS. Having several additional years of development and experiences outside of academic settings may have enabled her to be more successful in establishing new health routines. Moreover, as an older student, the participant did not live on campus and lived with a partner. This means that the participant did not have to move when the university closed, and the partner offered accountability for the daily walks. Some participants began or resumed therapy sessions, which helped them better manage their mental health. Others were able to use campus closures as an opportunity to reflect and "spend a lot of time with" themselves. One participant shared that they became more comfortale with themselves, while another "learned more about how [they] handled situations" related to stress or social interactions with their family.

Beyond its relationship to physical health, participants' mental health also suffered during the pandemic. Many participants shared struggles with depression and anxiety that were exacerbated by pandemic conditions. For some, moving back in with family introduced new stressors that aggravated their mental health. One participant described the oppressive nature of the pandemic as "hovering over all of us and our families" while another shared that she had been suffering from panic attacks and needed to be hospitalized shortly after returning home. A participant shared the drastic ways in which the pandemic exacerbated issues they had already been dealing with:

> I have struggled with depression and anxiety for years ... I would say the pandemic has triggered a lot of things that I went through in my childhood

... my depression got a lot worse. Once it started, I started having hallucinations and seeing things ... I think the isolation made me slip off a little bit.

For others, the fear of contracting COVID-19 caused increased anxiety. Several participants felt that other students were not taking social distancing policies seriously, nor were their universities being strict enough in enforcing the policies. One participant, whose interview took place in fall 2020, when campuses were reopened in a limited capacity, shared:

Just being on campus always came with a level of anxiety about, "I don't want to get too close to [other people.]" ... I really cannot trust what you're doing when you are in your own personal space.

Elsewhere in the interview, the participant shared that a baseline anxiety she felt was not being able to keep up academically as an FGCS, something that had plagued her before the pandemic. Many interview participants echoed this concern. One respondent, in an open-ended survey response, described an obstacle unique to low-income and FGCS: aging out of the foster care system at the beginning of his undergraduate career had added considerable strain to his mental health and well-being, making it hard to focus on anything else. As the findings from Research Question 2 will show, the transition to distance learning added a new set of challenges for FGCS' academic performance.

2. How Did University Closures and the Transition to Distance Learning Impact FGCS' Academic Engagement and Ability to Succeed in College?

Although students indicated that they understood what was expected of them as distance learners, across both data strands, students overwhelmingly reported low levels of engagement in their classes during university closures. Only 15.25% of respondents agreed or strongly agreed that they felt connected to fellow students, and 31.96% agreed or strongly agreed that they felt connected to their professors during remote instruction. Feeling disconnected from their courses may have contributed to the decline in students' academic performance during university closures. As part of the survey, respondents were asked to rate their concerns about their academic performance before and during university closures. These concerns included grades, academic eligibility, study habits, preparedness, and studying environment. As shown in Table 4.3, more students agreed or strongly disagreed that they were performing well across these six academic concerns. Notably, 15.11% fewer respondents reported that they strongly

First Generation College Students' Health and Well-Being 95

agreed that their grades were lower than expected during the pandemic. Only 3.81% of respondents reported that their grades were lower than expected before the pandemic, compared to 18.92% during university closures.

Table 4.3

FGCS' Concerns about Academic Performance

Before the COVID-19 Pandemic

	Level of Agreement			
Statement	Strongly Agree	Agree	Disagree	Strongly Disagree
My grades are lower than expected.	3.81%	17.07%	55.03%	24.09%
I am not concerned about my academic eligibility.	25.11%	33.69%	25.73%	15.47%
I have poor study habits.	5.95%	32.16%	44.97%	16.92%
I like school.	29.20%	56.73%	10.55%	3.52%
I feel prepared for college.	17.48%	54.45%	24.54%	3.53%
I have a great study environment.	18.78%	52.98%	24.58%	3.66%

During University Closures due to the Pandemic

	Level of Agreement			
Statement	Strongly Agree	Agree	Disagree	Strongly Disagree
My grades are lower than expected.	18.92%	34.34%	35.93%	10.81%
I am not concerned about my academic eligibility.	21.14%	35.45%	27.03%	16.38%
I have poor study habits.	18.35%	37.03%	34.65%	9.97%
I like school.	14.94%	45.47%	27.03%	12.56%
I feel prepared for college.	9.55%	40.29%	35.51%	14.65%
I have a great study environment.	9.18%	34.02%	36.87%	19.94%

One factor that may have impacted participants' grades was their ability to access a study environment conducive to virtual learning. The percentage of respondents who strongly agreed that they did have such a study environment fell by half to just 9.18% during closures from 18.78% before the pandemic. Not having access to such a study environment may have influenced participants' reports of their study habits. During university closures, 55.38% of respondents agreed or strongly agreed that they had poor study habits, compared with 38.11% prior, an increase of nearly 20%. One possible reason why students may have had poor study habits during closures may have been that they did not enjoy the experience of distance learning. More than 25% fewer respondents said that they liked school during closures, a decrease from 85.93% to 60.41%.

The open-ended survey responses and interview data sheds considerable light on why students struggled with their academic performance when schools were not open and why fewer survey respondents reported that they liked school. To begin with, many students described feeling disappointed about losing out on formative experiences due to the pandemic, such as studying abroad, hands-on lab experiences, and working on research with faculty. One participant shared that he was unable to collect data for a project he hoped to use on graduate school applications. Participants also talked about missing the day-to-day opportunities going to school in person afforded them. Some students were frustrated by having to deal with attending classes online, as one participant explained:

> definitely miss … interacting with the other students in person and interacting with the professor. It's definitely different to do that over a screen. Especially if someone's Internet's not really working, or the connection is bad. Then, you only hear every other word they're saying, which can be frustrating.

Another participant described attending face-to-face classes at her school as "much richer and more dynamic" and expressed disappointment that the online experience was less engaging while another added that they "would definitely be focusing a lot better" if their classes had been in person. Other participants added that it was more difficult to ask questions during classes because getting a professor's attention online was less efficient than raising one's hand in a classroom. One participant shared how the move to remote instruction changed their experience with classes related to their major:

> I feel like in my major in my classes, I'm finally taking things I'm passionate about and I was excited for. But…. It doesn't feel exciting, like learning. It doesn't feel like learning at all, it feels like we are, like, this is a job that I have to go to.

Since participants shared that the quality of their online classes was poorer than their in-person classes, they also shared that, by extension, they struggled to be engaged and enthusiastic about them. Participants' descriptions of the quality of their remote learning is best characterized as apathetic. Across the interviews, there was a general languidness about distance learning. One participant shared that there is "less accountability" when attending a virtual class, which led him to watch Netflix during lectures. Consequently, the participant said he learned "half or even a third as much as I would have in a regular semester." Another participant explained that her mindset about learning changed when classes transitioned online. She said:

> The pandemic really affected [my mindset] because I just found myself not as motivated as I normally am. I'm just literally cramming before a test, and I'm not retaining the information that's kind of important to me, especially my major.

Interview participants, aligned with quantitative survey findings, affirmed that diminished study habits and decreased attentiveness during online classes led to lower grades and less learning.

Some interview participants also shared that they felt unsupported by their universities and faculty during closures, such as poor communication around class or semester break schedules and that universities "needed[ed] to be much more transparent about how they" made decisions. Some participants shared that they were responsible for looking after younger siblings during the day while parents worked, making it difficult for them to attend their own classes or complete their own schoolwork. Other participants said their family homes or the other places they were living in did not have adequate spaces for them to work without distractions.

As another example, one participant, who returned to a low-wealth rural region during university closures, did not have access to reliable Wi-Fi at home. As a result, she was forced to drive to her local library and sit in the parking lot to access the Internet for her classes. This participant felt her university's transition to online learning did not equitably acknowledge the needs of its low-income and FGCS, partly as a result of the university comprising a largely affluent student population.

Another participant who returned to a small house with many siblings said he felt uncomfortable having his camera on during class. However, in one of his classes, he was forced to because otherwise the professor would kick students out. The participant felt the professor's policy was unfair and inequitable, given the wide array of environments students may be living and learning in. Also, in line with the quantitative survey data, interviews with FGCS demonstrated that learning environments were not always conducive to quality learning either, with one participant expressing that learning from home:

> Can be very chaotic at times … you can hear everything that's going on around you. It's kind of hard when you're in a Zoom class and there's so much going on around you, people yelling or whatever. And it makes it harder to focus [on coursework] at home.

98   M. K. RAUCH GRIFFARD, R. A. LONG, and C. R. DAVIS

Echoing this point, one participant shared that it was difficult to study and focus on school when he was currently experiencing homelessness. Although he was couching surfing between friends' and family members' homes, the participant said it was challenging to find quiet places to log onto classes and to study.

3. How Did the Disruptions to Their Living and Learning Environments and Other Challenges FCGS Encountered Related to the Pandemic Influence Their Sense of Self?

Despite the many obstacles FGCS faced health-wise, academically, and due to a lack of support from their universities, study participants overwhelmingly remained steadfast in their determination to finish their undergraduate educations. As prior research found, FGCS are typically resilient in the face of challenges and hardships (Verdín et al., 2018). Nearly all survey respondents (94.28%) said they were either returning to higher education in fall 2020 or graduating from their universities. Less than 6% of respondents reported that they were either taking time off or were unsure of their plans for the upcoming academic year. This finding suggests that FGCS have what Flury and Ickes (2007) called a strong sense of self, which means that their determination to persist in their educational endeavors was not derailed by the difficulties they faced because of the pandemic.

Indeed, as part of the interviews, participants were asked whether the pandemic made them reconsider their current educational trajectories and timelines. While many participants admitted that they had thought about making changes to their current plans, they all ultimately decided not to alter their academic or professional goals or the time it would take them to reach these goals. Nearly all interview participants said they were confident they would still graduate from college. When asked to elaborate on why they felt confident about graduating, participants said things like, "I made it this far. I don't see anything stopping me" and "I'm fighting for something." One participant added that the pandemic and move to remote learning affected their sense of resiliency:

> I think it's made me more resilient. I think [I'm] able to handle last minute changes a lot better, and just kind of roll[ing] with whatever is really thrown at you ... [I have] more confidence in myself ... because, in a way, you're more independent when you're doing classes remotely ... so I think it's definitely improved my resilience and motivation, interacting with a screen versus in a classroom.

The concept of resilience came up in many interviews and open-ended survey responses, and participants frequently described themselves as resilient. When asked on the survey what she would like her university administration to know, one participant shared the following:

> I would like them to know more about my background, my pitfalls, and how I am trying to accept life's many adversities and continue in stride.... Of course, COVID-19 has thrown a major wrench in my plans since I am now the only financial source of income in my household, but I would like to think that the resiliency I learned along the way in dealing with other adversities will help me overcome my current obstacles.

Because of their experiences as FGCS and the personal difficulties they overcame outside of college, participants' sense of self was often characterized by their ability to successfully navigate challenging circumstances. Even if they were currently facing tremendous obstacles, such as food and housing insecurity, worsened mental and physical health, financial worries, and academic struggles, participants overwhelmingly felt they possessed the determination and work ethic necessary to overcome them.

DISCUSSION

This study investigated how FGCS' physical and mental health and academic experiences and performance were impacted by the university closures due to the COVID-19 pandemic. Despite attending different types of universities, we found minimal variation in students' experiences during pandemic-related closures across campuses. Rather, their experiences can be characterized by two factors. First, FGCS encountered many problems common to both people living through the COVID-19 pandemic, such as increased stress and anxiety, and to university students, such as dealing with suboptimal learning experiences during school closures. Second, and perhaps more importantly because of the circumstances associated with their FGCS status, many study participants also encountered many more challenges during the pandemic, especially related to their health and well-being, academic engagement, and sense of self. Nevertheless, despite these challenges, participants were determined to continue their education. Their senses of self were defined by their determination and resilience.

For Research Question 1, the quantitative results showed that most participants reported increased challenges with their health and well-being. Unhealthy habits and stress both increased. Qualitatively, the findings explained more deeply what these new behaviors were. Some participants described being caught on a slippery slope of not having the energy or desire to exercise, eating poorly, gaining weight, and then not feeling energized enough to exercise or eat healthier because they had gained weight. FGCS also had unique circumstances, such as aging out of the foster care system, that added to their stress and anxiety. In addition to problems with maintaining physical and mental fitness that were common among many people living through the pandemic, study participants also faced challenges unique to their status as FGCS and/or low-income students that increased their stress. Increased stress hampered both their physical and mental health.

The pandemic also influenced students' academic engagement. The survey results showed that respondents who said their grades were lower than expected increased by more than 15% during the pandemic compared with before. The percentage of respondents who said they liked school fell by half. In interviews, participants described a lack of enthusiasm for online learning, disconnectedness from professors and classmates, and lost learning opportunities were just some of the problems participants said they had academically during closures. Some participants also had challenges with juggling personal responsibilities, such as taking care of siblings and academics. Overall, the transition to online instruction was not smooth. For a variety of intrinsic and extrinsic factors (e.g., motivation, having a good study space, etc.), FGCS found distance learning was not conducive to their academic success.

Despite these hardships, FGCS in the study thought of themselves as resilient and capable of overcoming obstacles. Flury and Ickes (2007) would characterize the participants as having a strong sense of self, meaning that their self-image was not suddenly or drastically altered by external factors. Participants remained confident in their ability to succeed in college. Nearly 95% of survey respondents said they were either returning to higher education or graduating from college. Interview participants described themselves as resilient in the face of obstacles both before and during the pandemic. Participants were confident they would still graduate. Participants' sense of self was primarily characterized by their ability to overcome obstacles. Despite the many difficulties the pandemic created their confidence in their ability to succeed was not hampered.

During convergence between the quantitative and qualitative analyzes, we found that there was considerable alignment between what the larger quantitative sample reported on the surveys and what interview participants shared in the qualitative data. We found that the qualitative findings provided more specific, detailed accounts of FGCS' experiences during school closures. For example, survey particpants were asked about how remote learning changed their study habits. More than half of particpants (55.38%) reported that they agreed or strongly agreed that they had poor study habits during the pandemic. Through interviews, we were able to learn what FGCS' poor study habits looked like in practice, such as not

First Generation College Students' Health and Well-Being   101

paying attention in class, procrastinating, and not engaging in authentic, deeper learning.

Overall, the findings from our study align with other studies investigating how FGCS were impacted by the pandemic (e.g., Barber et al., 2022; Davis et al., 2021; Soria et al., 2020; Soria et al., 2022; Umeda et al., 2023). Our study adds to this growing body of research in several important ways. Foremost, by using a mixed methods research design, we looked beyond survey data to provide in-depth, firsthand accounts from FGCS that spoke specifically to their experiences as FGCS during the pandemic. The qualitative data provide a narrative that expounds upon the quantitative findings from the study. Second, in addition to capturing the hardships that FGCS experienced during the pandemic, we were also able to explore how these hardships shaped their sense of self and their outlook toward their future.

Limitations

While we believe that the study offers important insights into the experiences and mindsets of FGCS during the pandemic, we recognize that there are several limitations to our study. First, the results of the survey used in the quantitative strand are likely limited by a low response rate. The total number of respondents on the survey unfortunately represents a very small proportion of the overall population of FGCS at the five universities, which we estimate to be in the thousands. However, we believe 659 fully completed surveys is no small number of responses in light of both the difficulties FGCS would have been preoccupied with during data collection and the difficulties many researchers encountered in collecting data during the pandemic.

Second, much of the data consists of study participants' retrospections on their experiences. In the survey, participants were asked to compare their experiences before and during university closures. In the interviews, which mainly occurred after schools had reopened in fall 2021, participants were asked to recall feelings and experiences they had during the closures. In both cases, individuals' recollections may not be accurate, or their perceptions may be colored by unrelated factors.

Policy Implications

According to participants, university resources aimed to address their needs as FGCS and students from low-income households were limited or poorly advertised. This lack of support contributed to students feeling even less connected to their schools than they had before the pandemic. Many participants criticized their universities for not recognizing the myriad of difficulties students grappled with outside of class due to the pandemic and for not requiring faculty to adjust their expectations of students during school closures. Participants wished for more flexibility and understanding from both faculty and administration.

Importantly, from a mental health perspective, our work is not alone in finding that students' mental health has been adversely influenced by COVID-19 and the related pandemic. While the focus here is first-generation students, undergraduate and graduate students more broadly have seen an increase in symptoms related to depression, anxiety, or suicidal thoughts (Wang et al., 2020), and other findings suggest such mental health distress among students has persisted well into the pandemic (Neal, 2021). As with the work presented here, these other studies indicate that academic success has been negatively hindered by mental health impacts. Colleges can also improve academic outcomes by better addressing mental health concerns. Policymakers and university leaders can develop and improve practices for future instances of distance learning and school closures through increasing the understanding on how the pandemic affected FGCS.

Policymakers and leaders can improve best practices for future instances of distance learning and school closures by considering the following recommendations. First, universities should acknowledge the interrelated impacts of the pandemic on students' health and academics. By having readily accessible and well-advertised resources to address student mental health and other concerns (i.e., food insecurity), colleges may also improve academic outcomes. Universities should reevaluate the availability and students' awareness of various supports during school closures. In particular, universities should also work to destigmatize seeking treatment for mental health concerns.

Second, faculty and administrators must recognize that students need greater flexibility and empathy, especially during school closures and periods of stress and uncertainty. Many faculty members want to better support their students' emotional needs and help them feel more connected. Expanding professional training to make online content more engaging and building social support networks services are essential. Universities could equip and train faculty to deliver high-quality instruction in a remote environment. Instructors could receive tools to address students' non-academic needs, such as their mental health needs (Neuwirth et al., 2021).

Last, universities should reflect on whether the resources they offered during the pandemic supported a diverse student population. Specifically, universities could ensure that both their academic policies and their financial support acknowledge the wide array of personal circumstances students

First Generation College Students' Health and Well-Being 103

face outside of school. It is imperative for universities to assess FGCS' external factors that may influence their ability to be successful in school.

Overall, our chapter contributes to the growing need for policymakers and educational leaders to understand the impacts of the COVID-19 pandemic on student experiences, especially for students from marginalized and underrepresented groups. Taken altogether, policymakers and university leaders have the opportunity to acknowledge how the pandemic has impacted FGCS and provide equitable support to their students in both pandemic and non-pandemic times. By caring for the whole student, universities give FGCS a better chance to reach graduation.

REFERENCES

Aristovnik, A., Keržič, D., Ravšelj, D., Tomaževič, N., & Umek, L. (2020). Impacts of the COVID-19 pandemic on life of higher education students: A global perspective. *Sustainability*, *12*(20), 8438.

Bandura, A. (2002). Social cognitive theory in cultural context. *Applied psychology*, *51*(2), 269 290.

Barber, P. H., Shapiro, C., Jacobs, M. S., Avilez, L., Brenner, K. I., Cabral, C., Cebreros, M., Cosentino, E., Cross, C., Gonzalez, M. L., Lumada, K. T., Menjivar, A.T ., Narvaez J., Olmeda, B., Phelan, R., Purdy, D., Salam, S., Serrano, L., Velasco, M. J., Zerecero E. M., & Levis-Fitzgerald, M. (2021). Disparities in remote learning faced by first-generation and underrepresented minority students during COVID-19: insights and opportunities from a remote research experience. *Journal of Microbiology & Biology Education*, *22*(1), ev22i1–2457.

Bettencourt, G. M., Mansour, K. E., Hedayet, M., Feraud-King, P. T., Stephens, K. J., Tejada, M. M., & Kimball, E. (2022). Is first-gen an identity? How first-generation college students make meaning of institutional and familial constructions of self. *Journal of College Student Retention: Research, Theory & Practice*, *24*(2), 271–289.

Bono, G., Reil, K., & Hescox, J. (2020). Stress and wellbeing in urban college students in the US during the COVID-19 pandemic: Can grit and gratitude help? *International Journal of Wellbeing*, *10*(3).

Brinkmann, S. (2020). Unstructured and semi-structured interviewing. In P. Leavy (Ed.), *The Oxford Handbook of Qualitative Research* (2nd ed., pp. 1–39). Oxford University Press.

Centers for Disease Control and Prevention. (2020, November 13). *Coronavirus disease: Long-term effects*. Retrieved December 2020, from https://www.cdc.gov/coronavirus/2019-ncov/long-term-effects.html

Centers for Disease Control and Prevention. (2021). *United States COVID-19 cases, deaths, and laboratory testing (RT-PCR) by state, territory, and jurisdiction*. https://covid.cdc.gov/covid-data-tracker/#cases_casesper100klast7days

Creswell, J. W., & Plano Clark, V. L. (2018). *Designing and conducting mixed methods research* (3rd ed.). SAGE.

Davis, C. R., Hartman, H., Turner, M., Norton, T., Sexton, J., Méndez, D., & Méndez, J. (2021). "Listen to the feedback of students": First-generation college students voice inequalities in schooling brought on by the COVID-19 pandemic. *Journal of College Student Retention: Research, Theory & Practice*. https://doi.org/10.1177/15210251211066302

Ettman, C. K., Abdalla, S. M., Cohen, G. H., Sampson, L., Vivier, P. M., & Galea, S. (2020). Prevalence of depression symptoms in US adults before and during the COVID-19 pandemic. *JAMA Network Open*, 3(9), e2019686.

Flury, J. M., & Ickes, W. (2007). Having a weak versus strong sense of self: The Sense of Self Scale (SOSS). *Self and Identity*, 6(4), 281–303.

Forbus, P. R., Newbold, J. J., & Mehta, S. S. (2011). First-generation university students: Motivation, academic success, and satisfaction with the university experience. *International Journal of Education Research*, 6(2), 34–56.

Fruehwirth, J. C., Biswas, S., & Perreira, K. M. (2021). The Covid-19 pandemic and mental health of first-year college students: Examining the effect of Covid-19 stressors using longitudinal data. *PloS One*, 16(3), e0247999.

Gonzalez-Ramirez, J., Mulqueen, K., Zealand, R., Silverstein, S., Mulqueen, C., & BuShell, S. (2021). Emergency Online Learning: College Students' Perceptions During the COVID-19 Pandemic. *College Student Journal*, 55(1), 29–46.

Gracia, J. (2020). COVID-19's Disproportionate impact on communities of color spotlights the nation's systemic inequities. *Journal of Public Health Management and Practice*, 26(6), 518–521.

Lichtenberg, J. D. (1975). The development of the sense of self. *Journal of the American Psychoanalytic Association*, 23(3), 453-484.

Lohfink, M. M., & Paulsen, M. B. (2005). Comparing the determinants of persistence for first-generation and continuing-generation students. *Journal of College Student Development*, 46(4), 409–428.

MacMillan, T., Corrigan, M. J., Coffey, K., Tronnier, C. D., Wang, D., & Krase, K. (2021). Exploring factors associated with alcohol and/or substance use during the COVID-19 pandemic. *International Journal of Mental Health and Addiction*, 1–10.

Neal, T., Quandt, E., Thornton, J., & Tucker, J. (2021). Understanding the mental health impact of pandemic on student-athletes and sports medicine staff. *College Athletics and the Law*, 18(2), 6–8.

Neuwirth, L. S., Jović, S., & Mukherji, B. R. (2021). Reimagining higher education during and post-COVID-19: Challenges and opportunities. *Journal of Adult and Continuing Education*, 27(2), 141–156.

North, C. S. (2020). Mental health and the Covid-19 pandemic. *The New England Journal of Medicine*, 383(6), 510–512.

Pascarella, E. T., Pierson, C. T., Wolniak, G. C., & Terenzini, P. T. (2004). First-generation college students: Additional evidence on college experiences and outcomes. *The Journal of Higher Education*, 75(3), 249–284.

Postsecondary National Policy Institute. (2021, February 1). *Factsheets: First-generation students*. Retrieved from PNPI: https://pnpi.org/first-generation-students/#

Prebble, S. C., Addis, D. R., & Tippett, L. J. (2013). Autobiographical memory and sense of self. *Psychological Bulletin*, 139(4), 815.

QSR International Pty Ltd. (2020). *NVivo* (Release 1).

Redford, J., & Hoyer, K. M. (2017). *First-generation and continuing-generation college students: A comparison of high school and postsecondary experiences*. National Center for Education Statistics. https://nces.ed.gov/pubs2018/2018009.pdf

Spiegel, L. A. (1959). The self, the sense of self, and perception. *The Psychoanalytic Study of the Child, 14*(1), 81–109.

Smith, J. A. (1995). Semi-structured interviewing and qualitative analysis. In J. A. Smith, R. Harré, & & L. Van Lagenhove (Eds.), *Rethinking methods in psychology,* (pp. 9–26). SAGE

Soria, K. M., Horgos, B., Chirikov, I., & Jones-White, D. (2020). *First-generation students' experiences during the COVID-19 pandemic*. SERU Consortium, University of California–Berkeley and University of Minnesota.

Soria, K. M., Kelling, C., Mossinghoff, M., & Beahm, R. (2022). First-Generation College Students' Mental Health During the COVID-19 Pandemic. *Journal of First-Generation Student Success, 2*(2), 97–117.

Taquet, M., Geddes, J. R., Husain, M., Luciano, S., & Harrison, P. J. (2021). 6-month neurological and psychiatric outcomes in 236,379 survivors of COVID-19: A retrospective cohort study using electronic health records. *Lancet Psychiatry, 8*, 416–427.

Teddlie, C., & Tashakkori, A. (2006). A general typology in research designs featuring mixed methods. *Research in the Schools, 13*, 12–28.

Terenzini, P. T., Springer, L., Yaeger, P. M., Pascarella, E. T., & Nora, A. (1996). First-generation college students: Characteristics, experiences, and cognitive development. *Research in Higher education, 37*(1), 1–22.

Toutkoushian, R. K., May-Trifiletti, J. A., & Clayton, A. B. (2021). From "First in Family" to "First to Finish": Does college graduation vary by how first-generation college status is defined? *Educational Policy, 35*(3), 481–521.

Umeda, M., Kim, Y., Park, S. W., Chung, E., & Ullevig, S. L. (2023). Food insecurity and academic function among college students during the COVID-19 pandemic: A moderating role of the first-generation college student status. *Journal of American College Health*, 1–7.

Vahratian, A., Blumberg, S., Terlizzi, E., & Schiller, J. (2021). Symptoms of anxiety or depressive disorder and use of mental health care among adults during the COVID-19 pandemic—United States, August 2020–February 2021. *MMWR Morb Mortal Wkly Rep, 70*, 490–494.

Verdín, D., Godwin, A., Kirn, A., Benson, L., & Potvin, G. (2018). *Understanding how engineering identity and belongingness predict grit for first-generation college students*. School of Engineering Education Graduate Student Series. Paper 75. https://docs.lib.purdue.edu/enegs/75

Wang, X., Hegde, S., Son, C., Keller, B., Smith, A., & Sasangohar, F. (2020). Investigating mental health of US college students during the COVID-19 pandemic: Cross-sectional survey study. *Journal of Medical Internet Research, 22*(9), e22817.

APPENDIX A

Interview Protocol

In this interview we are interested in finding out how you are doing today, how you have been doing since March or since the coronavirus has turned into a pandemic, what has changed for you during this period and how you've managed with these changes.

1. Before we begin, please tell me about yourself,

   a. What year are you?
   b. How many years have you been at [NAME OF UNIVERSITY]?
   c. What is your major? Minor?

2. Are you the first person in your family who's gone to college?

   a. (If no) Who else in your family has gone to college? (Where/what kind of college? Degree/field? When—how long ago?)
   b. (If yes) How do you think being the first in your family to go to college has impacted your college experience? (Positive ways, negative ways, challenges)

For my next few questions, I want to ask you about changes you may have experienced since March, such as changes to your school, living situation, health, work, and social life.

3. Tell me a little about your living situation: where were you living before the pandemic, and how has that situation changed? (where were you living? Proximity to campus? With friends or family? Proximity to home? Where are you living now?—)

4. To what extent have you experienced any changes to your health, including your physical, mental, or emotional well-being?

   a. Can you tell me more about how these changes to your health have affected you?
   b. To what extent has COVID-19 affected you indirectly? (e.g., have any of your close friends or relatives had experiences with COVID-19?)

First Generation College Students' Health and Well-Being   107

5. To what extent has COVID-19 disrupted your job?
   (Has it changed your working hours? Do you have more or fewer
   responsibilities? Have you been laid off? Do you have a new job?
   Are you working remotely?)

   a. How about the work of members in your immediate
      family?

6. In what ways has your social life been impacted?
   (Close relationships, family, friends)

*For this next set of questions, I'll be asking about your educational experiences at
[NAME OF UNIVERSITY].*

7. What led you to pick your school?
   (Proximity to home? Financial aid/scholarship/ affordability?
   Field of study? Friends?)

8. How do you think the pandemic has affected your education?
   (Your readiness for college education—academically, emotional/
   mental readiness; your willingness or eagerness to go to college;
   your sense of belongingness or connection to the university/
   major? your ability to continue—financially, family obligations,
   ability to complete enough credits; how much you feel you
   belong at college)

9. Have you made any or considered making any changes regarding your college education since the pandemic began?
   (Changing major—why; changing colleges—why: to be closer
   to home, to save money, to work more, to help out family, is
   this temporary—do you anticipate coming back to [NAME OF
   UNIVERSITY] in the future? When? Taking a semester off—
   why: $, job, online/remote learning, family responsibilities, etc;
   dropping out—why)

   a. If you transitioned to remote learning, how, if at all, has it
      affected your experience at the university? Your personal
      life?
   b. How confident are you that you will graduate with a de-
      gree in your current major?
   c. More generally, what do you think is your primary
      barrier(s) to making it to graduation?
   d. How has COVID influenced these barriers?

> a. What kinds of financial support (e.g., scholarships, fellowships, etc.) do you have/have you had for your undergraduate experience? Has that changed during the pandemic?

10. What other kinds of support have you had that are important in your life? How has the pandemic changed any of these?
11. If you could change one thing about how your school has handled the pandemic, what would it be?
12. Thinking about next semester, will you be coming back even if classes are remote, or do you prefer remote learning?
13. Where do you see yourself in 5 years? Has that changed as a result of COVID-19?
14. For our last question, what can [NAME OF UNIVERSITY] do to best support you academically and personally right now?
15. Do you have any additional comments, or is there anything that I've missed that you would like to share?

Thank you for time today, and I hope you stay well!

CHAPTER 5

RELATIONSHIPS BETWEEN STUDY CONDITIONS, STRESS, AND PERCEIVED HEALTH

Studying at University After the COVID-19 Lockdown

**Knut Inge Fostervold, Silje Endresen Reme,
Helge I. Strømsø, and Sten R. Ludvigsen**
University of Oslo, Norway

ABSTRACT

This study investigates how university students perceived the state of affairs after the sudden campus lockdown in Norway due to the COVID-19 outbreak, and how those perceptions affected students' experiences of stress and self-perceived mental health. We report the results of a survey study among 8,907 students at a large Norwegian university. As indicators of their perceptions of the new study situation, we asked about their feelings of loneliness, the physical study conditions, and their tendencies to procrastinate. Analyzes based on structural equation modeling (SEM) showed that all three indicators were directly associated with students' experienced levels of stress, their self-perceived health, sleep problems, and well-being. The relationships between the predictor variables and the outcome variables on mental health were also partly mediated through students' self-perceived stress. Loneliness was the strongest predictor of students' mental health, but physical study conditions and procrastination were also significantly related to the mental health

---

Research on College Stress and Coping: Implications From the COVID-19 Pandemic and Beyond, pp. 109–134
Copyright © 2024 by Information Age Publishing
www.infoagepub.com
All rights of reproduction in any form reserved.

indicators. To be better prepared for similar situations, universities need to provide a digital infrastructure for students' social activity and help students develop skills in self-regulated learning.

Keywords: COVID-19, university students, study conditions, stress, health

INTRODUCTION

Quite suddenly, Norwegian society was shut down on March 12, 2020 due to the rapid spread of COVID-19. Consequently, university campuses were locked down, and teaching was swiftly switched to a digital remote mode. Thus, students no longer had access to reading halls, seminar rooms, laboratories, or the ability to have face-to-face discussions with teachers and fellow students. The imposed restrictions have raised concerns about the students' study progress and their psychosocial well-being. In a survey conducted by NOKUT (Norwegian Agency for Quality Assurance in Education, 2021) related to the lockdown during the spring term 2020, a substantial portion (39%) of the students reported that they did not have access to a suitable place to study. A majority reported that they found emergency remote digital teaching to be less motivating than on-campus teaching. The majority of the students felt lonelier, missed the social and physical study environment on campus, and found it more difficult to organize their study routines. In another study following Norwegian bachelor's students during the fall term of 2020, Fretheim et al. (2021) found that remote teaching was negatively associated with students' well-being. Study conditions seemed to affect students' experience of life negatively, independent of their more general anxiety related to the pandemic. On the other hand, a couple of large-scale Norwegian studies seem to indicate that adolescents' and young adults' mental health, in general, was not severely affected by the outbreak of the pandemic (Hansen et al., 2021; von Soest et al., 2022). Hence, in a study based on data from a probability-based sample of adults from two Norwegian counties, results from participants in age group 18–24 did not indicate a significant change in participants' feeling of loneliness three months after the lockdown (Hansen et al., 2021). Neither did results from a nationwide Norwegian survey among students in junior and senior high schools show substantial changes in participants' response on measures of mental health and loneliness one year after the lockdown (von Soest et al., 2022). Thus, although younger people, in general, seem to have managed the lockdown fairly well, a majority of higher education students seem to have experienced somewhat challenging situations due to changed study conditions and lack of face-to-face contact with teachers and fellow students. As also indicated in other studies (e.g., Loda et al., 2020), students may experience more stress due to the new study situation characterized by the lockdown and remote teaching, than to the COVID-19 pandemic in general. In the present study, we will investigate how students' perceptions of the new study situation predict their perceived level of stress and how stress, in turn, might mediate the potential effect of those features on indicators of students' psychosocial well-being. Specifically, we will examine how students' physical study conditions, experienced loneliness, and tendencies for procrastination might affect perceived stress and indicators of health and well-being.

Theoretical Introduction

Stress is a healthy and necessary response to a threat (stressor). The same bodily activation occurs whether the stress is caused by a physical threat (e.g., being chased by a lion) or by a social threat (e.g., being involuntarily isolated due to a pandemic). However, the individual variability in response to a social threat is considerably larger than that in response to a physical threat (Sapolsky, 2015). While most of us react to a situation of physical stress with high-stress activation, there is great variability in the stress activation in response to social stress. Several factors influence this variability, including genetic predispositions, previous experiences, social support, and contextual factors (Rab & Admon, 2021; Sapolsky, 1994). Nevertheless, while short-term stress serves as a necessary alarm and typically does not affect one's long-term health, the sustained activation of long-term stress can negatively influence one's health and well-being (Ursin & Eriksen, 2010). The level and duration of the stress response depend largely on our expectations of being able to cope with our situation. While an expectation of being able to cope is followed by a marked reduction in activation (healthy "strain" situation), negative expectations in the form of helplessness and hopelessness sustain the activation (unhealthy "strain" situation; Eriksen et al., 2005; Neuner, 2023). Sustained activation, or chronic stress, is consistently associated with adverse health outcomes in the literature (McEwen, 2017).

Potential Stressors in the Student Population

There are indications that university students' perceived level of stress might be somewhat higher than that of the general population (Stallman, 2010; Zhu et al., 2021). Potential stressors in students' lives are related to transitions to new social contexts and learning environments, often involving deadlines, examinations, and more expectations related to students' time management skills (Robotham, 2008). Accordingly, students' tendency to procrastinate has also been considered a potential stressor. For example, Sirois and colleagues demonstrated how procrastination predicts stress and how stress partly mediates the relationship between procrastination and students' sleep quality (Sirois, 2014; Sirois et al., 2015). Recently, von Keyserlingk et al. (2022) showed that the association between students' perceived stress and their tendencies to procrastinate increased after the COVID-19 outbreak. A shift to remote learning implies that those students also experienced changes regarding features of their physical study conditions, for example, in the amount of space, type of furniture, noise level, and/or appropriate information and communication technology (ICT). The results from studies on stress in working life indicate that workplace stressors might negatively affect both biological and psychological processes, specifically when complex tasks are required (Danquah & Asiamah, 2022; Kazlauskaitė et al., 2022; Vischer, 2008). Thus, it seems plausible that students' working conditions after the COVID-19 lockdown could affect stress and other mental health indicators.

Loneliness is another phenomenon closely linked to stress. It is commonly described as a negative cognitive state that influences the perception of life events and surroundings. More formally, it is defined as "a distressing feeling that accompanies the perception that one's social needs are not being met by the quantity, or especially the quality, of one's social relationships" (Hawkley & Cacioppo, 2010, p. 1). Thus, loneliness is commonly understood as being equivalent to the perception of social isolation, rather than objective social isolation (Hawkley & Cacioppo, 2010; Wheeler et al., 1983;). While being "alone" is a factual situation, "lonely" is a feeling, and social connectedness is therefore defined by quality and not by numbers. In other words, it is the individual's perception that matters. For some individuals, perhaps as much as 30% of the population, loneliness is a chronic state (Heinrich & Gullone, 2006). Inherent in loneliness is a lack of coping. A chronic state of loneliness, therefore, implies a chronic state of stress, with serious consequences for health and well-being. In support of that, a strong relationship between loneliness and atypical stress reactivity has been documented (Brown et al., 2018), suggesting that loneliness results in lasting physiological changes and that these changes accumulate over time to adversely influence health. Several health consequences of loneliness have been documented, including an increased risk for morbidity and mortality, as well as compromised mental health and well-being (Hawkley & Cacioppo, 2010). Loneliness is an important social determinant of health and addressing it is now being increasingly recognized as a public health priority (Pitman et al., 2018; WHO, 2021).

Consequences of Stress and Stressors Among Students

Several studies indicate loneliness to be prevalent among university students and to be related to indicators of both psychological and mental health in student populations (Diehl et al., 2018; Hysing et al., 2015). Reduced sleep quality seems to be a worrisome outcome of students' feelings of loneliness, and the association between loneliness and sleep quality appears to be independent of a number of lifestyle and social factors (Hayley et al., 2017). However, other mental health indicators, such as rumination and anxiety, could mediate the effect of loneliness on students' sleep problems (Werner et al., 2021; Zawadzki et al., 2013).

This association does not apply only to loneliness. Stress in general is considered a major cause of disrupted sleep, and associations between perceived stress and insomnia are generally high (Han et al., 2012; Yang et al., 2018), and this also affects student populations (Gardani et al., 2022). Sleep problems are consistently associated with subjective reports of emotional volatility (Horne, 1985; Simon et al., 2020) and emotional dysregulation (Yoo et al., 2007), and evidence points toward a causal and bidirectional relationship between sleep and emotional brain function (Goldstein & Walker, 2014; Vandekerckhove & Wang, 2018).

Whereas the transition to a higher education context, in general, seems to involve challenges to students' mental health, it seems plausible that those challenges were reinforced when the COVID-19 lockdown occurred. Several recent longitudinal studies confirm the assumption of an immediate increase in students' level of stress and feelings of loneliness after the lockdown. For example, Werner et al. (2021) found a substantial increase in feelings of loneliness from 2019 to March/April 2020 among 443 German students. The results also showed an increase in symptoms of depression, whereas participants' subjective health status did not change significantly from 2019 to 2020. Similar results were demonstrated in a study including a cohort from the Swiss Student Life study, with a significant increase in participants' scores on measures of loneliness, stress, and depression (Elmer et al., 2020). In a study based on data from 10 Polish universities on the trajectories of COVID-19-related mental health problems among university students, there was a steep increase in perceived stress and depression from before (March 2020) to after the lockdown (April 2020) (Debowska et al., 2020). Interestingly, the results from a large study including Swedish university students with data collected before the onset of the pandemic, with follow-ups three and six months after the outbreak (Johansson et al., 2021), did not demonstrate the same kind of increase in mental health problems as in the aforementioned studies. One possible explanation could be that, although Swedish universities switched to online education in March 2020, there were no general lockdowns. Thus, the contextual factors initiating stress activation might have varied somewhat across nations. However, the general picture seems to be that the lockdown initiated in March 2020 seemed to have affected many university students' mental health negatively, more or less immediately. Although there are no longitudinal data on the immediate effects of the lockdown on students' mental health in Norway, there are data supporting the assumption of an increase in students' mental health problems. The results from a Norwegian student survey carried out since 2010 showed a marked deterioration from 2018 to 2021 (spring) in students' subjective health status, sleep problems, and feelings of loneliness (Sivertsen, 2021). Accordingly, our aim was to investigate the relationships between different mental health variables a couple of months after the COVID-19 lockdown was implemented.

The Current Study

In accordance with our review of prior research, we formulated three hypotheses:

a. Students' feelings of loneliness, their satisfaction with the physical study conditions, and their tendencies to procrastinate will predict the perceived level of stress, self-perceived health, sleep problems, and well-being.
b. Students' perceived level of stress will predict their self-perceived health, sleep problems, and well-being.
c. Students' perceived level of stress mediates the effect of the three stressors on students' self-perceived health, sleep problems, and well-being.

The three hypotheses represent a model, with the three stressors included as exogenous predictor variables. We believe those variables may represent significant challenges in the new study environment. Students' social activity was severely restricted after the lockdown, and their feelings of loneliness increased. While they were denied access to campus facilities, they had to rely on facilities in their home (e.g., shared apartment, parents' home), which varied from excellent to unsuitable. Finally, opportunities for procrastination increased when they had to stay at home, where the boundaries between study and leisure time are less obvious. Together, these three stressors probably affected many students more severely during the lockdown than previously, with possible consequences for perceived stress, which again could have consequences for other aspects of mental health. Finally, we also hypothesize that each of the three stressors will predict each of the three endogenous mental health variables directly.

METHODS

Design and Procedures

The study was a cross-sectional survey conducted at a large university in Oslo, the capital of Norway. Data were collected from May–June 2020, approximately two months after the Norwegian government declared a general lockdown on March 12, 2020, in response to the COVID-19 pandemic. Student accommodation is not located on the university campus but scattered throughout the city. A minority of the student population lives in student dormitories, while the majority rent a flat, shared or alone, or live with their parents. After the lockdown, only grocery stores and pharmacies were accessible, and social gatherings were strictly regulated. Remote teaching was offered by the universities, and university campuses were closed. Students had to cope with a new learning environment characterized by several potential stressors, such as less social contact, no access to learning spaces at the university, and more opportunities to procrastinate studying.

All registered full-time students (25,325) at the eight different faculties/schools at the university received an email that stated the purpose of the study, that participation was voluntary, and that participation was anonymous. The email also comprised a link to an electronic questionnaire located at a secure website (Nettskjema.no) hosted by the University of Oslo. A written informed consent was electronically signed by all participants before answering the questionnaire. According to Norwegian legislation, collecting non-clinical anonymous data from adults are exempt from formal ethical approval. All procedures involving human participants were in accordance with the national ethical standards and with the Helsinki declaration. The study was approved by the data protection officer and endorsed by the leadership team of the university.

Participants

A total of 9,490 students responded to the questionnaire, with a response rate of 37.5%. Students more than 40 years old (583) were considered atypical for the student body at the university and removed before data were analyzed, leaving a valid sample of 8,907 respondents ($M_{Age} = 25.1$, $SD = 4.4$; females: 67.2%; nonbinary: 0.6%). The sample consisted of students following different study programs; 36.8% of the students enrolled in different bachelor's programs, 52.1% in master's programs, and 11.1% in shorter programs (one-year programs or single subjects). Compared to the total student population at the university, the present sample contained

116 K. I. FOSTERVOLD, S. E. REME, H. I. STRØMSØ, and S. R. LUDVIGSEN

6.3% more females, while the distribution of students across study programs (undergraduate (BA) and postgraduate (MA) and different faculties/schools was approximately similar.

Measures

The first part of the survey contained background variables (age, gender, faculty/school, and study program). For the remaining parts of the survey, the participants were asked to think specifically about the period after the COVID-19 lockdown when responding to the items, and they were reminded to do so before each section of the survey.

Procrastination

The subjectively perceived tendency to procrastinate was measured by the Irrational Procrastination Scale (IPS; Steel, 2010). The IPS consists of nine statements assessed on a 5-point Likert scale, ranging from "Not true of me" to "True of me." Sample items were "When I should be doing one thing, I will do another" and "I do everything when I believe it needs to be done." The coefficient alpha (α) was .91, which is comparable to the original norm data (Steel, 2010).

Physical Study Condition

Satisfaction with the physical study condition was measured by five items assessing satisfaction with the lighting conditions, the size of the workspace, the computer equipment, the opportunity to study in a quiet place, and the possibility of adjusting chairs and tables. The items were adapted from acknowledged work environmental scales to fit the present purpose (Carlopio, 1996; Kim & de Dear, 2012). Each item was rated on a seven-step interval scale ranging from "Very satisfied" to "Dissatisfied". Cronbach's alpha (α) in the current sample was .80.

Loneliness

Loneliness was measured by the Three-Item Loneliness Scale (TILS; Hughes et al., 2004). Participants were asked how often they felt that they (1) lacked companionship, (2) were left out, and (3) were isolated from others. Each item was rated on a 5-point Likert scale ranging from "Never" to "Very often." The coefficient alpha (α) was .85.

Self-Perceived Stress

Self-perceived stress (SPS) was measured by three items adapted for the present purpose from previously validated single-item measures of self-perceived stress (Houdmont et al., 2019). The first item asked, "How stressful do you usually find your studies?", whereas the second item asked, "How stressful have you found your studies after the COVID-19 lockdown?" Both questions were rated on a 5-point Likert scale ranging from "Very good" to "Bad." The third question asked, "How stressful do you rate your studies compared to others at your age?" This item was rated from "More stressful" to "Much less stressful." The question was reverse coded before being analyzed. The coefficient alpha (α) was .70.

Self-Perceived Health

Three items measured participants' self-perceived health (SPH). The items were sampled from previously validated single-item measures of self-perceived health (DeSalvo et al., 2006; Idler & Benyamini, 1997)

Two of the items concerned students' perception of their general health. The first item asked, "How do you rate your health in general?", whereas the second item asked, "How do you rate your health after the closing of the university?" (the COVID-19 lockdown). The participants responded on a 5-point Likert scale ranging from "Very good" to "Poor." The third item asked how they perceived their health compared to that of others in the same age group. The question ranged from "Much worse" to "Much better" and was reverse coded before being analyzed. The coefficient alpha (α) of the three questions was .80.

Sleep Problems

Sleep problems were assessed by the Bergen Insomnia Scale (BIS; Pallesen et al., 2008). The scale includes six items concerning nocturnal and daytime sleep problems in the last month. Four items accord with the A criteria of insomnia in the fourth edition of the *Diagnostic and Statistical Manual of Mental Disorders* (DSM-IV; American Psychiatric Association [APA], 1994), while the remaining two items concur with the B criteria. The criteria were unchanged in the later text revision of DSM-IV (DSM-IV-TR;

APA, 2000) and only slightly amended in DSM-V (APA, 2013). The most significant change was that the minimum duration of the criteria for being diagnosed with insomnia changed from one to three months.

Each item is rated on an 8-point scale, ranging from zero to seven days per week (e.g., difficulties with sleep initiation). The coefficient alpha (α) for the total scale was .85.

Subjective Well-Being

To measure participants' subjective well-being, we used a Norwegian single-item version of Cantril's ladder (Cantril, 1965). Students were instructed to imagine a ladder with steps numbered from 1 "worst possible life for you" to 10 "best possible life for you" and to mark on the ladder where they stood at the present time. The measure has been used in numerous studies, with results showing satisfactory reliability and validity (see review in Tov et al., 2023).

Statistical Analyzes

Descriptive statistics and analyzes of reliability and bivariate intercorrelations among the study variables were conducted with IBM SPSS statistics for windows version 26. IBM Amos version 26 was used for structural equation modeling (SEM). Maximum likelihood parameter estimation was used in analyses of measurement models and structural relationships between predictor and outcome variables.

Following Kline (2016), the goodness-of-fit was evaluated using the model chi-square (χ^2), the comparative fit index (CFI), the root mean square error of approximation (RMSEA), including the 90% confidence interval for RMSEA, and the standardized root mean square residual (SRMR). A CFI $>.95$, RMSEA $<.06$, and SRMR $<.08$ were considered indications of good model fit (Hu & Bentler, 1999). Bootstrap estimation, based on 5,000 bootstrap samples, using bias-corrected 95% confidence intervals, was conducted to examine the indirect effects (Shrout & Bolger, 2002).

Confirmatory factor analyzes (CFAs) were conducted for scales containing more than three items. As depicted in Table 5.1, the goodness-of-fit was considered satisfactory for procrastination and the physical study condition. The results for the BIS revealed a poor fit, especially for the RMSEA. An inspection of the residuals, factor loadings, and regression coefficients indicates that the BIS is a multidimensional construct. The fact that the BIS consists of items pertaining both to nocturnal and daytime sleep problems and represents two different sets of diagnostic criteria (A and B in the DSM-IV; APA, 1994) corroborates this interpretation. According to Little et al. (2013), the shared variance of a latent variable only represents the unidimensional part of a multidimensional construct. The multidimensional part of the variance is not accounted for, which may increase the possibility of residual covariance among the items.

Table 5.1

Goodness-of-Fit Statistics for Confirmatory Factor Analyzes of Measurement Models

Latent variable	χ^2	df	CFI	RMSEA	[90% CI]	SRMR
Physical Study Condition	183.755**	5	.99	.063	.056, .071	.023
Procrastination Scale	1506.512**	27	.97	.078	.075, .082	.034
Bergen Insomnia Scale	2002.6753**	9	.91	.158	.152, .164	.064

Note. $**p < .01$

Poorly fitted measurement models may compromise the goodness-of-fit of the structural model (Williams et al., 2009). To maintain psychometric rigor and preserve the structure of the scale, three parcels were calculated based on the mean of item pairs. Two of the parcels (Items 1, 2 and 3, 4) represented category A criteria of insomnia, while the third parcel (Items 5, 6) represented category B criteria.

Potential Moderating Effects of Gender and Years of Study Experience

The strength of the relationships between predictors and outcome variables may be affected by moderator variables. Gender and years of study experience are of special interest in the current context. Recent studies have demonstrated gender differences in mental health problems both among Norwegian university students (Hysing et al., 2015; Sivertsen, 2021) and in other countries (Prowse et al., 2021; Werner et al., 2021). Recent research also indicates that undergraduate students may experience reduced well-being, increased anxiety, and more negative feelings during the pandemic compared to postgraduate students (Camacho-Zuñiga et al., 2021; Dodd et al., 2021).

Two multigroup analyzes were fitted to investigate the possible moderating effect of gender and years of study experience. When analyzing the influence of gender, all parameters were first allowed to vary freely across gender (female/male). In the second step, the structural paths were constrained to be equal, and the difference in goodness-of-fit between the unconstrained and constrained models was calculated and evaluated following the recommendations of Chen (2007). Corresponding analyzes

120 K. I. FOSTERVOLD, S. E. REME, H. I. STRØMSØ, and S. R. LUDVIGSEN

were conducted across years of study experience (undergraduate ≤ 3 years of study experience/postgraduate ≤ 6 years of study experience).

RESULTS

Descriptive Analyzes

We first checked whether students' perceived level of stress had changed from what they considered being typical after the campus lockdown. The results indicate a higher level of stress after the lockdown ($M = 3.30$, $SD = 1.15$) than their usual stress level ($M = 2.97$, $SD = .89$). However, 36.9% of the participants reported no change in perceived stress level, 19.5% reported a lower level after the lockdown, and 43.6% reported an increased stress level due to the lockdown. Loneliness, defined as a mean higher than 3 (sometimes), were experienced by 47.3% of the students.

Means, standard deviations, and bivariate correlations between all variables included in the analysis are shown in Table 5.2. The results showed low-to-moderate zero-order correlations between the variables. Well-being had the strongest relationship with all the other variables, and those relationships were negative. Thus, students' perceived well-being decreases when scores on the other variables increase.

Testing the Proposed Structural Equation Model

Based on the theoretical considerations outlined in the introduction, a structural equation model containing seven variables was drawn. Three

Table 5.2

Means, Standard Deviations, and Zero-Order Correlations (r) Among Variables

Variable	M	SD	1.	2.	3.	4.	5.	6.	7.
1. Procrastination	3.15	.90	–						
2. Physical conditions	3.56	1.51	.19**	–					
3. Loneliness	3.05	1.03	.22**	.27**	–				
4. Perceived stress	3.11	.78	.16**	.20**	.31**	–			
5. Perceived health	2.51	.80	.29**	.22**	.41**	.31**	–		
7. Well-being	6.23	1.96	–.31**	–.30**	–.50**	–.32**	–.54**	–.40**	–

Note. **$p < .01$

latent constructs, loneliness, physical work condition, and procrastination, were considered exogenous predictor variables. Self-perceived stress was entered as an endogenous (mediating) latent predictor variable, while self-perceived health and sleep problems were drawn as latent outcome variables. Being a single item, well-being was modeled as an observed outcome variable. Hypothesized direct causal paths were drawn between each predictor variable and the outcome variables. Bidirectional paths were added to the model between the exogeneous predictor variables and between the outcome variables to represent the intercorrelations between these variables.

The model's goodness-of-fit measures revealed a significant chi-square ($\chi2(304) = 6147.257, p < .001$), which implies that the hypothesis of exact fit is rejected. This result should be expected, however, provided the sample size of the study. The other fit measures, CFI (.95), RMSEA (.046, 90% CI [.045, .047]), and SRMR (.038), indicated good fit with the empirical data. The model, presented in Figure 5.1, explained 36% of the variance in sleep problems and 37% of the variance in self-perceived health and well-being.

Figure 5.1

Proposed Theoretical Model Depicting Structural Relationships Among Exogenous Predictor Variables, Endogenous Predictor Variables, and Outcome Variables

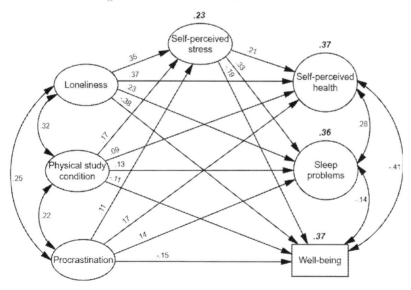

Note. Numbers on arrows are standardized regression coefficients. Large, bold, italicized numbers are R^2 (explained variance). Empirical indicators and error terms are omitted to enhance readability.

Direct Effects

As shown in Figure 5.1, the path coefficients varied from quite small to rather large. It should be noted, however, that all displayed direct effects were significant (p <.001) due to the large sample size. Loneliness was associated with increased self-perceived stress (β = .35), reduced self-perceived health (β = .37), increased sleep problems (β = .23), and reduced well-being (β = –.38). Dissatisfaction with the physical study condition was associated with increased self-perceived stress (β = .17), reduced self-perceived health (β = .09), increased sleep problems (β =.13), and reduced well-being (β = –.11). A tendency to procrastinate was associated with increased self-perceived stress (β = .11), reduced self-perceived health (β = .17), increased sleep problems (β = .14), and reduced well-being (β = –.15). Direct associations were also found between increased self-perceived stress and reduced self-perceived health (β = .21), increased sleep problems (β = .33), and reduced well-being (β = –.19). Both the exogenous predictor variables and the endogenous outcome variables were moderately correlated.

Indirect Effects

Indirect effects were modeled from all exogenous predictor variables to all outcome variables through self-perceived stress. Table 5.3 shows the bootstrapped indirect effects as both standardized regression coefficients (β) and unstandardized regression coefficients (b), as well as their associated standard errors (SE), 95% CIs, and probability values (p).

Table 5.3

Indirect (Mediated) and Total Effects. Standardized Regression Coefficients (β), Unstandardized Regression Coefficients (b), Standard Errors (SE), Their Associated 95% CIs, and Probability Values (p)

Path	β	b	SE	95% CI		p
				LL	UL	
Indirect effect						
Lon→SPS→SPH	.074	.036	.003	.031	.041	< .001
Lon→SPS→SP	.114	.134	.008	.121	.149	< .001
Lon→SPS→WB	–.066	–.117	.009	–.133	–.103	< .001

(Table continued on next page)

Relationships Between Study Conditions, Stress, and Perceived Health   123

Table 5.3 (Continued)

Indirect (Mediated) and Total Effects. Standardized Regression Coefficients (β), Unstandardized Regression Coefficients (b), Standard Errors (SE), Their Associated 95% CIs, and Probability Values (p)

Path	β	b	SE	95% CI		p
				LL	UL	
PSC→SPS→SP	.056	.051	.005	.043	.061	< .001
PSC→SPS→WB	−.032	−.045	.005	−.054	−.037	< .001
Pro→SPS→SPH	.023	.018	.003	.013	.022	< .001
Pro→SPS→SP	.036	.065	.009	.050	.081	< .001
Pro→SPS→WB	−.021	−.057	.009	−.072	−.043	< .001
Total effect						
Lon→SPH	.443	.220	.007	.208	.232	< .001
Lon→SP	.348	.409	.016	.382	.435	< .001
Lon→WB	−.444	−.793	.021	−.828	−.759	< .001
PSC→SPH	.121	.047	.005	.039	.055	< .001
PSC→SP	.186	.171	.012	.151	.191	< .001
PSC→WB	−.147	−.205	.016	−.231	−.179	< .001
Pro→SPH	.191	.146	.010	.130	.161	< .001
Pro→SP	.178	.322	.022	.287	.358	< .001
Pro→WB	−.173	−.476	.027	−.523	−.433	< .001

Note. Lon = loneliness, PSC = physical study conditions, Pro = procrastination, SPS = self-perceived stress, SPH = self-perceived health, SP = sleep problems, WB = well-being, LL = lower limit, UP = upper limit.

Due to the large sample size, all indirect effects displayed in Table 5.3 were significant. The most pronounced effects were found for loneliness, where high loneliness seems to be associated with reduced self-perceived health, increased sleep problems, and reduced well-being, all mediated through self-perceived stress. The indirect effect of loneliness on sleep problems (β = .144) seems especially high. The indirect effects of the physical study condition were more intermediate, but for all three relations, dissatisfaction with the physical study condition seems to be associated with reduced health and well-being. The highest association was found for sleep problems (β = .056). The same pattern was also present for indirect effects of procrastination on the outcome measures, although the associations were somewhat weaker. The highest indirect effect was again present for the association of procrastination with sleep problems ($\beta = .036$).

Total Effects

The total effects of the three predictor variables, loneliness, physical study condition, and procrastination, are displayed in Table 5.3. The most prominent effect was found for loneliness, where high loneliness yielded reduced well-being ($\beta = -.444$), reduced self-perceived health ($\beta = .443$), and increased sleep problems ($\beta = .348$). Although somewhat smaller, the total effects of physical study condition and procrastination corroborate this pattern. Both dissatisfaction with the physical study conditions and increased procrastination were associated with reduced health and well-being. The smallest total effect was observed for the physical study condition on self-perceived health ($\beta = .121$), while the strongest effect was procrastination on self-perceived health ($\beta = .191$).

Stability of the Structural Model Across Gender and Years of Study Experience

The results showed that the chi-square of the unconstrained cross-gender model was significant ($\chi2(608) = 6367.429$, $p < .001$). All other fit measures indicated a good fit with the data (CFI = .95, RMSEA = .033, 90% CI [.032, .033], SRMR = .038). The difference between the unconstrained model and the model with the structural path coefficients constrained to be equal revealed a significant Chi-square ($\Delta\chi2 = 54.764$, $\Delta df = 11$, $p < .001$). As such, this result indicates that gender moderated the relationships shown in Figure 5.1. Inspections of the model parameters show mostly minor unsystematic changes in path values (β_{diff} between 0 and .03). The effect of loneliness might represent an exception, indicating a somewhat stronger relationship for males compared to females (max $\beta_{diff} = .07$). On the other hand, the effect of physical study condition on stress ($\beta_{diff} = .09$) indicated a stronger relationship for females.

However, the effect size was very low (w = .02) and changes in the other fit measures were minor (ΔCFI =.001, ΔRMSEA < .001 ΔSRMR < .001). The explained variance for all three outcome variables were also comparable. Considering the large sample size, the observed moderating effect of gender is hardly of any practical importance, which implies that the model shown in Figure 5.1 is better interpreted as stable across gender.

Analysis of the unconstrained model across study experience revealed a significant chi-square ($\chi2(608) = 6528.860$, $p < .001$). All other fit measures

Relationships Between Study Conditions, Stress, and Perceived Health   125

indicated good fit (CFI = .95, RMSEA = .033, 90% CI [.034, .049], SRMR = .037). The difference between the unconstrained model and the constrained model was significant ($\Delta\chi2$ = 22.626, Δdf = 11, p = .02). Changes in the other fit measures were minimal (ΔCFI <.001, ΔRMSEA <.001, ΔSRMR <.001), and the effect size was very low (w = .02). Inspection of the model parameters indicated mostly minor unsystematic differences between the two groups. The largest difference (β_{diff} = .06) was observed for the effect of stress on sleep problems, indicating a stronger relationship for undergraduates than for postgraduates. The explained variance showed only minor differences. The most plausible interpretation is therefore to consider the model shown in Figure 5.1, stable also across years of study experience.

DISCUSSION

The aim of the present study was to investigate how loneliness, the physical study condition, and procrastination affected self-perceived health, sleep problems, and well-being of students during the initial COVID-19 lockdown of the University of Oslo. To this end, three hypotheses were put forward (a, b, and c). (a): Students' feelings of loneliness, their satisfaction with the physical study condition, and their tendencies to procrastinate will predict the perceived level of stress, self-perceived health, sleep problems, and well-being. (b): Students' perceived level of stress will predict their self-perceived health, sleep problems, and well-being. (c): Students' perceived level of stress mediates the effect of the three stressors on students' self-perceived health, sleep problems, and well-being, by showing indirect associations between the three predictor variables and the three outcome variables through self-perceived stress. The suggested structural path model showed a satisfactory fit with the empirical data, confirming all the three hypotheses (a, b, and c). The structural path model was stable across potential moderator variables, as neither gender nor years of study experience seemed to moderate the structural relationships.

The strongest effect was found for loneliness, where feeling lonely seemed to adversely influence health, sleep problems, and well-being, both directly and indirectly. Dissatisfaction with the physical study condition and a tendency toward procrastination also negatively influenced sleep, health, and well-being, although the associations were somewhat weaker. Moderate correlations were observed between the three predictor variables, as well as between the three outcome variables. The model explained between 36 and 37% of the variance in the outcome variables. Despite representing a substantial proportion, most of the variance is thus explained by other unknown factors.

The adverse effects of loneliness on health and well-being are well known from the literature (Brown et al., 2018; Hawkley & Cacioppo, 2010). We therefore hypothesized that loneliness would play an important role in the context of the new study situation of COVID-19, where social distancing and isolation were enforced by law. Indeed, loneliness did play a particularly important role in our study, exerting a strong influence on all the outcome variables, both directly and mediated by self-perceived stress. From a theoretical point of view, loneliness represents a serious threat to the individual, namely, the threat of social exclusion (Vanhalst et al., 2015). The perception of a threat will trigger a stress response that will likely be sustained as long as the stressor is perceived as threatening (Ursin & Eriksen, 2010) (i.e., for as long as the student feels lonely). Clearly, students also experienced loneliness prior to the pandemic, but a salient difference between the study situation before and three months into the lockdown is the accessibility of coping strategies that could mitigate the risk of loneliness or buffer its negative effects. Enforced isolation deprived students of most of the means and strategies for coping with loneliness (e.g., volunteering in student organizations). This was further aggravated by the student housing situation, which is generally more restricted in Oslo, both socially (many live alone) and environmentally (many do not have direct access to nature). We therefore argue that university students represent a particularly vulnerable group (Sivertsen et al., 2022). Whereas individuals staying in families had other family members to socialize with and people living in the suburbs and rural areas had access to nature as a recreational space (Soga et al., 2021), the university students had fewer of these opportunities. Moreover, many of them were new to the city, with little or no social network. Social situations such as lectures, seminars and parties are thus crucial arenas for students where they can connect and get to know each other. These arenas disappeared during lockdown.

Students located in other places in the world also experienced greater stress due to the new extraordinary study situation imposed by COVID-19 (Elmer et al., 2020; Loda et al., 2020). In our study, more than 40% of the students at the University of Oslo reported experiencing more stress than before the pandemic, and the prevalence of loneliness was high (43.7%). This sets the stage for a negative cascade of physical and mental health deterioration, which our structural model, to a large degree, supports. Interestingly, however, a significant proportion of the students experienced *less* stress than before the pandemic in our study. This illustrates how a stressful situation is experienced differently across individuals, probably due to complex interactions between individual and contextual factors (Sapolsky, 1994, 2015). Nevertheless, whether the negative effects of the lockdown will be reversed in the post-pandemic phase where student life normalizes remains to be seen and is a topic for future studies.

Relationships Between Study Conditions, Stress, and Perceived Health   127

Whereas loneliness turned out to be the strongest predictor in the model, satisfaction with the physical study condition and students' tendencies for procrastination were also significantly related to mental health outcome measures. Stress has been defined as a result of individuals' lack of appropriate resources to master a challenging situation (Lazarus & Folkman, 1984). The new study situation could certainly represent challenging changes in students' learning environments because of the unavailability of campus-based resources. Likewise, scaffolds provided at campus related to study routines and schedules were not available, allowing more room for procrastination. Hence, progress relied more on students' ability to independently organize their study environment, and because of the added responsibility in their study routines, the perceived level of stress was increased for many students. Universities could potentially reduce the impact of those stressors by emphasizing the teaching of self-regulated learning, such as time management, and by establishing more structured learning settings in remote teaching modes. For example, Carpenter et al. (2012) show the advantage of spreading work on the learning content over time (*spacing*). In line with this, Gonzalez et al. (2020) found that students improved their performance under COVID-19 confinement when they studied continuously, in contrast to the pre-COVID-19 strategy of cramming in the last days before an exam. Thus, both the increase in structured learning settings and a greater emphasis on the development of students' self-regulated learning skills could potentially have contributed to a reduced impact of the stressors related to the study condition and procrastination.

Strengths and Limitations

The current study was based on a large sample with a relatively high response rate, and although both should be considered methodological strengths, they do not necessarily ensure representativity of the population (Hendra & Hill, 2019). Analyzes of the sampling frame (all students at the university) did not indicate substantial nonresponse bias across university faculties/schools, age, gender, or years of study. The structural model tested in the study was also shown to be stable across gender and years of study. The use of SEM should also be considered advantageous compared with the regression analyzes often used in previous research. Taken together, this indicates that the structural model depicted in Figure 5.1 is robust and provides a valid picture of the situation at the university two months after the lockdown.

The cross-sectional design makes it difficult to draw firm conclusions about causality. Although the paths depicted in Figure 5.1 are modeled in accordance with theory and previous findings within the field, they should be regarded as substantiated hypotheses. It is also impossible to discern how much the COVID-19 pandemic has affected the observed relationships. In both cases, the causal relationships should be subject to further investigation, preferably utilizing longitudinal designs.

Conclusion

To our knowledge, this is the first study to empirically test a model that specifies direct and indirect relationships between individual variables collectively in an ecologically valid stressful situation. Thus, we believe it represents a unique extension of prior work in the field.

The study identifies loneliness as the strongest predictor of students' mental health. Given the high degree of confinement experienced by many students during the lockdown and the prominence of social contact, social cohesion, and belongingness during this transitional period of life, this finding emphasizes the importance of developing a digital social infrastructure for students. In the wake of the pandemic, this finding also accentuates the responsibility of health authorities to carefully consider cost-benefit calculations for youths and other vulnerable groups before implementing intrusive measures. Considering that limited—or none— access to university campuses seems to have a negative and significant impact on students' mental health (Fretheim et al., 2021; Sivertsen et al., 2022), universities should emphasize availability to common spaces both for social contact and for study work. When remote learning is the sole alternative, study programs should provide digital environments and tasks requiring students to be socially involved.

Apart from loneliness, the study also deemed addressing physical study condition and procrastination to be important for mental health during the initial phase of the lockdown. To be better prepared for similar situations, universities and society should further strengthen students' skills in self-regulated learning. Such skills seem to be particularly important in less structured learning environments, as students must rely more on their own study routines and schedules. There are indications that self-regulation skills might have a buffering effect on students' perceived stress (von Keyserlingk et al., 2022), and that students have profited from taking part in learning modules on self-regulated learning during the pandemic. For example, did Hadwin and colleagues (2022) demonstrate that students participating in a one semester online learning (self-regulation) module during the fall 2020 experienced fewer academic challenges than peers not taking the module. Hence, by providing opportunities for students to acquire a repertoire of learning strategies, universities can help facilitate students' adaptation to new learning contexts, tasks, and situations.

REFERENCES

American Psychiatric Association. (1994). *Diagnostic and statistical manual of mental disorders* (4th ed.).

American Psychiatric Association. (2000). *Diagnostic and statistical manual of mental disorders* (4th ed., text rev.).

American Psychiatric Association. (2013). *Diagnostic and statistical manual of mental disorders* (5th ed.).

Brown, E. G., Gallagher, S., & Creaven, A. M. (2018). Loneliness and acute stress reactivity: A systematic review of psychophysiological studies. *Psychophysiology*, 55(5), e13031. https://doi.org/10.1111/psyp.13031

Camacho-Zuñiga, C., Pego, L., Escamilla, J., & Hosseini, S. (2021). The impact of the COVID-19 pandemic on students' feelings at high school, undergraduate, and postgraduate levels. *Heliyon*, 7(3), e06465. https://doi.org/10.1016/j.heliyon.2021.e06465

Cantril, H. (1965). *The pattern of human concerns*. Rutgers University Press.

Carlopio, J. R. (1996). Construct validity of a physical work environment satisfaction questionnaire. *Journal of Occupational Health Psychology*, 1(3), 330–344. https://doi.org/10.1037/1076-8998.1.3.330

Carpenter, S. K., Cepeda, N. J., Rohrer, D., Kang, S. H. K., & Pashler, H. (2012). Using spacing to enhance diverse forms of learning: Review of recent research and implications for instruction. *Educational Psychology Review*, 24, 369–378. https://doi.org/10.1007/s10648-012-9205-z

Chen, F. F. (2007). Sensitivity of Goodness of Fit Indexes to Lack of Measurement Invariance. *Structural Equation Modeling: A Multidisciplinary Journal*, 14(3), 464–504. https://doi.org/10.1080/10705510701301834

Debowska, A., Horeczy, B., Boduszek, D., & Dolinski, D. (2020). A repeated cross-sectional survey assessing university students' stress, depression, anxiety, and suicidality in the early stages of the COVID-19 pandemic in Poland. *Psychological Medicine*, 1–4. https://doi.org/10.1017/S003329172000392X

DeSalvo, K. B., Fisher, W. P., Tran, K., Bloser, N., Merrill, W., & Peabody, J. (2006). Assessing measurement properties of two single-item general health measures. *Quality of Life Research*, 15(2), 191–120. https://doi.org/10.1007/s11136-005-0887-2

Diehl, K., Jansen, C., Ishchanova, K., & Hilger-Kolb, J. (2018). Loneliness at Universities: Determinants of Emotional and Social Loneliness among Students. *International Journal of Environmental Research and Public Health*, 15(9), 1865. https://www.mdpi.com/1660-4601/15/9/1865

Dodd, R. H., Dadaczynski, K., Okan, O., McCaffery, K. J., & Pickles, K. (2021). Psychological wellbeing and academic experience of university students in Australia during COVID-19. *International Journal of Environmental Research and Public Health*, 18(3), 866. https://www.mdpi.com/1660-4601/18/3/866

Danquah, E., & Asiamah, N. (2022). Associations between physical work environment, workplace support for health, and presenteeism: A COVID-19 context. *International Archives of Occupational and Environmental Health*, 95, 1807–1816. https://doi.org/10.1007/s00420-022-01877-1

Elmer, T., Mepham, K., & Stadtfeld, C. (2020). Students under lockdown: Comparisons of students' social networks and mental health before and during the COVID-19 crisis in Switzerland. *PLoS One*, *15*(7), e0236337. https://doi.org/10.1371/journal.pone.0236337

Eriksen, H. R., Murison, R., Pensgaard, A. M., & Ursin, H. (2005). Cognitive activation theory of stress (CATS): From fish brains to the Olympics. *Psychoneuroendocrinology*, *30*(10), 933–938. https://doi.org/10.1016/j.psyneuen.2005.04.013

Fretheim, A., Helleve, A., Løyland, B., Sandbekken, I. H., Flatø, M., Telle, K., Viksmoen, S. W., Schjøll, A., Helseth, S., Jamtvedt, G., & Hart, R. K. (2021). Relationship between teaching modality and COVID-19, well-being, and teaching satisfaction (campus & corona): A cohort study among students in higher education. *Public Health in Practice*, *2*, 100187. https://doi.org/10.1016/j.puhip.2021.100187

Gardani, M., Bradford, D. R. R., Russell, K., Allan, S., Beattie, L., Ellis, J. G., & Akram, U. (2022). A systematic review and meta-analysis of poor sleep, insomnia symptoms and stress in undergraduate students. *Sleep Medicine Reviews*, *61*, 101565. https://doi.org/10.1016/j.smrv.2021.101565

Goldstein, A. N., & Walker, M. P. (2014). The role of sleep in emotional brain function. *Annual Review of Clinical Psychology*, *10*, 679–708. https://doi.org/10.1146/annurev-clinpsy-032813-153716

Gonzalez, T., de la Rubia, M. A., Hincz, K. P., Comas-Lopez, M., Subirats, L., Fort, S., & Sacha, G. M. (2020). Influence of COVID-19 confinement on students' performance in higher education. *PLoS One*, *15*, e0239490. https://doi.org/10.1371/journal.pone.0239490

Hadwin, A.F., Sukhawathanakul, P., Rostampour, R., & Bahena-Olivares, L. M. (2022). Do self-regulated learning practices and intervention mitigate the impact of academic challenges and COVID-19 distress on academic performance during online learning? *Frontiers in Psychology*, *13*, 813529. https://doi.org/10.3389/fpsyg.2022.813529

Han, K. S., Kim, L., & Shim, I. (2012). Stress and sleep disorder. *Experimental Neurobiology*, *21*(4), 141–150. https://doi.org/10.5607/en.2012.21.4.141

Hansen, T., Nilsen, T. S., Yu, B., Knapstad, M., Skogen, J. C., Vedaa, Ø., & Nes, R. B. (2021). Locked and lonely? A longitudinal assessment of loneliness before and during the COVID-19 pandemic in Norway. *Scandinavian Journal of Public Health*, *49*(7), 766–773. https://doi.org/10.1177/1403494821993711

Hawkley, L. C., & Cacioppo, J. T. (2010). Loneliness matters: a theoretical and empirical review of consequences and mechanisms. *Annals of Behavioral Medicine*, *40*(2), 218–227. https://doi.org/10.1007/s12160-010-9210-8

Hayley, A. C., Downey, L. A., Stough, C., Sivertsen, B., Knapstad, M., & Øverland, S. (2017). Social and emotional loneliness and self-reported difficulty initiating and maintaining sleep (DIMS) in a sample of Norwegian university students [hein]. *Scandinavian Journal of Psychology*, *58*(1), 91–99. https://doi.org/10.1111/sjop.12343

Heinrich, L. M., & Gullone, E. (2006). The clinical significance of loneliness: A literature review. *Clinical Psychology Review*, *26*(6), 695–718. https://doi.org/10.1016/j.cpr.2006.04.002

Hendra, R., & Hill, A. (2019). Rethinking response rates: New evidence of little relationship between survey response rates and nonresponse bias. *Evaluation Review*, *43*(5), 307–330. https://doi.org/10.1177/0193841x18807719

Horne, J. A. (1985). Sleep function, with particular reference to sleep deprivation. *Annals of Clinical Research*, *17*(5), 199–208.

Houdmont, J., Jachens, L., Randall, R., Hopson, S., Nuttall, S., & Pamia, S. (2019). What does a single-item measure of job stressfulness assess? *International Journal of Environmental Research and Public Health*, *16*(9), 1480. https://doi.org/10.3390/ijerph16091480

Hu, L. t., & Bentler, P. M. (1999). Cutoff criteria for fit indexes in covariance structure analysis: Conventional criteria versus new alternatives. *Structural Equation Modeling: A Multidisciplinary Journal*, *6*(1), 1–55. https://doi.org/10.1080/10705519909540118

Hughes, M. E., Waite, L. J., Hawkley, L. C., & Cacioppo, J. T. (2004). A short scale for measuring loneliness in large surveys: Results from two population-based studies. *Research on Aging*, *26*(6), 655–672. https://doi.org/10.1177/0164027504268574

Hysing, M., Pallesen, S., Stormark, K. M., Jakobsen, R., Lundervold, A. J., & Sivertsen, B. (2015). Sleep and use of electronic devices in adolescence: Results from a large population-based study. *BMJ Open*, *5*(1), e006748. https://doi.org/10.1136/bmjopen-2014-006748

Idler, E. L., & Benyamini, Y. (1997). Self-rated health and mortality: A review of twenty-seven community studies. *Journal of health and social behavior*, *38*(1), 21–37. https://doi.org/10.2307/2955359

Johansson, F., Côté, P., Hogg-Johnson, S., Rudman, A., Holm, L. w., Grotle, M., Jensen, I., Sundberg, T., Edlund, k., & Skillgate, E. (2021). Depression, anxiety and stress among Swedish university students before and during six months of the COVID-19 pandemic: A cohort study. *Scandinavian Journal of Public Health*, *49*(7), 741–749. https://doi.org/10.1177/14034948211015814

Kazlauskaitė, R., Martinaitytė, I., Lyubovnikova, J., & Augutytė-Kvedaravičienė, I. (2022). The physical office work environment and employee wellbeing: Current state of research and future research agenda. *International Journal of Management Reviews*, 1–30. https://doi.org/10.1111/ijmr.12315

Kim, J., & De Dear, R. (2012). Nonlinear relationships between individual IEQ factors and overall workspace satisfaction. *Building and Environment*, *49*, 33–40. https://doi.org/10.1016/j.buildenv.2011.09.022

Kline, R. B. (2016). *Principles and practice of structural equation modeling* (4 ed.). The Guilford Press.

Lazarus, R. S., & Folkman, S. (1984). *Stress, appraisal, and coping*. Springer.

Little, T. D., Rhemtulla, M., Gibson, K., & Schoemann, A. M. (2013). Why the items versus parcels controversy needn't be one. *Psychological Methods*, *18*(3), 285–300. https://doi.org/10.1037/a0033266

Loda, T., Löffler, T., Erschens, R., Zipfel, S., & Herrmann-Werner, A. (2020). Medical education in times of COVID-19: German students' expectations—A cross-sectional study. *PLoS One*, *15*(11), e0241660. https://doi.org/10.1371/journal.pone.0241660

McEwen, B. S. (2017). Neurobiological and systemic effects of chronic stress. *Chronic stress, 1*, 1–11. https://doi.org/10.1177/2470547017692328

Neuner, F. (2023). Physical and social trauma: towards an integrative transdiagnostic perspective on psychological trauma that involves threats to status and belonging. *Clinical Psychology Review, 99*, 102219. https://doi.org/10.1016/j.cpr.2022.102219

NOKUT (Norwegian Agency for Quality Assurance in Education). (2021). *Studiebarometeret 2020—Hovedtendenser* [The National Study Survey 2020—Main trends]. https://www.nokut.no/globalassets/studiebarometeret/2021/hoyere-utdanning/studiebarometeret-2020_hovedtendenser_1-2021.pdf

Pallesen, S., Bjorvatn, B., Nordhus, I. H., Sivertsen, B., Hjørnevik, M., & Morin, C. M. (2008). A new scale for measuring insomnia: The Bergen Insomnia Scale. *Perceptual and Motor Skills, 107*(3), 691–706. https://doi.org/10.2466/pms.107.3.691-706

Pitman, A., Mann, F., & Johnson, S. (2018). Advancing our understanding of loneliness and mental health problems in young people. *The Lancet Psychiatry, 5*(12), 955–956. https://doi.org/10.1016/S2215-0366(18)30436-X

Prowse, R., Sherratt, F., Abizaid, A., Gabrys, R. L., Hellemans, K. G. C., Patterson, Z. R., & McQuaid, R. J. (2021). Coping with the COVID-19 pandemic: examining gender differences in stress and mental health among university students. *Frontiers in Psychiatry, 12*. https://doi.org/10.3389/fpsyt.2021.650759

Rab, S. L., & Admon, R. (2021). Parsing inter-and intra-individual variability in key nervous system mechanisms of stress responsivity and across functional domains. *Neuroscience & Biobehavioral Reviews, 120*, 550–564. https://doi.org/10.1016/j.neubiorev.2020.09.007

Robotham, D. (2008). Stress among higher education students: Towards a research agenda. *Higher Education, 56*(6), 735–746. https://doi.org/10.1007/s10734-008-9137-1

Sapolsky, R. M. (1994). Individual differences and the stress response. *Seminars in Neuroscience, 6*(4), 261–269. https://doi.org/10.1006/smns.1994.1033

Sapolsky, R. M. (2015). Stress and the brain: Individual variability and the inverted-U. *Nature Neuroscience, 18*(10), 1344–1346. https://doi.org/10.1038/nn.4109

Shrout, P. E., & Bolger, N. (2002). Mediation in experimental and nonexperimental studies: New procedures and recommendations. *Psychological Methods, 7*(4), 422–445. https://doi.org/10.1037/1082-989X.7.4.422

Simon, E. B., Vallat, R., Barnes, C. M., & Walker, M. P. (2020). Sleep Loss and the socio-emotional brain. *Trends in Cognitive Sciences, 24*(6), 435–450. https://doi.org/https://doi.org/10.1016/j.tics.2020.02.003

Sirois, F. M. (2014). Procrastination and stress: Exploring the role of self-compassion. *Self and Identity, 13*(2), 128–145. https://doi.org/10.1080/15298868.2013.763404

Sirois, F. M., Kitner, R., & Hirsch, J. K. (2015). Self-compassion, affect, and health-promoting behaviors. *Health Psychology, 34*(6), 661–669. https://doi.org/10.1037/hea0000158

Relationships Between Study Conditions, Stress, and Perceived Health 133

Sivertsen, B. (2021). *Studentenes helse og trivselsundersøkelse: Tilleggsundersøkelse 2021* [Students' health and well-being survey: Supplementary survey 2021]. Norwegian Institute of Public Health. https://sioshotstorage.blob.core.windows.net/shot2018/SHOT2021.pdf

Sivertsen, B., Knapstad, M., Petrie, K., O'Connor, R., Lønning, K. J., & Hysing, M. (2022). Changes in mental health problems and suicidal behaviour in students and their associations with COVID-19-related restrictions in Norway: A national repeated cross-sectional analysis. *BMJ Open*, *12*, e057492. https://doi.org /10.1136/bmjopen-2021-057492

Soga, M., Evans, M. J., Cox, D. T., & Gaston, K. J. (2021). Impacts of the COVID-19 pandemic on human–nature interactions: Pathways, evidence and implications. *People and Nature*, *3*(3), 518–527. https://doi.org/10.1002/pan3.10201

Stallman, H. M. (2010). Psychological distress in university students: A comparison with general population data. *Australian Psychologist*, *45*(4), 249–257. https://doi.org/10.1080/00050067.2010.482109

Steel, P. (2010). Arousal, avoidant and decisional procrastinators: Do they exist? *Personality and Individual Differences*, *48*(8), 926–934. https://doi.org/10.1016/j.paid.2010.02.025

Tov, W., Keh, J. S., Tan, Y. Q., Tan, Q. Y., & Indra Alam Syah, A. (2023). Assessing subjective well-being: A review of common measures. In W. Ruch, A. B. Bakker, L. Tay, & F. Gander (Eds.), *Handbook of positive psychology assessment* (pp. 38–57). Hogrefe.

Ursin, H., & Eriksen, H. R. (2010). Cognitive activation theory of stress (CATS). *Neuroscience and Biobehavioral Reviews*, *34*(6), 877–881. https://doi.org/10.1016/j.neubiorev.2009.03.001

Vandekerckhove, M., & Wang, Y. L. (2018). Emotion, emotion regulation and sleep: An intimate relationship. *AIMS neuroscience*, *5*(1), 1–17. https://doi.org/10.3934/Neuroscience.2018.1.1

Vanhalst, J., Soenens, B., Luyckx, K., Van Petegem, S., Weeks, M. S., & Asher, S. R. (2015). Why do the lonely stay lonely? Chronically lonely adolescents' attributions and emotions in situations of social inclusion and exclusion. *Journal of Personality and Social Psychology*, *109*(5), 932–948. https://doi.org/10.1037/pspp0000051

Vischer, J. C. (2008). Towards an environmental psychology of workspace: How people are affected by environments for work. *Architectural Science Review*, *51*(2), 97–108. https://doi.org/10.3763/asre.2008.5114

von Keyserlingk, L., Yamaguchi-Pedroza, K., Arum, R., & Eccles, J. S. (2022). Stress of university students before and after campus closure in response to COVID-19. *Journal of Community Psychology*, *50*(1), 285–301. https://doi.org/10.1002/jcop.22561

von Soest, T., Kozák, M., Rodríguez-Cano, R., Fluit, D. H., Cortés-García, L., Ulset, V. S., Haghish, E. F., & Bakken, A. (2022). Adolescents' psychosocial well-being one year after the outbreak of the COVID-19 pandemic in Norway. *Nature Human Behaviour*, *6*(2), 217–228. https://doi.org/10.1038/s41562-021-01255-w

Werner, A. M., Tibubos, A. N., Mülder, L. M., Reichel, J. L., Schäfer, M., Heller, S., Pfirrmann, D., Edelmann, D., Dietz, P., Rigotti, T., & Beutel, M. E. (2021). The impact of lockdown stress and loneliness during the COVID-19 pandemic on mental health among university students in Germany. *Scientific Reports, 11*(1), 22637. https://doi.org/10.1038/s41598-021-02024-5

Wheeler, L., Reis, H., & Nezlek, J. B. (1983). Loneliness, social interaction, and sex roles. *Journal of Personality and Social Psychology, 45*(4), 943. https://doi.org/10.1037/0022-3514.45.4.943

WHO. (2021). *UN Decade of Healthy Ageing 2021–2030.* https://www.who.int/initiatives/decade-of-healthy-ageing

Williams, L. J., Vandenberg, R. J., & Edwards, J. R. (2009). Structural equation modeling in management research: A guide for improved analysis. *The Academy of Management Annals, 3*(1), 543–604. https://doi.org/10.1080/19416520903065683

Yang, B., Wang, Y., Cui, F., Huang, T., Sheng, P., Shi, T., Huang, C., Lan, Y., & Huang, Y. N. (2018). Association between insomnia and job stress: A meta-analysis. *Sleep and Breathing, 22*(4), 1221–1231. https://doi.org/10.1007/s11325-018-1682-y

Yoo, S.-S., Gujar, N., Hu, P., Jolesz, F. A., & Walker, M. P. (2007). The human emotional brain without sleep—A prefrontal amygdala disconnect. *Current Biology, 17*(20), R877–R878. https://doi.org/10.1016/j.cub.2007.08.007

Zawadzki, M. J., Graham, J. E., & Gerin, W. (2013). Rumination and anxiety mediate the effect of loneliness on depressed mood and sleep quality in college students. *Health Psychology, 32(2),* 212–222. https://doi.org/10.1037/a0029007

Zhu, J., Racine, N., Xie, E. B., Park, J., Watt, J., Eirich, R., Dobson, K., & Madigan, S. (2021). Post-secondary student mental health during COVID-19: A meta-analysis. *Frontiers in Psychiatry, 12,* 777251. https://doi.org/10.3389/fpsyt.2021.777251

CHAPTER 6

COLLEGE STUDENTS, STRESS, AND COVID

Lessons and Potential for the Future

Shannon C. Mulhearn, Megan Adkins, and Stefanie Neal
University of Nebraska at Kearney

ABSTRACT

The coronavirus disease (COVID-19) caused a high infectious and fatality rate and impacted the health and wellness of persons of all ages. Of particular interest in this study was the impact on university students. Guided by the health belief model and Lazarus and Folkman's stress and coping theory, researchers evaluated students' mental well-being and resilience. College students' perceptions of COVID-19 (susceptibility and severity), perceived stress, perceived wellness across six dimensions of wellness, and ability to cope with the stress were measured across three semesters (spring 2020, fall 2020, and spring 2021). Cross-sectional data were collected through two separate web-based questionnaires sent to students from two U.S. universities: one in the Southwest and the other in the Midwest. Researchers received 354 responses, of which a majority identified as white and female. The sample included students from all years of undergraduate and graduate programs. Results indicated high perceived levels of stress, however, students indicated feeling positive about control of their academic responsibilities. Early in the pandemic (fall, 2020), stressors were individual in nature while later into the second semester (spring, 2021), students reported feeling more stress related to health and wellness of friends and family. Connections to peers/friends/family and high perceived resilience were protective against perceived stress

---

Research on College Stress and Coping: Implications From the COVID-19 Pandemic and Beyond, pp. 135–159
Copyright © 2024 by Information Age Publishing
www.infoagepub.com
All rights of reproduction in any form reserved.

levels. As universities continue to educate through global challenges, college students' overall well-being should be considered along with their academic responsibilities.

Keywords: holistic wellness, resilience, questionnaire, peer support

INTRODUCTION

The mental and physical health burdens which follow disaster events negatively and significantly impact outcomes for young adults (North, 2016). College students have been impacted by the COVID-19 pandemic through loss, uncertainty, uncontrollable change in social, academic, occupational, housing and food resources, and unpredictable outcomes in physical and mental health challenges (Paterson, 2020). Although responses are bound to vary as individuals navigate disasters, to improve outcomes for young adult populations, more research focused on their experiences is warranted.

Several negative effects have already been identified as stemming from the stress and trauma related to this recent global health challenge. The COVID-19 pandemic has caused emotional struggle, which echoes research conducted from the 2014 Ebola virus disease outbreak (Schultz et al., 2016). Post-traumatic stress disorder (PTSD) has been linked to the chronic psychological stress, anxiety, and depression associated with COVID-19 due to the pandemic being considered a collective trauma (Boyraz & Legros, 2020; Hirschberger, 2018). Collective traumas associated with PTSD can occur first or second-hand. For example, trauma can be considered second hand when someone has seen another suffer, or from watching media and news outlets report about traumatic events. In these instances, the individual observing the trauma also suffers from post-traumatic stress symptoms (Pfefferbaum et al., 2001; Tomaszek & Muchacka-Cymerman, 2022). Additionally, beyond simply watching the pandemic affect the world, there is the fact that persons living in the United States have not had to deal with either stay-at-home or shelter-in-place policies in this generation. Emotional expressions such as irritability, insomnia, fear, anger, and even boredom have been attributed to the unique stresses such as during the pandemic (Pfefferbaum & North, 2020).

In this chapter, mental health refers to social, emotional, and psychological well-being. In a recent letter to the editor, Zhai and Du (2020) pointed out that universities carry the responsibility of supporting and accommodating students beyond simply their collegial or academic roles, but also in terms of their mental health. In this call to action, they related challenges facing college students' mental health due to COVID-19, such as feelings of loneliness, frustration, and anxiety. In consideration of components taken

College Students, Stress, and COVID   137

to indicate positive states of mental health, the concept of dimensions of wellness are used to indicate levels of holistic wellness. The purpose of this two-phase study was to better understand the experiences of college students navigating the university experience and maintaining academic success during the COVID-19 pandemic in terms of their holistic wellness.

The initial phase took place in the fall of 2020, and was driven by the research question, "What are college students' perceptions of their holistic wellness during the COVID-19 pandemic?" This first phase of the study was prompted by a desire to understand and address potential issues at a single, regional university. After gaining insight into perceptions, the research team became interested in how these findings might compare to other students in the United States and if these perceived states were, in fact, more generalizable than just to one location. Therefore, the next phase of the study posed the research question, "With the continued state of the pandemic, what are students' current perceived states regarding stress and coping?" Results from Phase I of the study were utilized to inform the design and methodology for Phase II.

Theoretical Foundation

The present study was grounded in the health belief model (HBM), a theoretical model built to guide health promotion and disease prevention programs (Rosenstock, 1974). Although the HBM is generally used in understanding individuals' health behaviors, it was utilized in this project to better understand the cognitive processes students traverse as they are within the midst of global health challenges. At the heart of the HBM is the idea that people want to avoid illnesses. This is paired with a belief that personal actions can prevent or cure illnesses. The HBM includes six constructs: (a) perceived susceptibility, (b) perceived severity, (c) perceived benefits, (d) perceived barriers, (e) cue to action, and (f) self-efficacy.

The first two constructs (perceived susceptibility and severity) have been suggested to work together to represent a person's perceived threat (Skinner et al., 2015). These constructs are critical to influencing behavior as it is the perception of threat that prompts consideration of the adoption of preventive measures which connect to the next two constructs. Once posed with the threat, a person considers both benefits and barriers to adopting healthy behavior. The construct of "cue to action" refers to the need for something to prompt the change in behavior. This could be internal such as personally feeling symptoms or external like seeing a commercial promoting vaccination. The final construct of self-efficacy is that after believing there is a threat and that taking action will be beneficial, the person must also believe they can overcome the barriers and they have the confidence to make the behavior change. HBM is often used in social science research and was recently referenced in relation to COVID-19 and vaccine hesitancy in a study which investigated students' perceptions of both *susceptibility* and *severity* of COVID-19 (Al-Metwali et al., 2021). Along with susceptibility and severity, the current study explored college students' *self-efficacy* related to coping with the stress of suddenly moving to online course work and isolation during a period of life that is normally thought of as quite social.

A second theory, Lazarus and Folkman's (1984) stress and coping theory, suggests a continual interplay between a person's appraisal of what is required of them and their perceived support and ability to meet the requirements. As this evaluation takes place, the internal process of determining appropriate stress management strategies begins. For example, Homa and colleagues (2022) considered this interaction of appraisal and support in cancer patients. Patients with breast and/or colorectal cancer reported their personal and familial health history, which was then compared to their personal views on cancer and survival. Researchers found that people who had previous experiences with health problems were less likely to use healthy coping strategies. They also noted these patients had stronger emotional responses to their current cancer diagnoses.

In order to understand the experiences college students were having during the initial months of COVID-19, the stress and coping theory (Lazarus & Folkman, 1984) was deemed critical. It was during the initial months of the pandemic that universities shut down and students were swiftly moved into virtual classroom formats. Applying the stress and coping theory (Lazarus & Folkman, 1984) to students' initial encounters with the unique stresses of the pandemic, students were likely going through the cognitive processes of comparing perceived demands to their perceived personal ability to manage these pressures.

Early research related to the pandemic suggested the need for continued evaluation of the psychosocial needs of the public (Pfefferbaum & North, 2020), more specifically the mental health of university students (Zhai & Du, 2020). Utilizing both the HBM (Rosenstock, 1974) and the stress coping theory (Lazarus-Folkman, 1984), this study took on the charge to learn about college students' experiences across a span of three semesters during the beginning of the COVID-19 pandemic. The remainder of this chapter is devoted to the two phases of the study with methods, results, and a discussion of lessons learned along with the connections between the phases of the study. Finally, suggestions are given for practical ways institutions of higher learning can provide positive support for college students moving forward.

METHODS

The present study included two phases (assessing spring 2020 and spring 2021), each with a separate population and online survey. Although a small portion of study participants may have participated in both Phase I and Phase II, intentional measures (described within the participants' sections to follow) were taken to target different populations in the two phases. All aspects of the study received approval from the University IRB prior to implementation. The methods are described separately based on the phase of the study and the two research questions.

Phase I— Spring 2020

Research Question: What Are College Students' Perceptions of Their Holistic Wellness During the COVID-19 Pandemic?

Participants

Recruitment was completed in the fall semester of 2020 through a general university email list of students attending a single regional university in the midwestern United States (hereafter referred to as University A). Due to restrictions at the institution which limits access to students' emails for research purposes, 500 randomly selected students received the invitation to participate in the study. The sample included students from all years of undergraduate and graduate programs (Please see Table 6.1 for a full description of participant demographics). The questionnaire was available for a total of five weeks online via Qualtrics. Two weeks after the initial email, a follow-up email was sent as a reminder of the request to participate in the study.

Instrumentation

Student Health and Wellness Questionnaire (SHAW-Q), a new instrument, was developed to meet the needs of the study. Although several measures exist for the constructs of interest, since the pandemic was a novel experience, no previously existing measure met our specific needs. Within this section, we will summarize the development of the 54-question SHAW-Q, followed by a description of each of the previously validated measures that were included within the final instrument.

First, a literature review was conducted to identify common stressors for college students. Using a university library-based multi-database search engine, a search for peer-reviewed articles was conducted using phrases including "college students" AND "perceived wellness," "college students" AND "common stressors," and "college students" AND "stress" AND "trauma." Articles were retained if they used college students as their sample, and if they provided information about common stressors. Following the review process, a list of the most common stressors was created, and an electronic questionnaire was developed, modeled after measures frequently found in the literature. Two measures, the General Health Questionnaire-28 (Goldberg & Hillier, 1979), and the Impact of Event Scale (Weiss & Marmar, 1996) were often used. The General Health Questionnaire-28 (Goldberg & Hillier, 1979) evaluates dimensions of psychological health within four categories of somatic symptoms, anxiety and insomnia, social dysfunction, and depression acted as a primary resource. The Impact of Event Scale-Revised questionnaire (Weiss & Marmar, 1996) assesses distress due to traumatic events.

In addition, the HBM (Rosenstock, 1974) served as the foundation for several questions aimed at learning about college students' perceived susceptibility to COVID-19 and their self-efficacy in coping with the related stresses. The wording of existing questions was tailored to better relate to the target population (college students) and to glean stressors and sense of control during the pandemic. The resulting questionnaire was sent to six experts in the areas of counseling, psychology, teacher education, and health and physical education. The experts all indicated the questions adequately measured the intended constructs. Suggested revisions such as condensing similar questions into matrices and using clear anchors on Likert-like questions were applied.

The final SHAW-Q included 54 questions with the following section breakdown: demographics ($n = 6$), perceived wellness ($n = 12$), protective factors ($n = 2$), stress and control ($n=20$), and COVID risk and anxiety ($n = 14$). The internal consistency reliability for the instrument was acceptable with $\alpha = .89$. Participants were asked to reflect on their experiences during the spring semester, which coincided with the start of the pandemic, and then were given the same criteria and asked to rate how they were feeling in the fall semester of 2020. The spring semester was unique in that there was a sudden change in course formats and new restrictions in social settings, such as social distancing and facemask requirements. The fall semester of 2020 marked the first full semester of COVID-19 of these ongoing restrictions for the campus.

Perceived Wellness. The first section of the questionnaire was based on the Perceived Wellness Scale (PWS; Adams, 1997) and focused on six dimensions of wellness: (a) emotional, (b) mental, (c) occupational,

College Students, Stress, and COVID   141

(d) physical, (e) social, and (f) spiritual. Three matrix-based questions were used to condense each dimension of wellness. This section asked participants to rate how they personally felt about each dimension of wellness during the COVID-19 experience. The matrix included sliding bars that participants moved to indicate rating from zero (not well) to 50% (moderate wellness) and 100% (extremely well). Each item was considered at the individual level to understand the six dimensions separately. Additionally, a mean of the six items was used as a composite variable titled, *Perceived Wellness* score.

Protective Factors. The next section of the questionnaire focused on factors protective against stress, including both Resilience and Social Connection. The Brief Resilience Scale (BRS; Smith et al., 2008) is a six-item instrument that asks participants about personal capacity for coping and optimism. In a single question, participants were presented with all six statements from the BRS and asked to select all with which they identified. The three positive statements, *I tend to bounce back quickly after hard times; It does not take me long to recover from a stressful event;* and *I usually come through difficult times with little trouble, and* three negative statements, *I have a hard time making it through stressful events; It is hard for me to snap back when something bad happens;* and *I tend to take a long time to get over set-backs in life,* were given. The positive statements were assigned +1 points while the negative statements were assigned –1. The added point total was used to indicate resilience (any positive total) or lack thereof (any negative total) of the participant. Student feelings about Connectedness with others on their campus was also inquired. Five statements such as "I feel like I belong," "I feel connected to other students," and "I feel connected to teachers." were provided for students to indicate all that applied to their thoughts with the range of possible answers from 0–5. Together, these two questions were summed to give a single score of Protective Factors with a range from 3 (lacking any connection or resilience) to 8 (both connected and resilient).

Stress and Control. This section of the questionnaire assessed common stressors for college students found in the literature including: (a) health and well-being of self, (b) ability to pay bills, (c) food and housing security, (d) access to emotional support, (e) access to resources to cope financially, (f) access to personal protection equipment, (g) exercise, (h) ability to adapt to academic changes, and (i) ability to adapt to community changes. Students were asked to rate to what extent they felt they experienced negative stress as well as their perception of control over the stressor in each semester. Each stressor was rated on a scale from 0 (no effect) to 100 (debilitating effect). In a separate question, participants were asked to mark which of the nine stressors they felt they had control over in the given semester.

COVID Risk and Anxiety. Using constructs from HBM (Rosenstock, 1974), questions in this section asked about personal exposure and perceived risk to the coronavirus. A single question inquired about how at-risk students felt about COVID-19 exposure while on campus with seven answer options ranging from 0 "*I feel totally safe*" to 5 "*No matter what I do I will get COVID.*" Another question asked about exposure risk off campus with questions like "*My job responsibilities require me to have increased exposure to COVID-19.*" Also included in this section of the questionnaire was a single composite question from the Coronavirus Anxiety Scale (CAS; Lee, 2020). The CAS includes 5 questions about anxiety that are specifically related to dysfunctional anxiety associated with the pandemic; this was converted to a single matrix question allowing responses ranging from 1 (never) to 5 (nearly every day) to describe characteristics of anxiety such as "*I felt dizzy or faint when reading or listening to the news.*" The resulting composite score of COVID-related anxiety ranged from 5 to 25.

Phase II—Spring 2021

Research Question: With the Continued State of the Pandemic, What Are Students' Current Perceived States Regarding Stress and Coping?

Participants

University A was included in both phases of the study. To provide intentional diversity, and thereby lending strength to the generalizability of the findings, a second university was included in this phase. University B is a large research institute in a major city in the Southwest United States and was targeted due to its geographically diverse setting from University A. However, in order to sample students who would have similar academic requirements or stresses for the purpose of comparisons between regions, purposeful recruitment was utilized to target students with similar academic responsibilities from both universities. Therefore, the recruitment email was sent through a single college program (College of Education) at both universities at the beginning of the spring semester of 2021. A representative from each College of Education was provided the email script and agreed to email 100 randomly selected majors within the college, resulting in a participant pool of 200. Participants ($n = 75$) identified as female (87%), male (12%), nonbinary (0%) or prefer not to answer (1.3%). Ethnicity was reported as mostly White (76%), followed by Hispanic (17%), Black (4.1%), and other (1.4%). Please see Table 6.1 for a full description of participant demographics by university and across both phases of the study. In line with the hope for a more diverse sample, Phase II resulted in more

College Students, Stress, and COVID 143

Hispanic and graduate student representation. All years of academic status were represented with the majority (60%) indicating undergraduate level.

Table 6.1

Participant Demographics Percentages

	University A		University B	Combined
	SHAW-Q N = 274	PSARQ N = 30	PSARQ N = 45	PSARQ Total N = 75
Student Level				
Undergraduate	76.7	63.3	57.8	60.0
Graduate	23.3	36.7	42.2	40.0
Gender				
Female	78.0	96.7	80.0	87.0
Male	18.9	3.3	17.8	12.0
Nonbinary	3.1	–	–	–
Prefer not to answer	–	–	2.2	1.3
Ethnicity				
Asian	3.56	–	–	–
Black	1.07	3.3	4.4	4.1
Hispanic	7.12	6.7	24.4	17.0
White	84.0	86.7	68.9	76.0
Other	–	3.3	–	1.4

Note: Participants were able to skip individual questions, therefore, all percentages may not add up to 100%.

Instrumentation

Due to the uncertainty and high number of changes that took place during the early months of the pandemic, the SHAW-Q utilized in Phase I provided data specifically asking students about their experiences during these dynamic months. On the other hand, by the spring semester of 2012, the research team felt it was important to take intentional measures related to stress and coping as related to the ongoing pandemic. By January 2021, many considered the pandemic to have created a "new normal" state during which students were simply continuing to cope with changes that had been made in their previous two semesters. Additionally, the research team wanted to be able to compare results from before the pandemic to future research beyond the pandemic. Therefore, in Phase

II, the electronic questionnaire consisted solely of previously validated measures, allowing researchers to focus more directly on specific characteristics of stress and coping commonly recognized in the literature. The final Perceived Stress and Resilience Questionnaire (PSARQ) included 43 questions with the following breakdown: demographics ($n = 6$), perceived stress ($n = 14$; $α = .88$), mindfulness ($n = 15$; $α = .91$), resilience ($n = 5$; $α = .89$), and connection ($n = 3$; $α = .83$). An explanation about each of the PSARQ sections of the questionnaire is provided next.

Perceived Stress. The Perceived Stress Scale (PSS, Cohen et al., 1983) includes 14 questions which ask respondents to consider their thoughts and feelings related to stress and how often they experienced stress in the past month. For trustworthiness, half of the questions are phrased in a negative way while the other seven are worded positively. For instance, one question asked, "*In the last month, how often have you felt nervous and 'stressed?'*" and another, "*In the last month, how often have you felt confident about your ability to handle your personal problems?*" Response options ranged from 1 (never) to 6 (very often); positively phrased questions were reverse coded. The sum of the 14 answers was analyzed with a possible range of 14–84. Higher scores indicated a higher level of perceived stress.

Mindfulness. The Mindful Attention Awareness Scale (MAAS, Brown & Ryan, 2003) is a 15-item instrument asking participants about mindfulness characteristics, such as attention and short-term memory. This scale has been used and validated on multiple populations (college students, cancer patients, adolescents) and across several language translations (Brown et al., 2003; Carlson & Brown, 2005; Lawlor et al., 2014). Response answer options ranged from 1 (almost always) to 6 (almost never). The average of the 15 ratings is used to indicate a level of mindfulness attention awareness, with a higher score suggesting a higher level of awareness.

Loneliness. The 3-Question Loneliness scale (L-3, Hughes et al., 2004) includes three questions to assess perceptions of social isolation. The 3-question version was adapted from the 20-item Revised UCLA Loneliness Scale (Russell et al., 1980) and has been validated for use in similar populations. Questions ask (a) *how often do you feel that you lack companionship*, (b) h*ow often do you feel left out*, and (c) h*ow often do you feel isolated from others*. Responses range from 1, Never to 4, Often. The sum of the three answers was used as a single score with higher scores indicating more loneliness/lack of social connection.

Resiliency. The Brief Resiliency Scale (BRS; Smith et al., 2008) was also utilized in Phase II. In this case, the six-item instrument was used as initially designed and validated by Smith and colleagues (2008). This scale includes three items with positive wording and three with negative wording in which participants rate their level of agreement from 1 (strongly disagree) to 5 (strongly agree). After reverse-coding the negative questions,

College Students, Stress, and COVID   145

the mean of the six questions was used to indicate a single resilience score of the participants in the study.

Data Analysis

All data from both questionnaires were entered into IBM SPSS (Version 27). To answer Research Question one, "What are college students' perceptions of their holistic wellness during the COVID-19 pandemic?", descriptive statistics and frequencies were run on the SHAW-Q data. Correlations were run across the variables within the SHAW-Q to consider relationships within the data. In answering Research Question two, "With the continued state of the pandemic, what are students' current perceived states regarding stress and coping?", descriptive statistics and frequencies were run on data from the PSARQ. Again, correlations were run in order to investigate connections between components of the questionnaire. Finally, data were considered across both phases to investigate any trends or changes over time. Threshold for significance was set at $p < .05$.

RESULTS

Table 6.2 displays the general overview of the descriptive results from both phases of the study and also provides a visual for how the sections of each questionnaire relate along the horizontal rows. For instance, only the SHAW-Q assessed Perceived Wellness, therefore, no similar variable is noted under the PSARQ. On the other hand, Protective Factors in the SHAW-Q aligned with the measures of Resilience in the PSARQ. As the initial research question was broad, researchers made use of a variety of measures. The second research question was more targeted to stress and coping and relied on only four measures. Results pertaining to each individual research question are discussed separately, followed by connections across all data.

Research Question One: Students' Perceptions of Early COVID-19 Challenges

In addressing the first research question, "What are college students' perceptions of their holistic wellness during the COVID-19 pandemic?", researchers investigated results from the SHAW-Q. As noted above, the questionnaire asked students to recall information from spring 2020

Table 6.2

General Descriptives From Both Questionnaires

	SHAW-Q			PSARQ		
Category	**Range**	**Spring 2020**	**Fall 2020**	**Category**	**Range**	**Spring 2021**
Perceived Wellness	0–100	$M = 55.49$ $SD = 19.76$	$M = 51.27$ $SD = 19.27$			
Protective Factors	–3 to 8		$M = 2.92$ $SD = 1.92$	Resilience	0–6	$M = 3.85$ $SD = 0.99$
Connection	1–5		$M = 2.83$ $SD = 1.46$	Loneliness	3–12	$M = 7.77$ $SD = 2.55$
Stress	0–100	$M = 58.26$ $SD = 20.55$	$M = 54.85$ $SD = 21.74$	Perceived Stress	14–84	$M = 47.80$ $SD = 9.87$
Control	0–15		$M = 4.77$ $SD = 4.11$	Mindfulness	1–6	$M = 3.59$ $SD = 0.99$
Perceived Risk	0 = Low risk 5 = High risk		$M = 2.23$ $SD = 1.45$			
COVID Anxiety	5–No anxiety 25–High anxiety		$M = 7.39$ $SD = 3.59$			

Note: Although different measures were used, the horizontal rows indicate similar measures, such as Protective Factors and Resilience, Connection and Loneliness, Stress and Perceived Stress, and Control and Mindfulness.

semester and for current reflections of experiences in the fall of 2020. The findings were compared to look at changes over the two semesters.

Figure 6.1 displays changes in the dimensions of wellness across the two semesters. The composite score of Perceived Wellness decreased from fall to spring of 2020, indicating students felt less well in the second semester of coping with COVID-19 changes. Examining each of the dimensions (see Figure 6.1), researchers found the Environmental dimension of wellness received the highest ratings in both semesters, indicating students perceived their wellness in this dimension to be high (spring $M = 63.60$, $SD = 28.64$; fall $M = 59.27$, $SD = 27.91$). The social dimension of wellness was rated the lowest for students in both semesters (spring $M = 46.24$, $SD = 28.57$; fall $M = 43.08$, $SD = 26.37$). Students reported feeling they were able to control an average of 1.92 ($SD = 2.00$) of the six dimensions of wellness with environmental selected most often, and mental and social wellness selected least often.

Figure 6.1

SHAW-Q Average Ratings of Perceived Wellness Categories by Semester

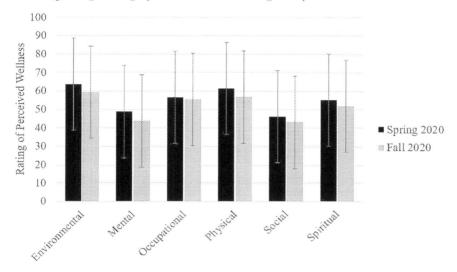

Note: Participants moved the sliding bar from zero (not well) to 100% (extremely well) in each dimension of wellness.

Reported negative effects from common stressors appeared to decrease from spring to fall 2020. However, by investigating the individual questions within this section, it was identified that students' stress increased from spring to fall relating to: (a) the well-being of family and friends, (b) food and housing security, and (c) access to resources to help cope. On the other hand, areas where stress was reported as less burdensome by fall were: (a) health and well-being of self, (b) ability to pay bills, (c) level of physical safety and exposure to coronavirus, (d) level of emotional support from others, and (e) ability to adapt to academic changes. With nine stressors posed, the average number of stressor students indicated feeling control over was 2.86 ($SD = 2.58$). Average self-reported effects of stressors were significantly correlated ($p < .05$; $r = .716$) between spring and fall 2020.

Smith and colleagues (2008) suggest that the resulting score from the BRS can be interpreted as 1 indicating low resilience, and 5 representing high resilience. Therefore, with a mean of 2.92 ($SD = 1.92$), students reported by fall 2020, they had a moderate level of protective factors. In both semesters, protective factors demonstrated a weak, negative relationship with perceived stress (see Table 6.3 for Phase I correlations). None of the respondents reported feeling they had zero connections with others

148 S. C. MULHEARN, M. ADKINS, and S. NEAL

or that they lacked any resilience. High scores for feeling connected were weakly, negatively associated with perceived stress for both semesters. Feeling connected was also weakly but negatively associated with anxiety overall.

Table 6.3

Phase I. Correlations Among the SHAW-Q Constructs

	Well Sp.	Well Fa.	Protect	Connect	Stress Sp.	Stress Fa.	Control	Risk	Anxiety
Well Sp.	1	.773*	.220*	.210*	.027	−.045	.422*	.081	−.231*
Well Fa.		1	.325*	.284*	−.062	−.157	.515*	.131	−.328*
Protect			1	.875*	−.088	−.150	.388*	.187*	−.239*
Connect				1	−.069	−.130	.318*	.224*	−.209*
Stress Sp.					1	.716*	−.236*	−.141	.274*
Stress Fa.						1	−.295*	−.198*	.295*
Control							1	.086	−.371*
Risk								1	−.084
Anxiety									1

Note: * denotes $p < .05$; Sp. = Spring; Fa.= Fall

Frequencies of responses were utilized to understand categorical responses within stressors. Participants ($n = 76$) indicated a past experience of having a loved one hospitalized or a close friend or family member who had been quarantined. Only 27 of participants had personally experienced being hospitalized due to COVID-19. The perceived risk of exposure was moderate ($M = 2.23$, $SD = 1.45$) with a rating of five suggesting a high perceived risk. Twelve percent of participants felt they would end up getting COVID-19 "*no matter what*" steps they took. Composite anxiety category scores out of 25 were low ($M = 7.39$, $SD = 3.59$). Within the CAS, the highest scoring item ($M = 1.65$, $SD = .971$) was "I've had trouble falling or staying asleep because I was thinking about Coronavirus" which received 17.4% of answers of 3 (several days), 4 (more than 7 days), or 5 (nearly every day over the last two weeks). There was a small and non-significant negative correlation between perceived risk and anxiety of getting COVID-19.

Research Question 2: Stress and Coping After Prolonged Exposure to the Pandemic

To address the second research question which asked, "With the continued state of the pandemic, what are students' current perceived states regarding stress and coping?", researchers focused on data from the PSRQ.

This data provided a snapshot of students' perceptions in the spring of 2021, which was the third semester affected by COVID-19. Beginning with their perceptions of stress, average PSS scores were 47.80 (SD = 9.87) with an available range of 14–84. To consider trends within each individual question from the PSS, means were also examined by question. The questions receiving the highest ratings, thereby suggesting highest sources of perceived stress, were: "In the last month, how often have you found yourself thinking about things that you have to accomplish?" (M = 5.21, SD = 1.06); and "In the last month, how often have you felt nervous and 'stressed'?" (M = 4.95, SD = 1.08). On the other side of the ratings, "In the last month, how often have you dealt successfully with day-to-day problems and annoyances?" (M = 2.34, SD = .83); this question was reverse-coded; therefore, the lower score actually represents a positive coping strategy, as opposed to higher perceived stress.

Average resilience scores were 3.85 out of 6 (SD = .99), which can be called moderate based on the scale provided in the BRS (Smith et al., 2008). Similarly, MAAS averages indicated positive outcomes, with mean scores trending towards the upper half of response options (M = 3.59, SD = 0.99). Again, considering individual questions, lower scores suggest less mindful attention and those questions which were rated lowest included: "I find myself preoccupied with the future or the past" (M = 2.61, SD = 1.43), "I find myself listening to someone with one ear, doing something else at the same time" (M = 2.68, SD = 1.23). MAAS responses demonstrating more mindful awareness with higher average scores included: "I break or spill things because of carelessness, not paying attention, or thinking of something else" (M = 4.91, SD = 1.25), and "I drive places on automatic pilot and then wonder why I went there" (M = 4.13, SD = 1.69).

The correlational data provided useful in answering the question of students' experiences during the prolonged pandemic (Table 6.4). Although the correlation coefficients indicate weak to moderate connections, the directions of these relationships are insightful to gain an understanding about the connections between the constructs. Students with higher perceived stress generally also reported higher loneliness and lower mindfulness scores. There was a moderate and inverse relationship between PSS and BRS (r = −.672, p = .000) further supporting that perceived resilience may be protective against perceived stress.

Connections Across All Data

Students' perceptions of stress were relatively consistent in both phases of this study, with scores hovering above the midline of the scales. PSARQ results, collected in spring 2021, demonstrated that the PSS results were

Table 6.4

Phase II. Correlations Among the PSRQ Constructs

	PSS	MAAS	BRS	L-3
PSS	1	−.480*	−.672*	.411*
MAAS		1	.347*	−.344*
BRS			1	−.342*
L-3				1

Note: * denotes $p < .05$

also higher than those observed in previous studies conducted with college students (González-Ramírez et al., 2013). Comparing how students responded to specific stressors in SHAW-Q, and the breakdown of PSS questions in the PSARQ, researchers noticed trends in types of stress. Near the beginning of the pandemic, students recalled feeling most stress due to individual stressors such as personal health, ability to pay bills, and adapting to academic changes, while in their second semester, there was a shift to stress that was related to external factors such as their concern for friends and family members' health and well-being. The data from the PSARQ, collected in spring 2021, suggested the level of coping changed from when SHAW-Q was administered. Students rated questions about experiencing worry and rumination over things they needed to accomplish higher. Even so, throughout the duration of the study, respondents reported positive self-efficacy as related to coping with the demands of their personal and academic lives.

Stressors perceived as controllable by students were: (a) ability to finish classes, and (b) ability to adapt to academic and community changes. The *Dimensions of Wellness* students most often reported as having control over were Environmental Wellness and Physical Wellness. Keeping in mind the internal balancing act individuals utilize related to stress as described in the Lazarus and Folkman stress and coping theory (1984), protective factors such as social connections and resilience appeared to stave off negative health and wellness outcomes such as stress and anxiety. This was observed in the inverse relationship between PSS and BRS. Unfortunately, there has been limited research prior to COVID-19 looking at BRS outcomes in college-aged students with which to compare this study with previous work. Many studies that have used this measure are focused on college students with eating disorders (Thurston et al., 2018; Whatnall et al., 2019). With increased interest in resilience across all ages, the hope is that more research with college students will consider this as a measure.

College Students, Stress, and COVID   151

Another stress and anxiety risk factor observed in this study was that of a "lack of social support." Trends were observed of low to moderate levels of connection in 2020 and moderate to high levels of loneliness in 2021. As social support may act as a protective factor against stress, it would come into play as a person weighs their stress and coping levels within Lazarus and Folkman's theory (1984). This suggests a need for increasing university awareness of how to help students find ways to make social connections with one another in this time of social distancing.

DISCUSSION

Given the COVID-19 pandemic and life stressors specifically impacting university students of today, the psychosocial needs which in turn can impact academic success continue to be a topic which should be brought to the forefront of research. The two guiding questions for this study addressed college students' perceptions of their stress levels during the initial and extended semesters affected by the pandemic. With a better understanding of students' perceptions and areas of need, institutions of higher learning can better prepare to provide aid during future large-scale traumatic events. Recent assessments of colleges' moves to meet students' needs during the pandemic appear to focus on offering tools for students to utilize online learning management systems and to access services for student success and services (Kelly, 2021). It is well accepted at this point that the pandemic has had deleterious effects on students of all ages and, in response, there is a need to focus on students' mental health and resilience in present times (Pandya, 2022). However, it has also been pointed out that if institutions are offering supports but students are unaware of the resources; they are underutilized (Bhowmik, 2021).

Lazarus and Folkman's stress and coping theory (1984), which defines stress as resulting from an imbalance between perceived demands and personal/social resources to deal with the stressors, was valuable in this study. The theory assisted in building an understanding of the participants in the study and their process of negotiating what was being asked of them and what they were able to cope with. Those aspects of students' lives most often appraised as within their control during the pandemic were their ability to finish classes and to adapt to academic and community changes. In terms of learning about students' perceptions of their stress and coping, being able to successfully manage some stresses seemed to have allowed students to feel capable of coping with the number of stresses encountered during the ongoing pandemic.

The HBM (Rosenstock, 1974) was conducive in understanding outcomes throughout the two-phase research conducted. In considering the findings of Al-Metwali et al. (2021), participants with higher perceived susceptibility and severity of COVID-19 infection were more likely to have already acted on getting the vaccine at the time of the study. No correlation was found between COVID-related anxiety and perceived risk of exposure, which was an unexpected outcome. Perhaps this is related to the number of students (12%) who indicated the feeling that no matter what steps they took, they would likely end up getting COVID-19. In this case, it may be college students observing the current pandemic do not feel behavior changes will result in a decreased risk of exposure, suggesting a lack of power or control over personal outcomes. Please see Table 6.5 for a supplement to this discussion, including actionable steps of development for universities and faculty to consider implementing.

Table 6.5

Application of Results

Study Result	Suggested Step Towards Support
Perceived Wellness: Early stress related to personal risk	Share resources with students so they can be properly informed of how to limit exposure to infection
Protective Factors: Need for recognizing protective factors earlier in a stressful situation	Early in every semester, guide students through a practice of listing their protective factors and skills, such as who is in their support system and how to be organized for planning study time
Connection: A sense of Connection was protective and Social Wellness was rated low	Create opportunities for students to connect with their peers even in virtual settings. Offer informal virtual office hours during which students can just drop in and connect
Perceived Stress: Later stress related to friends and family members' risk	Check in with students about how they can share their experiences and what worked for them in their personal coping experiences with their loved ones
Perceived Stress: Stress levels overall for college students is high during the COVID-19 epidemic	Integrate simple stress-relieving strategies such as having a mindful minute at the start of class, before exams, or midway through a tough topic. Teach students to be aware of their state of mind throughout the day
Perceived Stress: Significant inverse relationship between Stress and Protective Factors	Provide students with problem-solving opportunities in class where they are given the chance to fail in a safe setting. Then point out to them how they were able to work together to bounce back and overcome initial challenges. Intentionally show them their resilience
Mindfulness: Negative effects from preoccupation with past and future	Share resources with students to help them stay focused on the present, such as mindful breathing

Limitations, Future Directions, and Next Steps

This section will address the limitations of the study and then focus on the practical application of the study's findings and recommendations for the next steps. This study was completed in response to the pandemic and lack of studies being completed on the university student population. Like so many other areas within academia, the initial research question focused on the broad state of students' perceived wellness as a result of the pandemic. The study was initiated by a desire to help a small, targeted student population at a single university, which stands as a limitation in terms of the generalizability of the results. As the pandemic continued into the second calendar year, the research team worked to decrease this limitation by expanding the population to include students from a second university in a different region of the country.

Since no personally identifying data were collected, it was not possible to send invitations specifically to students at University A who had not participated in the initial questionnaire, therefore, there is a possibility of some participants being in both phases. An additional limitation in both phases of the study is the sample size. It is understandable that institutions limit the number of research recruitment emails students are presented with. However, this led to limiting the pool of potential study participants. Based on current standards, surveys are classified as "good" with a 25% or more response rate (Ramshaw, 2019). Both phases had an above average response rate by participants who completed the electronic questionnaires (55 and 37%, respectively). A smaller sample in the second phase of the study which researchers believe to be possibly associated with students feeling burned out from an excess of email and online communications by the third semester of the pandemic, spring, 2021.

Lessons learned from the results of the two-phase study include an understanding that, when faced with unfamiliar stresses, college students thought of themselves first. While this self-centeredness may be related to age, educators should consider that self-centered student conduct extends beyond the ego-driven activities of youth and adolescence. As universities look towards supporting students moving forward, administration should focus their attention on communication with students. Administration needs to encourage faculty to reach out directly to students and continue to build authentic relationships to learn about individual needs to provide resources on campus to assist on a personal level. For instance, students who participated in this study noted needing resources to help with personal finances. Communications to the student body about available options related to financial issues, like outstanding fees, and what help may be available regarding financial burdens during hard times would have been beneficial to learn about which may have assisted in decreasing stress levels felt by students.

Perceived stress of participants was also connected with the unpredictable susceptibility to COVID-19. This parallels recent research that indicated the COVID-19 pandemic strongly contributed to anxiety (Rajkumar, 2020). Similarly, Atchison and colleagues (2021) noted perceptions of severity of COVID-19 drive the adoption of specific health change behaviors which aligns with the HBM (Rosenstock, 1974). Universities need to increase the priority of providing social support to students and assist in eliminating the stigma associated with psychiatry and assistance with mental health problems. He and colleagues (2022) found that social support improves resilience and perceived risk of COVID-19.

Another area of stress indicated by participants stemmed from personal wellness. Personal wellness encompasses a wide variety of areas of well-being both physically and mentally. Communication related to available resources such as the campus medical clinic and recreation facility hours of operation were not readily available. The psychosocial benefits of being physically active and the inability to socialize or know when the recreation center was open to assist in an individual personal wellness journey may have contributed to individualized stress. Stress levels may have been decreased for students if announcements were made about student services available, even in an online only setting, such as counseling services, testing capabilities, and even tips for at-home best practices for staying healthy. As the world continues to live in an atypical learning environment due to the various unknowns of current and future COVID outbreaks, communication plans should be created and an increase of communication to students needs to be developed. Researchers believe the offices of financial and health services would be ideal platforms to begin increased communication and awareness for students moving forward.

According to the findings, in the second semester, students' stress was more extrinsically motivated. They became concerned with those they care about. As suggested by Twenge (2013), adolescents are quite self-centered, however, with the passage of time and the extended challenge of COVID-19, students' concern switched from self to others. The shift to recognizing a concern for others and realizing that loved ones may also be at risk for sickness or death is an emotional experience in and of itself. As the COVID-19 trauma evolved, students in this study indicated a need for more support in coping with the bigger picture beyond themselves. Universities should consider programming, involve faculty in professional development training to provide students with opportunities to learn about coping strategies and how to apply those strategies to second-hand trauma and areas of life out of their control. The program, Creating Opportunities for Personal Empowerment ([COPE] Hart et al., 2019) is an example of a coping training available to teachers. Hart and colleagues found an increase in academic success in students from classrooms where teachers completed the COPE training. However, there is currently a lack of trauma-based professional development for those teaching in higher education settings.

Resilience was positively connected to feelings of control over stress. This is similar to findings from Jenkins and colleagues (2021) who related students' viewing stress as a stepping-stone to positive outcomes of markers of physical health. In this study, students who reported ample coping skills also reported lower perceived stress. The results of this study indicated that students felt their level of resilience was moderate (Smith et al., 2008). This may be that students who were willing to share their experiences within the study through the questionnaires were also those who felt more resilient in the first place. However, this does suggest that there are students in university classes who recognize ways to cope. Taking this under consideration, the authors suggest using class time to engage in open discussions about challenges, failures, and fears to create dialogue and consider coping strategies. This strategy could encourage students to take stock of their support systems and to recognize their networks related to the academic topic as well as recognize there are other students and faculty who can provide support or guidance to improve their overall well-being. The approach is similar to a study completed by university students using the Resilience and Coping Intervention Program, in which the intervention reduced stress and helped students develop coping skills and strategies (First et al., 2018).

The research team had access to university communications from both institutions associated with the present study. Neither university offered prior instruction related to integrating themes of coping or resilience in courses to faculty. Similarly, no campus-related student emails in the three semesters during which the research took place provided students with strategies of this nature. Based on previous work (Coiro et al., 2017) and the findings from this study, it is the recommendation of the authors that institutions of higher learning should recognize the importance of teaching resilience and coping skills and consider training faculty to incorporate these concepts into their coursework. University staff and faculty have the opportunity to share coping strategies with students through providing resources, integrating relevant discussions into our content, and modeling for students how to practice these strategies in daily situations. As university administration moves forward, they should focus on providing professional development and encouragement for faculty and teaching staff in the area of facilitating discussions about coping and resilience.

Challenges will continue to pervade the student experience, whether on local or global levels. The unique circumstances of the global pandemic provided serious stressors in a short amount of time. With little time to plan and take account of coping strategies, students' resilience was tested. As a precursor to future negative experiences, educators have an opportunity to make changes to benefit current and future students through communication and by arming students with coping skills. Future research is recommended in these areas, including assessing specific changes to communications and resources universities have adopted in response to the pandemic. Investigating administration and faculty perceptions of responses and resources is also needed in order to identify any gaps in alignment between what university personnel are providing versus what students believe is needed. Qualitative inquiries are also needed for a deeper understanding of the layers of stresses and coping that students and faculty experienced during the pandemic as well as to identify areas of need for the training of future faculty.

CONCLUSION

This study investigated college students' perceptions of constructs related to holistic wellness across three semesters affected by the COVID-19 pandemic. Students reported feeling less control of their mental, occupational, and social dimensions of wellness. They also reported a lack of perceived control in their ability to pay bills, find emotional support, their personal health, and the health of their family and/or friends. Student levels of resilience seemed to increase when resources, support, a sense of value and a sense of connection were positively perceived by the students. Consistent academic routines have previously been shown to positively benefit mental health and psychological resilience in university students with severe mental illness (Drake & Whitley, 2014). The findings of the current study provide further support of the need for consistency, as demonstrated by students indicating feeling positive about control of their academic responsibilities. Finding ways to help students continue their school-related routines, create connections with their peers, and provide resources for support for students, even in times of quarantine or distance learning, is paramount. Future research should focus on conducting a longitudinal study of the change and/or development of university programs and resources, faculty/staff perceptions of change of wellness of self, classroom dynamics, and student interactions based upon the continued COVID-19 pandemic. Additionally, student change in wellness related to the dimensions based on continual COVID variants and outbreaks throughout their college career and within their transition to employment after college.

REFERENCES

Adams. T., Bezner, J., & Steinhardt, M. (1997). The conceptualization and measurement of perceived wellness: Integrating balance across and within dimensions. *American Journal of Health Studies, 14*(4), 380–388.

Al-Metwali, B. Z., Al-Jumaili, A. A., Pharm, Z. A. A., & Sorofman, B. (2021). Exploring the acceptance of COVID-19 vaccine among healthcare workers and general population using health belief model. *Journal of Evaluation in Clinical Practice, 27*(5), 1112–1122. https://doi.org/10.1111/jep.13581

Atchison C., Bowman L. R., Vrinten. C., Redd, R., Pristtera, P., Eaton, J., & Ward, H. (2021). Early perceptions and behavioural responses during the COVID-19 pandemic: A cross-sectional survey of UK adults. *BMJ Open, 11,* e043577. https://doi.org/10.1136/bmjopen-2020-043577

Bhowmik, S. (2021, November, 16). *Essential needs of university students during COVID-19 pandemic*. News Medical Life Sciences. https://www.news-medical.net/news/20211116/Essential-needs-of-university-students-during-COVID-19-pandemic.aspx

Boyraz, G., & Legros, D. N. (2020). Coronavirus disease (COVID-19) and traumatic stress: Probably risk factors and correlates of posttraumatic stress disorder. *Journal of Loss and Trauma, 25*(6), 503–522. https://doi.org/10.1080/1525024.2020.1763556

Brown, K., W., West, A., M., Loverich, T., M., & Biegel, G., M. (2011). Assessing adolescent mindfulness: validation of an adapted mindful attention awareness scale in adolescent normative and psychiatric populations. *Psychological Assessment, 23*(4), 1023–1033. https://doi.org/10.1037/a0021338

Brown, K. W., & Ryan, R. M. (2003). The benefits of being present: Mindfulness and its role in psychological well-being. *Journal of Personality and Social Psychology, 84*(1), 822–848. https://doi.org/10.1037/0022-3514.84.4.822

Carlson, L., E., & Brown, K., W. (2005). Validation of the mindful attention awareness scale in a cancer population. *Journal of psychosomatic research, 58*(1), 29–33. https://doi.org/10.1016/j.jpsychores.2004.04.336

Cohen, S., Kamarck, T., & Mermelstein, R. (1983). A global measure of perceived stress. *Journal of Health and Social Behavior, 24*(1), 385–396.

Corio, M. J., Bettis, A. H., & Compas, B. E. (2017). College students coping with interpersonal stress: Examining a control-based model of coping. *Journal of American College Health, 65*(3), 177–186. https://doi.org/10.1080/07448481.2016.1266641

Drake, R. E., & Whitley, R. (2014). Recovery and severe mental illness: Description and analysis. *Canadian Journal of Psychiatry, 59*(5), 236–242. https://doi.org/10.1177/070674371405900502

First, J., First, N. L., & Houston, B. (2018). Resilience and coping intervention (RCI): A group intervention to foster college student resilience. *Social Work with Groups, 41*(3), 198–210. https://doi.org/10.1080/01609513.2016.127231

Goldberg, D. P., & Hillier, V. F. (1979). A scaled version of the General Health Questionnaire. *Psychol Med, 9*(1), 139–145. https://doi.org/10.1017/s0033291700021644

González-Ramírez, M .T., Rodríguez-Ayan, M. N., & Hernández, R. L. (2013). The perceived stress scale (PSS): normative data and factor structure for a large-scale sample in Mexico. *Spanish Journal of Psychology, 16*(E47). https://doi.org/10.1017/sjp.2013.35

He, T. B., Tu, C. C., & Bai, X. (2022) Impact of social support on college students' anxiety due to COVID-19 isolation: Mediating roles of perceived risk and resilience in the postpandemic period. *Frontiers of Psychology, 13*, online 948214. https://doi.org/10.3389/fpsyg.2022.948214

Hart Abney, B. G., Lusk, P., Hovermale, R., & Melnyk, B. M. (2019). Decreasing depression and anxiety in college youth using the Creating Opportunities for Personal Empowerment Program (COPE). *Journal of the American Psychiatric Nurses Association, 25*(2), 89–98. https://doi.org/10.1177/1078390318779205

Hirschberger, G. (2018). Collective trauma and the social construction of meaning. *Frontiers in Psychology, 9*, Article 1441. https://doi.org/10.3389/fpsyg.2018.01141

Homa, M., Ziarko, M., & Litwiniuk, M. (2022). Impact of previous health-related events on coping with cancer. *Annals of Oncology, 33*(Supplement 7), S1198. https://doi.org/10.1016/j.annonc.2022.07.1532

Hughes, M. E., Waite, L. J., Hawkley, L. C., & Cacioppo, J. T. (2004). A short scale for measuring loneliness in large surveys: Results from two population-based studies. *Research on Aging, 26*(6), 655–672. https://doi.org/10.1177/0164027504268574

Jenkins, A., Weeks, M. S., Hard, B. M., & Wang, Z. (2021). General and specific stress mindsets: Link with college student health and academic performance. *PLoS ONE, 16*(9). http://dx.doi.org/10.1371/journal.pone.0256351

Kelly, R. (2021, June16). *How institutions met student needs during the pandemic.* Campus Technology. https://campustechnology.com/articles/2021/06/16/how-institutions-met-student-needs-during-the-pandemic.aspx

Lazarus, R., & Folkman, S. (1984). *Stress, appraisal and coping.* Hemisphere.

Lawlor, M. S., Schonert-Reichl, K. A., Gadermann, A. M., & Zumbo, B. D. (2014). A validation study of the mindful attention awareness scale adapted for children. *Mindfulness, 5*(6), 730–741. https://doi.org/10.1007/s1267-013-0228-4

Lee, S. A. (2020). Coronavirus anxiety scale: A brief mental health screener for COVID-19 related anxiety. *Death Studies, 44*(7), 393–401. https://doi.org/10.1080/07481187.2020.1748481

North, C. S. (2016). Disaster mental health epidemiology: Methodological review and interpretation of research findings. *Psychiatry, 79*(2), 130–146.

Pandya, A., & Lodha, P. (2022). Mental health consequences of COVID-19 pandemic among college students and coping approaches adapted by higher education institutions: A scoping review. *Social Science & Medicine—Mental Health, 2*, 100122. https://doi.org/10.1016/j.ssmmh.2022.100122

Paterson, J. (2020). Amplified anxiety. *The Journal of College Admission, 248*(28), 28–32.

Pfefferbaum B., Nixon, S.J., Tivis, R. D., Doughty, D. E., Pynoos, R. S., Gurwitch, R. H., & Foy, D. W. (2001). Television exposure in children after a terrorist incident. *Psychiatry 64*(3), 202–211. https://doi.org/10.1521/psyc.64.3.202.18462

Pfefferbaum, B., & North, C. S. (2020). Mental health and the COVID-19 pandemic. *The New England Journal of Medicine, 383*(6), 510–512. https://doi.org/10.1056/NEJMp2008017

Ramshaw, A. (2019). *The complete guide to acceptable survey response rates.* Genroe Blog. https://www.genroe.com/blog/acceptable-survey-response-rate-2/11504

Rajkumar, R. P. (2020). COVID-19 and mental health: A review of the existing literature. *Asian Journal of Psychiatry, 52,* 102066. https://doi.com/10.1016/j.ajp.2020.102066

Roenstock, I. M. (1974). Historical origins of the health belief model. *Ealth Education Monograph, 2*(1), 328–335.

Russell, D., Peplau, L. A., Cutrona, C. E., & Hogan, R. (1980). The revised UCLA loneliness scale: Concurrent and discriminant validity evidence. *Journal of Personality and Social Psychology, 39*(3), 472–480.

Schultz, J. M., Althouse, B. M., Baingana, F., Cooper, J. L., Espinola, M., Greene, M. C., Espinel, Z., McCoy, C. B., Mazurik, L., & Rechkemmer, A. (2016). Fear factor: The unseen perils of the Ebola outbreak. *Bulletin of the Atomic Scientists, 72*(5), 304–310. https://doi.org/10.1080/00963402.2016.1216515

Skinner, C. S., Tiro, J., & Champion, V. L. (2015). The health belief model. In K. Glanz, B. K. Rimer, & K. Viswanath (Eds.), *Health behavior: Theory, research, and practice.* Jossey-Bass.

Smith, B. W., Dalen, J., Wiggins, K., Tooley, E., Christopher, P., & Bernard, J. (2008). The brief resilience scale: Assessing the ability to bounce back. *International Journal of Behavioral Medicine, 15*(3), 194–200. https://doi.org/10.1080/10705500802222972

Thurston, I. B., Hardin, R., Kamody, R. C., Herbozo, S., Kaufman, C. (2018). The moderating role of resilience on the relationship between perceived stress and binge eating symptoms among young adult women. *Eating Behaviors, 29*(1). 114–119. https://dio.org/10.1016/j.eatbeh.2018.03.009

Tomaszek, K., & Muchacka-Cymerman, A. (2022). Student burnout and PTSD symptoms: The role of existential anxiety and academic fears on students during the COVID-19 pandemic. *Depression Research and Treatment*, 1–9 https://doi.org/10.1155/2022/6979310

Twenge, J. M. (2013). The evidence for generation me and against generation we. *Emerging Adulthood, 1*(1), 11–16. https://doi.org/10.1177/2167696812466548

Weiss, D. S., & Marmar, C. R. (1996). The impact of event scale (Revised). In J. Wilson & T. M. Keane (Eds.), *Assessing psychological trauma and PTSD* (pp. 399–411). Guilford.

Whatnall, M. C., Patterson, A. J., Siew, Y. Y., Kay-Lambkin, F., & Hutchesson, M. J. (2019). Are psychological distress and resilience associated with dietary intake among Australian university students? *International Journal of Environmental Research and Public Health, 16*(21), 4099. https://doi.org/10.3390/ijerph16214099

Zhai, Y., & Du, X. (2020). Addressing collegiate mental health amid COVID-19 pandemic. *Psychiatry Research*, 288. https://doi.org/10.1016/j.psychres.2020.113003

CHAPTER 7

STRUGGLES AND STRESS

Impact of the COVID-19 Pandemic on STEM Preservice Teachers

Seema Rivera
Clarkson University

Preethi Titu
Kennesaw State University

Katie Kavanagh
Clarkson University

Jan DeWaters
Clarkson University

Ben Galluzzo
Clarkson University

Mike Ramsdell
Clarkson University

ABSTRACT

The COVID-19 pandemic created significant disruption to the Spring semester of 2020 and beyond, including how we think about instructional practices in our nation's classrooms. Educators were forced to reinvent their courses to online teaching caused by the COVID-19 pandemic, simultaneously

Research on College Stress and Coping: Implications From the COVID-19 Pandemic and Beyond, pp. 161–182
Copyright © 2024 by Information Age Publishing
www.infoagepub.com
All rights of reproduction in any form reserved.

navigating a public health crisis. As the summer progressed, many K–12 educators were nervous about how the fall of 2020 would start off. Would the students be in person? Would they be online? Would they be doing both? While both higher education and K–12 faculty were forced to transition into online teaching quickly, preservice teachers (PSTs) who are both students and teachers were vulnerable to the other pandemic stressors in ways that were not visible to their professors and mentor teachers. These include financial stressors, future job prospects, technology, Wi-Fi access, new family responsibilities, and economic insecurity (Beaunoyer et al., 2020). As the first full school year within the pandemic continues, we recognize that our PSTs are experiencing teaching in a completely different way than their peers in the past. Our paper highlights the experiences and challenges of PSTs amid the COVID-19 pandemic.

Keywords: preservice teachers, STEM, COVID-19, challenges, and teacher education

INTRODUCTION

Educators were forced to reinvent their courses in March 2020 with the emergency shift to online teaching caused by the COVID-19 pandemic, simultaneously navigating a public health crisis. While a myriad of research on the COVID-19 pandemic is now being published, there is limited research on how crises impacted teacher's teaching prior to the pandemic. Typically, that research focused on acute trauma such as school shootings, natural disasters, terrorist attacks, and so on, emphasizing student outcomes (Elbih, 2013; Foster, 2006; Nickerson & Sulkowski, 2021).

Studies on preservice teachers (PSTs) stress have focused almost exclusively on the teaching practice placement and may have contributed to an underestimation of the pressures on such individuals. Typically, students who are completing a student-teaching residency are also not able to work at a job. The financial hardships worsened during the COVID-19 pandemic. Students experienced stress related to loss in family income, household income, and an increase in food and housing insecurity (Jones et al., 2021). In addition, students also faced many other stressors, including mental health disorders (Soria & Horgos, 2021). However, this chapter on PSTs is in the context of the pandemic, a long-running cultural disruption.

As the summer progressed, many K–12 educators were nervous about how the new school year would start. PSTs were also significantly impacted by this pandemic, both in their learning as a student and also in their development to becoming new teachers. The quick shift from traditional to remote learning and virtual teaching affected both teachers and PSTs, which made teaching and learning much more challenging in a completely unprepared and sudden environment. Muacevic and Adler (2020) stated that the rapid increase in the number of confirmed COVID-19 cases has created a sense of anxiety and panic among students and teachers alike about the situation, including those at higher educational settings. There were some concerns about the quality of online teaching and the teachers' capability to adjust and effectively deliver their lessons during the pandemic (Auxier & Anderson, 2020). The challenges faced by teachers, and PSTs in particular, are just a reality (Hill, 2021). PSTs faced varied challenges during their practicum because of the quick shift to online teaching and learning that included, but not limited to, the content knowledge delivery; redesign of the teaching styles, assessments, and evaluation procedures. Though stressful, the sudden destabilization of schools has also offered an opportunity for reflection, collaboration, and reinvention of one's mentality toward teaching. The practicum in preservice teacher education programs, whether in the form of field experience, student teaching, clinical teaching, or mentoring programs, typically constitutes the longest and most intensive exposure to the teaching profession experienced by prospective teachers (Cohen et al., 2013). The major difficulty with the COVID-19 pandemic was to continue providing an interactive learning experience to model constructivist approaches for PSTs (Wu et al., 2020). An added challenge to this was that students were not able to complete their field experience in a regular/traditional setting; this was particularly challenging for science, technology, engineering, and mathematics (STEM) teachers who heavily rely on hands-on learning, group work, equipment, and safety measures.

Teacher preparation programs in general aim to assist candidates with the pedagogical, theoretical, and practical application of teaching and learning (Hill, 2021). Darling-Hammond and colleagues (2000) described quality teacher education programs as having four key features that align pre-service preparation and professional practice: (a) a clear, shared vision of what good teaching looks like across all aspects of the program, (b) clear standards, (c) a curriculum centered on child development, and (d) learning theories, pedagogy, content knowledge, and applied practice. "Quality programs have both a clinical component and an informative curriculum. They teach pre-service teachers to turn theory into practice by their application of skill-building" (Darling-Hammond, 2010, p. 40).

Until March 2020, the typical teaching situation at school was characterized by students who convened in classrooms according to their timetables and teachers who covered their subjects' standard content, frequently through formal lecturing (König et al., 2020). Teacher education was at the beginning of a digital and monumental pedagogical shift that disconnects teacher preparation from its history of classroom instruction in favor of online teaching and learning (Hill, 2021). Field experiences, an essential component of teacher preparation (Zeichner, 2010), have historically included a range of activities related to teaching practice, such as teaching a stand-alone lesson or observing in K–12 classrooms that provides opportunities to practice classroom instruction contributing to teacher readiness and relationship building (Hill, 2021). The immediate closure of educational institutions led to online remote teaching and learning where teacher educators were expected to use available technological affordances (learning platforms and social media) to ensure learning continuity for the student teachers, who were expected to adopt online remote learning.

Traditionally, the practicum experience has been situated in school-based contexts that serves as the culminating experience before PSTs complete their preparation program and prerequisites for licensure. The practicum experiences are to be designed, monitored, and structured by the teacher education programs, which align with and integrate them into its courses (Hammerness, 2006; Hayes, 2002; Otaiba, 2005; Vacc & Bright, 1999; Vuchic & Robb, 2006). In the practicum, PSTs act relatively independently under the guidance of a mentor, supervisory teachers, or supervisors from a university/college of education. This is the typical training structure that provides theoretical studies in the teacher education programs and hands-on experience on the school premises (Graham & Thornley, 2000). Preservice educators are usually being prepared to support student learning in this environment, but the conditions and environments changed due to the spread of the novel coronavirus in early 2020. Practicum experience has long been adopted to provide PSTs with an opportunity to practice and reflect on teaching and translate theoretical ideas into practice (Zeichner, 2010). However, the recent COVID-19 pandemic has prompted higher educational institutions to conceptualize the practicum experience and explore alternative ways to ensure that PSTs are classroom ready. This study is important and timely because it will provide much-needed information on how and in what ways PSTs addressed the challenges to their job demands during the shift in teaching and learning.

While PSTs faced challenges, equally important are the stories of PSTs who were particularly successful during these unprecedented times. A study by Whiteside and Colleagues (2020), for instance, suggested that the pandemic served as a vehicle of "disruptive innovation," creating an opportunity for empathy, collaboration, and support. This opportunity can provide us with insight on how to better prepare our PSTs. In this study, we focus on the challenges of STEM PSTs during their teaching practice in an educational setting. The PSTs wrote about their student teaching experience in the context of the pandemic, where they had varied student teaching experiences with various modalities face-to-face, online, and hybrid. Our research question guiding this study is: *How did STEM PSTs' job demands change during the pandemic?*

Theoretical Framework

Our study was guided by the interpretivist paradigm whose belief is that multiple realities are constructed by individuals based upon their personal experiences, values and beliefs (Dayal & Tiko, 2020). Interpretivism as a paradigm assumes that reality is subjective and can differ among individuals. Interpretivist paradigm allows researchers to view the world through the perceptions and experiences of the participants. According to Willis (2007), interpretivism usually seeks to understand a particular context, and the core belief of the interpretive paradigm is that reality is socially constructed. With the interpretivism perspective, we aim to gain a deeper understanding of the phenomenon and its complexity in its unique context instead of trying to generalize the base of understanding for the whole population (Creswell, 2007). Since individuals tend to have their own opinions and experiences about the pandemic and its impact on education based on the context they are in, we used the interpretivist paradigm to help us understand PSTs views towards their job demands during the pandemic.

METHODOLOGY

Setting and Context

The setting for this study is a 14-month Master of Arts in Teaching (MAT) program in a small, predominantly white institution in the northeast United States. The PSTs in this study enter the MAT program with bachelors in a STEM field. This is significant because during "normal-non-pandemic" times, the program is intensive and, for most students, it is their first glimpse into the field of education. Almost all the students in this MAT program have not taken education courses before, so few students have background knowledge in pedagogy or education theory. Additionally, as an undergraduate STEM student, these MAT students were very likely to not have taken a course on diversity, equity, inclusion, belonging, or other similar topics. There are a handful of students who have substitute teaching experience, but otherwise many of these MAT students have not been in a middle or high school since they were students themselves. So, for many of these PSTs, their first experience as a teacher in a school was during a global pandemic.

The MAT students complete an intensive summer course load focused on pedagogy and then continue their coursework while simultaneously working in their entire year of student teaching residency. From September to June, they are placed in one school with one mentor, to work with all

166   S. RIVERA ET AL.

year. Their MAT coursework is generally three or four days of the week in the evening following their day in school. During pre-COVID times, the MAT students would not have any courses dedicated to teaching online, but instead in one course, there is some practice with online tools and teaching with technology. However, due to the changing environment with COVID and not knowing how they would teach during their residency, all the MAT students completed their summer pedagogy coursework with the expectation of learning some pedagogy for online teaching and this was not optional. As a result, students were feeling the stress of an intensive master's program, starting a new profession, and coping with an unprecedented global pandemic.

Another significant context related to these MAT students is that they will all become STEM teachers. Through the MAT program, they will end up being certified in either earth science, living environment, chemistry, physics, mathematics, technology, or computer science. It is important to note this because all teachers, but particularly science and technology teachers, require specific tasks such as conducting laboratory experiments, using manipulatives, working in groups, conducting demonstrations, using equipment, and many other hands-on activities. In this particular state, secondary students are required to have completed a certain number of laboratory work minutes to be eligible for taking the discipline-specific science state test; this is usually tied to graduation requirements. In other words, there is a potential that PSTs may become certified science teachers with no experience teaching science laboratories.

Participants

The participants include four PSTs who were all Noyce Scholars (a program through the National Science Foundation that prepares students for teaching in high-need schools), who had the same programmatic experience, both the regular MAT program and also some additional support from the scholarship program that included regular meetings with the Noyce faculty. Due to their similar programming and teaching goals, purposive sampling was utilized. While data was collected from all PSTs, here we draw the responses from four PSTs. The participants are described in Table 7.1.

Study Design

This study focuses on the challenges of STEM PSTs during their teaching practice in an educational setting. The PSTs reflected on their student

Table 7.1

Participant Description

Name	Demographics	Experience	Residency
Participant 1	25, white female, BS in math, grew up in rural area	Taught in a private school for 3 yrs before starting MAT program, found it challenging but rewarding, no prior teaching experience online.	Large, racially diverse suburban school district, hybrid setting, half of the class virtual, other half of the class virtual, other half in person with masks, physically spaced apart.
Participant 2	24, white female, BS in biology	Taught in a private Hebrew school for 2 years then returned to program to become a teacher, grew up in a very rural area of the northeast United States. No prior online teaching experience.	Large, racially diverse, urban city school, full school year was online.
Participant 3	22, white male, BS in math	Undergraduate teaching assistant, with a pre-teaching minor participated in STEM outreach as an undergraduate, entered college not knowing what he wanted to do, grew up in a suburban area of Northeastern U.S., no prior online teaching experience.	Small suburban school district, students in a hybrid setting so half of class attended virtually while the other half in person with masks on and physically spaced apart.
Participant 4	25, white male, BS in engineering	Worked as an engineer for 2 years then returned to school/MAT program to be math teacher, felt that engineering was not fulfilling, grew up in suburbs, no prior online teaching.	Large, racially diverse suburban school students in a hybrid setting so half of class attended virtually while the other half in person with masks on and physically spaced apart.

teaching experiences during the pandemic throughout the academic year (September 2020–June 2021). According to Yin (2009), case-study research deals with real-life contexts and settings and provides a holistic understanding of the phenomenon under investigation. Case studies are not meant to be generalized to larger populations, but instead they provide a deeper understanding of a phenomenon. In the context of the COVID-19 pandemic, using case studies provides a more extensive understanding of what happened in schools and pre-service teachers. The ability to generalize this data to another situation is not plausible because of the distinctiveness of the COVID-19 pandemic. As such, the case-study research approach matches well with our study where we sought to explore individual PSTs challenges during the COVID-19 situation.

A single embedded case study design has been employed (Yin, 2009). According to Yin (2014), a single embedded case study may involve more than one unit of analysis when, within a single case, attention is given to subunits. While this case study is specific to one institution in one degree program, this case study will be helpful by allowing comparisons to occur with different contexts during the same period of time. As a case study, there are no claims made here about generalizability. This design is also appropriate because PSTs as a group are considered a case while each of the individual PSTs is identified as subunits. One of the significant characteristics of this research design is that it captures the "meaning" of how PSTs describe, in their own words, the personal challenges/opinions in a hybrid classroom setting during the pandemic.

Data Collection

For this study, the authors focused on the reflection journals as they provided details and opinions of the PSTs regarding the challenges that they were facing in their classrooms. Reflection journals are intended to capture the progressions and challenges that one encounters in the process. It acts as a source to learn from experiences that may be interpreted as processes of action learning-learning not just from the literature or lectures of "authorities" but from reflection on their engaged experiences (Stringer & Aragon, 2020). The reflective journal is a "free write" space where PSTs are merely asked to reflect on their practice in meaningful ways.

Journal reflections were introduced to the PSTs before the school year started and after their summer program ended, approximately late August 2020. The principal investigator, the first author, met with the PSTs, both first year PSTs and PSTs about to start their residency, to talk about the upcoming school year, and described the format of the journal reflections. The first author reminded the PSTs that these reflections were part of the scholarship program, however, they are not required to keep the scholarship. The purpose of the reflections was to support their own practice as a teacher and to help provide insight to the Noyce team on how to better support our Noyce scholars. Of the eight PSTs of the group, only one PST opted to not participate in the journal reflections, while all the other students gave consent to this IRB-approved research. The PSTs were required to write a reflection every other week throughout the school year, from September to May, approximately 15–20 reflections for each PST. The journals were completed on Google Docs, each PST had their own Google Doc that was set to be shared only with the faculty associated with the Noyce program. None of these faculty was an instructor to these PSTs. The faculty read through the reflections during the school year with two main purposes, first was to remind scholars to write their reflections so they were completed in a timely manner and reflected the teaching time period of their year. Second was to make sure there were no major concerns with the PSTs; sometimes the PSTs reach out for support when they need it. This is one of many ways faculty "check on" with the PSTs during their full year residency. To help PSTs reflect on their experiences meaningfully, they were given prompts to help guide their thoughts. Several of the reflection prompts included: *What did you learn this past month about yourself as a teacher? What has been the most challenging part of your residency? What students stand out to you and why? Describe your relationship with your mentor.*

Data Analysis

Using the journal reflections, codes were developed, inductively by each researcher. Codes were kept in a "living codebook" (Reyes et al., 2021), a table that was continuously updated and adjusted as new data was analyzed. While coding individually, the researchers worked in different sections of the codebook. Then, the researchers shared individual interpretations of the data by conversing, explaining, and resolving different interpretations. Codes that had to be negotiated were then shared with faculty members of the Noyce team; this strategy is consistent with other teams conducting qualitative research (Cornish et al., 2014; Richards & Hemphill, 2018). Next, the codebook was consolidated with the work from researchers and any additional notes or details. Several examples from the project's codebook are presented in Table 7.2, placed with the themes they represent. Themes were developed by identifying similarities across codes and their connections to one another. The researchers uncovered the themes together while working on the living codebook and re-reading the codes. In addition, each code's strengths in identifying the participants' experiences was also addressed (Castleberry & Nolen, 2018). Throughout this process, each researcher wrote comments, or analytic memos, on the documents analyzing the codes. Writing analytic memos to clarify conceptual clusters was essential in clarifying and developing ideas (Saldaña, 2015). The most salient themes that were representative of the PSTs' views and challenges of teaching during the pandemic were *technology, equity, and student engagement*. In an effort to establish the validity of our claims and analyses, we also shared an earlier draft of this manuscript with the participants to seek their feedback. The follow-up communications helped to triangulate the data and confirm findings (Patton, 2002).

Table 7.2

Codebook Sample Showing Relevant Themes Including One Example Code for Each Theme
Full Code Book Available in Appendix 1

		Theme	Example Code	Code Definition
Research Question 1		**Theme 1** *Technology*	Teaching Online	Instances of any online teaching, this includes hybrid teaching
		Theme 2 *Equity*	Resource	Instances that refer to access or availability of any resources, including time
		Theme 3 *Student Engagement*	Hybrid	Any reference to connecting with students in a hybrid classroom environment

Author Positionality

Like many studies investigating experiences during the COVID-19 pandemic, the researchers were also experiencing many of the same challenges that were faced by our participants. The researchers are faculty members who work with preservice teachers and wanted to reconsider the hierarchical relationship with their students and instead focus on compassion and support for the students. The researchers could empathize with the students experiencing having to learn to teach online in a relatively short period of time. The empathy also included opening up their homes when they logged on for class and also felt the uncertainty of the time period. However, the researchers acknowledge their privilege as they were working while their students were trying to finish their education.

FINDINGS

The four PSTs' journal reflections provided great insight into their experiences of student-teaching during the pandemic. Several categories or themes emerged from the PSTs reflections of those who wrote about their individual experiences. In this section, findings are organized thematically according to subtopics revealed as we explored the reflections to address the research question. Here, we unravel the ways in which PSTs expressed their challenges and the job demands while student teaching during the pandemic. The three common challenges that emerged from the reflection journals which we identify here as themes are *technology, equity, and student engagement.*

Technology

Technology was often the only way to connect and engage students, so it became a lifeline to these PSTs. Knowing the pandemic would completely transform how these PSTs would teach during their full-year teaching residency, online teaching strategies were heavily incorporated into the summer intensive program during their MAT program. Participant 3 wrote:

> Over the summer, we learned a lot about possible online teaching strategies.... The biggest takeaway from the summer in terms of strategies was definitely the importance of total participation. Since we are not always in front of the students, we need a way to check how they are doing and how they are feeling.

While generally optimistic about their experience with technology, they had many frustrations during the school year regarding the heavy use of technology, which was the case mainly for Participant 2, who had experienced her teaching residency entirely online. Participant 2 shares in her journal

> It is challenging to teach a bunch of active 12- and 13-year-old students through a computer screen, when I know during a "normal" year we would be able to be doing hands on activities and out of our seats, moving around the classroom. The difficulty is finding those other students who either don't show up at all, or just sign in for the Google Meet.... But currently we will send emails, write private comments on Google Classroom, try to talk to them at the start or end of class and get nothing in return. It is important to remember though that there is only so much we can do, and we can't forget the majority of the students who are in class, ready to learn.

Participant 2 went on to describe ways of trying to figure out how to teach a science course fully online. There were no plans or discussion about if and when the school would return to face to face, so it was planning for a science course to be fully virtual. Additionally, this biology course normally has a required lab component that is attached to the state test. At the time, it was not clear what would be waived and what was still required. Participant 2 adds:

> I'm not really sure how confident I will be doing biology labs in person one day when I am not going through the "normal" experience now. If I'm a certified biology teacher, I will need to teach lab, that means using lab equipment, and ordering specimens, and helping students figure out how and what to do with hands on lab experience. The online lab will be okay to help go over the concepts but it won't be like doing a lab in person. I am grateful for [Mentor's Name] though, because I know she will still help me even after the program ends.

Participant 1 also pointed out that using technology and teaching online made her more sympathetic to her professors that semester. She wrote:

> They [instructors] had to change their courses too, and I think that most of them did not want to, so I could feel their pain. I had to be a student and a teacher online. Being on the computer all day long was exhausting:

Participant 4 also wrote about his experience with technology:

> When I had initially enrolled in the program, the idea of my residency was significantly different; I didn't expect the virtual environment, nor the difficulties in engagement from our students in this atmosphere. By understanding that I will have to learn, grow, and adapt, as well as that my mentor will have to learn, grow, and adapt had me excited to contribute to the team. Of course, I did not expect to be an expert teacher right away, but the fact that my mentors are also striving to improve helped me see that this is a continuous learning process, and we can always improve.

Unsurprisingly, the technology theme was prevalent throughout the data and impacted the participants in multiple ways, particularly as STEM teachers.

Equity

While equity issues always existed in K–12 classrooms before the pandemic, according to the PSTs' experiences, the pandemic highlighted the existing inequities in classrooms. Issues regarding equity appeared in

Struggles and Stress 173

different ways and throughout the school year with all four PSTs. Here they share their reflections on equity during their teaching residency. Participant 1 writes

> Some of my students have consistent internet struggles, and others refuse to turn on the camera (I do not make any of my students do so, but some choose to) because of distractions around them. I need to be aware that not every student is fortunate to have a quiet learning environment free of distractions at home, and I am trying to amend my expectations. It is definitely hard though, because I am not sure how to help a student if I can't see them. Our school did have some mobile hot spots, but were trying to find more so students could borrow them if they needed to so they would have more consistent internet. I think everyone was trying, but it was harder for some students than others, for sure.

Participant 2 writes:

> Because of the drastic budget cuts and reduction of financial support from the state, my district had to go all virtual before school even started. Some students are sharing devices with siblings, which can result in them missing classes. Additionally, some students are sharing a Wi-Fi network with many other devices and have trouble staying connected during class. Most of the districts around us are not fully virtual so I think our students have it even harder this year. Taking a biology class and never doing a biology lab is definitely a problem. The other schools around us that will still have some in person learning will be able to provide students with this experience.

Participant 4 also reflected on issues related to equity. He wrote:

> A few of my students have told me that they were not able to come to virtual class or finish some of their work because they had to help their younger sibling. Normally, I would not allow that excuse unless there was some other underlying issues. However, because of the pandemic and not knowing what was going on at home, I just allowed my students to take care of what they needed to so there was not an added burden of me adding to their stress of the situation. Not everyone in class had obligations to help family like this, so it was clear some students were able to spend more time on schoolwork.

Participant 4 also wrote:

> I am teaching two classes, one a remedial geometry class with extra class time, and the other an advanced level Regents class. I have noticed that the students in my remedial class (in general) require much more support and guidance when I am delivering content than the advanced pace class. I understand the need to spend more time working with my remedial class, but I have to remember to not let that time difference impact my

174 S. RIVERA ET AL.

dedication to my advanced class. I have one student who struggles with anxiety almost daily, and I have realized the importance of making that student feel welcomed and comfortable every single day, and for this reason, this student has stood out to me. I understand how this could be perceived by other students in the classroom, so I ensure that I am checking in with each student every day.

Participant 2 also wrote:

When I initially met my mentor, she told me about their school's structure—each grade was split into two teams that would meet on a daily basis to discuss how students were doing. Now there aren't enough teachers to make two teams and to my knowledge there aren't any meetings among teachers to discuss how things are going with the students. The lack of support staff also makes me worry about students who may be trying to reach out for help but may not get it. It is a difficult situation, and all the teachers are working as hard as possible to make sure this doesn't happen but it must be hard to keep track of everyone when you have over 130 students.

Issues of equity appeared in different ways throughout the PSTs' journal reflections during the year.

Student Engagement

All the PSTs talked about how difficult it was to create community and connect with their students this past year. Many were in hybrid situations, seeing their students every other day or more or entirely virtual. All the PSTs discussed how some of the strategies they learned could continue in a post-pandemic world, but there was a lot of trial and error during the year. Participant 3 states:

I think the most challenging part of my residency has been getting students engaged, and in turn really helping their performance. At the beginning of the year we focused on getting the class into a schedule so that they hopefully felt more comfortable and prepared for class, which included watching EdPuzzles and following very similar class structure every day. While this worked for a while, recently it has become clear that students are getting burnt out, both of our class and school in general ... we are having trouble keeping students engaged and working, especially those that just do not want to work in class. With this upcoming unit, we're changing things up again and are going to try to focus more on live teaching. But I still feel like keeping the online students engaged will be difficult, and need to focus more on trying to ensure those students are learning too.

Struggles and Stress 175

Participant 4 also reflected on student engagement writing:

> The biggest challenge without question is treating students equitably who are exclusively virtual. It is challenging to get to know your students who are virtual due to them not typically having their cameras turned on and preferring to type everything in the chat rather than actually speak to me. I am working on brainstorming ideas to build community in my classrooms, particularly with respect to involving the online students more. I like the idea of doing a virtual or in person show-and-tell so students can display something they are proud of and hope to open some lines of communication due to me caring about what they choose to display.

Participant 2 wrote:

> Another challenge we've had to deal with is attendance. I was actually surprised by how many of the students had been showing up for the first week of school virtually, but that has started to dwindle in the second week. We are still doing well, with about 80–90% of the students showing up. However, there are cases of chronic absenteeism. In order to get to the bottom of the issue, my mentor teacher reached out to the parents of students who had consistently been absent or arriving late/leaving early. In some cases, the students lack a reliable device. In other cases, there isn't a parent at home during the day or the student might be at a friend's house because their parent has to work. And some parents have just not responded to any attempts at communication. My mentor explained her philosophy which I tend to agree with: we can try everything in our power to get students to come to class but at the end of the day, we need to be there for the students who did show up.

Participant 4 discussed engagement, but in reference to his own experience as an MAT student, he wrote:

> When I had initially enrolled in the program, the idea of my residency was significantly different; I didn't expect the virtual environment, nor the difficulties in engagement from our students in this atmosphere. By understanding that I will have to learn, grow, and adapt, as well as that my mentor will have to learn, grow, and adapt had me excited to contribute to the team. Of course, I did not expect to be an expert teacher right away, but the fact that my mentors are also striving to improve helped me see that this is a continuous learning process, and we can always improve. The difficulty with engaging students pushed me to be more of an active participant in the MAT program. Having no response or little interaction from students online is tough on the teacher's side, so I try to speak up more in my courses.

Participant 1 wrote about how she noticed her mentor teachers engage students in their own way:

176 S. RIVERA ET AL.

> Because I have two mentors, I get to experience two different approaches to teaching. One of my mentors provides the students with plenty of time to practice individually and loves to tell dad jokes in the middle of every lesson. While he doesn't fully know all the students' names yet, you can tell they already appreciate him and his teaching method. My other mentor loves to sing Hamilton songs for them and even checks their work by drawing smiley faces on their papers. While these are two very different approaches, I've realized there's no right or wrong way to teach, it's the way that works best for you and the students.

The engagement theme appeared in several different ways throughout the data, both in the K–12 setting and institute of higher education.

DISCUSSION AND LIMITATIONS

This study explored a small group of STEM teachers and how they navigated their student teaching residency through the COVID-19 pandemic. The study was guided by an interpretivist framework that allows researchers to answer research questions through the lens of their participants. The focus is not to generalize these results to the larger population, but instead have a deeper understanding and learning of a particular phenomenon. The pandemic provided a backdrop that impacted all individuals, but in an individually unique way, therefore this framework is appropriate for this study. The discussion is framed around the major findings which elaborate how our findings shed light on future teaching and learning experiences, particularly for preservice STEM teachers.

Both PSTs and their students were in this new nontraditional classroom setting and rendered vulnerable in previously hidden ways. Being forced to rethink their teaching, PSTs learned different lessons to take with them as new teachers from this past year. Their job demands as teachers changed in ways they never had before. This prolonged traumatic event impacted teachers differently than an acute traumatic event.

First, these PSTs learned what technologies worked best for different teaching aspects at the beginning and throughout the school year. During a typical summer for the MAT program, PSTs do not receive direct instruction or focus on their pedagogy class about teaching online. Due to the pandemic, the MAT program created online teaching pedagogy and made it part of their required classwork in the summer before their teaching residency. This allowed for the participants to have at least minimal exposure to online teaching and learning before their residency. It was unknown how different schools would handle the online teaching aspect due to their own individual factors, particularly finances, so teaching all PSTs about online teaching and allowing them some practice over the summer gave PSTs some useful tools going into their teaching residency. The residents learned that they would not always be directly in front of students physically, so they learned different ways to help encourage participation. Participant 2, for example, had a completely different residency than she expected when entering the MAT program. Her teaching residency was completely online, and she had to learn how this would work and also had to think about how she would teach biology labs in the future without having done it in person this particular year. All the PSTs entered the program before COVID-19 and knew the residency year would be challenging and unpredictable to some degree, but like most people, could not have expected this challenge. The PSTs did learn more technology during their residency regardless of what level of technology experience they had while entering the MAT program. The PSTs also learned how dynamic and surprising teaching can be to a more extreme level. The PSTs realized that, even with their little teaching experience, they had much to offer to their colleagues because of the different technological tools that were shared with others. While teaching during the pandemic was extremely difficult for these PSTs, they did learn about many different technologies and online pedagogical tools that supported their STEM teaching. Participant 2 learned about different types of virtual biology labs and Participant 3, Participant 1, and Participant 4 all shared their use of Desmos during the school year, an online advanced graphing calculator that is supportive in teaching math.

The PSTs seeing firsthand how equity impacted their students gives more insight into their students and their role as teachers. During pre-COVID years, PSTs would see this in their classroom. However, during COVID times, PSTs had a window into many of their students' homes. Some students kept their cameras off, and others kept them on. Some of those students who kept cameras off shared that they did not have a quiet, distraction free place to learn or sit in for their virtual class. One of the PSTs shared that their student attended class from the doghouse because it was a quieter spot than inside the house. At the same time, other students had more comfortable and supportive learning environments, emphasizing the inequities that exist among their students. The PSTs had a more personal understanding of equity than in a typical school year, due to prevalence of online teaching. Teacher preparation programs may consider when classrooms go back to "normal," how can they help their PSTs understand equity at a closer level than just what they see in the classroom. This may include having to be more proactive in getting to know their students as people and emphasizes that their students are more than just the person they see sitting in front of them.

It also became apparent that students, depending upon which school district they resided in and who they had as a teacher, could have drastically different experiences with STEM, particularly science. For example,

Participant 2's students, who were in a fully virtual biology class, would never have any experiences with biology labs firsthand. For other biology students, they could be exposed to many different types of labs, including those that are part of the required list for New York State and more elaborate labs such as dissections. Inequities have always existed in school, particularly in STEM, but the COVID-19 pandemic only exacerbated the existing inequities.

As Darling-Hammond and colleagues (2000) stated before, a quality teacher education program needs to have a clear understanding of what good teaching looks like in addition to the standards and curriculum that is centered around child development. During the COVID-19 pandemic, there was nothing teachers could look at to understand what "good teaching" was supposed to look like. They were just getting by.

Experiencing firsthand how important it is to engage directly with their students was evident for all PSTs. The PSTs who had many students online or completely online felt the challenge of how to keep students engaged, even when they were not able to see some of their students' faces. PSTs shared how it was difficult to keep students engaged, not only online, but in person as well. Students in person were spaced apart and unable to work in groups like they had in the past and when the PST attended to the students online (in the hybrid classrooms), students in person would lose focus. This emphasized the importance of learning in social contexts and also how to create routines, so students were still engaged and focused when the teacher was helping others. The PSTs and their mentors may have known the importance of this before COVID-19, but these experiences stressed the importance of them when teaching students. Based on the journal reflections, it was apparent that PSTs were assessing what was working and what was not working in their classroom and adjusting accordingly with their pedagogy and expectations. PSTs may have been more attuned to paying attention to this because of the overall care for students during the pandemic. Using strategies to get to know their online students better can be carried over to in person as well, supporting the positive impact of building classroom community.

These three themes were dominant, and therefore it should be emphasized how valuable their role is in the classroom environment and as developing teachers. We also elaborate on how teacher educators can now better prepare our PSTs. This case study is limited to just four STEM PSTs during the pandemic at different schools. The interpretivist paradigm enabled us to treat the context of the research and its situation as unique considering the given circumstances associated during the pandemic as well as participants involved. This allowed us to focus on the whole experience as a highly important aspect. The declarations of this study must be considered in the context of several limitations. Our sample is small and

Struggles and Stress   179

from a single institution, and the journal reflections were written mainly during the busy school year, which did not provide substantial time for thorough reflection.

CONCLUSION AND IMPLICATIONS

The COVID-19 pandemic created a major disruption to the spring of 2020 and beyond, including how we think about instructional practices in our nation's classrooms. On top of being stressed as a student and teacher, PSTs were also subject to the other pandemic stressors as others were—this includes feeling anxious about their family's safety, caregiving challenges as K–12 schools also shifted online, financial stressors, and future job prospects.

These accounts from PSTs help us learn as educators how to better prepare our PSTs for what they may face as new teachers and, like most qualitative research, not generalizable. The PSTs share what technology they plan on using in the future and how they plan on using it; in other words, a silver-lining from the pandemic. Inequities have always existed in school and in STEM; knowing that outside situations such as the pandemic can magnify the inequities, schools can start to be creative on how to reduce these impacts when disasters hit. Having one pandemic in our lifetime shows that, as a society, we are vulnerable, and that in these situations, schools are expected to just continue. Going forward, schools can think about how to provide students with more equitable science or lab access ahead of time. There are other situations where students may need to be outside of the classroom, but what can be done to prepare for these situations or how can they be made up if possible. Planning this ahead of time can help create somewhat more equitable learning conditions for students, especially in STEM. PSTs have always considered student engagement to be of utmost importance. However, PSTs may have been more attuned to paying attention to this because of the overall care for students during the pandemic. This attentiveness to student engagement can be carried forward though, regardless of outside situations like the pandemic. As Participant 4 suggests, having a show-and-tell just to see what students select to share about can be done to build community.

Our findings demonstrate the complex situations PSTs faced amid their teaching residency and the multifaceted ways that they were successful at maintaining stability, consistency, and development as teachers. Further, teacher preparation programs must increase their technology integration in order to prepare PSTs to be ready for an online teaching and learning environment complete with active student engagement, assessment, responsive instruction, and effective communication. Additionally, research is needed to determine how teachers can assess their students effectively

180   S. RIVERA ET AL.

and how they should provide responsive instruction. In addition to this, future research should investigate what effect a shift to online learning might have on the mental, social, and emotional development of students. Although the COVID-19 pandemic created a significant disruption to students and schooling, it has also created many opportunities to examine, critique, and question the status quo, including in education and teacher preparation, and for sure has provided us an opportunity to learn to prepare PSTs for different learning environments.

REFERENCES

Auxier, B., & Anderson, M. (2020). *As some schools close due to the coronavirus, U.S. students face a digital 'homework gap'*. Pew Research Center.

Beaunoyer, E., Dupéré, S., & Guitton, M. J. (2020). COVID-19 and digital inequalities: Reciprocal impacts and mitigation strategies. *Computers in Human Behavior, 111*, 106424. https://doi.org/10.1016/j.chb.2020.106424

Castleberry, A., & Nolen, A. (2018). Thematic analysis of qualitative research data: Is it as easy as it sounds? *Currents in Pharmacy Teaching and Learning, 10*(6), 807–815.

Cohen, E., Hoz, R., & Kaplan, H. (2013). The practicum in preservice teacher education: A review of empirical studies. *Teaching Education, 24*(4), 345-380.

Cornish, F., Gillespie, A., & Zittoun, T. (2014). Collaborative analysis of qualitative data. In F. Uwe (Ed.), *The SAGE handbook of qualitative data analysis* (pp. 79–93). SAGE.

Creswell, J. W. (2007). *Research design. Qualitative and mixed methods approaches*. SAGE.

Darling-Hammond, L. (2010). Teacher education and the American future. *Journal of Teacher Education, 61*(1–2), 35–47.

Darling-Hammond, L., Macdonald, M. B., Snyder, J., Whitford, B. L., Ruscoe, G., & Fickel, L. (2000). *Studies of excellence in teacher education: Preparation at the graduate level*. American Association of Colleges for Teacher Education.

Dayal, H. C., & Tiko, L. (2020). When are we going to have the real school? A case study of early childhood education and care teachers' experiences surrounding education during the COVID-19 pandemic. *Australasian Journal of Early Childhood, 45*(4), 336–347. https://doi.org/10.1177/1836939120966085

Elbih, R. (2013). *Pedagogy of post 9/11 United States: Muslim American students' experiences, teachers' pedagogies, and textbooks' analysis* [Unpublished doctoral dissertation]. University of New Mexico.

Foster, K. M. (2006). Bridging troubled waters: Principles for teaching in times of crisis. *Penn GSE Perspectives on Urban Education, 4*(2).

Graham, S., & Thornley, C. (2000). Connecting classrooms in preservice education: Conversations for learning. *Asia-Pacific Journal of Teacher Education, 28*(3), 235–245.

Hammerness, K. (2006). From coherence in theory to coherence in practice. *Teacher College Record, 108*, 1241–1265.

Hayes, M. T. (2002). Assessment of a field-based teacher education program: Implications for practice. *Education, 122*(581), 700–705.

Hill. J. B. (2021). Pre-service teacher experiences during COVID 19: Exploring the uncertainties between clinical practice and distance learning. *Journal of Practical Studies in Education, 2*(2), 1–13.

Jones, H. E., Manze, M., Ngo, V., Lamberson, P., & Freudenberg, N. (2021). The impact of the COVID-19 pandemic on college students' health and financial stability in New York City: Findings from a population-based sample of City of University of New York (CUNY) students. *Journal of Urban Health, 98*(2), 187–196. https://doi.org/10.1007/s11524-020-00506-x

König, J., Jäger-Biela, D. J., & Glutsch, N. (2020) Adapting to online teaching during COVID-19 school closure: teacher education and teacher competence effects among early career teachers in Germany. *European Journal of Teacher Education, 43*(4), 608–622.

Muacevic, A., & Adler, J. (2020). Closure of universities due to coronavirus disease 2019 (COVID-19): Impact on education and mental health of students and academic staff. *Cureus, 12*(4).

Nickerson, A. B., & Sulkowski, M. L. (2021). The covid-19 pandemic as a long-term school crisis: Impact, risk, resilience, and crisis management. *School Psychology, 36*(5), 271–276.

Otaiba, S. A. (2005). How effective is code-based reading tutoring in English for English learners and preservice teacher-tutors? *Remedial and Special Education, 26*, 245–254.

Patton, M. Q. (2002). *Qualitative research and evaluation methods* (3rd ed.). SAGE.

Reyes, V., Bogumil, E., & Welch, L. E. (2021). The living codebook: Documenting the process of qualitative data analysis: *Sociological Methods & Research, 53*(1). https://doi.org/10.1177/0049124120986185

Richards, K. A. R., & Hemphill, M. A. (2018). A practical guide to collaborative qualitative data analysis. *Journal of Teaching in Physical Education, 37*(2), 225–231

Saldaña, J. (2015). *The coding manual for qualitative researchers* (3rd ed.). SAGE.

Soria, K. M., & Horgos, B. (2021). Factors associated with college students' mental health during the COVID-19 pandemic. *Journal of College Student Development, 62*(2), 107–113. https://doi.org/10.1353/csd.2021.0024

Stringer, E., & Aragon, A.O. (2020). *Action research* (5th ed.). SAGE.

Vacc, N. N., & Bright, G. W. (1999). Elementary preservice teachers' changing beliefs and instructional use of children's mathematical thinking. *Journal for Research in Mathematics Education, 30*, 89–110.

Vuchic, R., & Robb, B. A. (2006). An integrative approach to FLES teacher training: The Delaware model. *Foreign Language Annals, 39*, 334–346.

Whiteside, A., Gomez-Vasquez, L., Ensmann, S., & Sturgill, R. (2020, November 10). *"We all had to become stronger together": Faculty experiences of disruption and innovation during the COVID-19 Pandemic.* OLC Accelerate Conference.

Willis, J. W. (2007). *Foundations of qualitative research: interpretive and critical approaches.* SAGE.

Wu, S. C., Pearce, E., & Price, C. J. (2020). Creating virtual engagement for preservice teachers in a science methods course in response to the COVID-19 pandemic. *The Electronic Journal for Research in Science & Mathematics Education, 24*(3), 38–44.

Yin, R. K. (2009). *Case study research: Design and methods* (4th ed.). SAGE.
Yin. R. K. (2014). Case study research design and methods (5th ed.). SAGE.
Zeichner, K. (2010). New epistemologies in teacher education. Rethinking the connections between campus courses and practical experiences in teacher education at the university. *Interuniversity Journal of Teacher Education*, *68*(24.2), 123–150.

APPENDIX 1

Codes

Parent Code	Definition
Teaching Online	Instances of any online teaching, this includes hybrid teaching
Resource	Instances that refer to access or availability of any resources, including time
Hybrid	Any reference to connecting with students in a hybrid classroom environment
Internet Struggles	Instances of internet or WiFi connection problems.
Videocamera	Any instance making reference to the camera being on or off for students.
Organized	Any reference to keeping lessons for both in person and online, or keeping track of students who were both in person and virtual.
English Language Learner	Any instances where the teacher made some adaptations for ELL students.
Quiet Student	Any reference to a student who was quiet, especially those who were virtual.
Connection with student	Any instance where a teacher connected with a student, does not necessarily have to be content-related.
Resources	Any reference to or lack of technology, materials, supports at home, etc.
Time spent with student	Any instance that discussed time spent with students in person or online, or how to balance that time.
Assessments	Any reference to any assessments, including ones made to be online, new types of technology used to assess.
Social Justice	Student making reference to something taking place politically, socially, etc. (e.g., student response to Breonna Taylor trial).
Support from Mentor	Any instance where teacher made reference to learning from their mentor teacher or receiving advice/feedback from their mentor teacher.

CHAPTER 8

A RAPID SCOPING REVIEW OF COLLEGIATE STUDENTS' STRESS, COPING, AND HELP-SEEKING DURING COVID-19

Caroline H. Weppner, Christopher J. McCarthy, Yijie Tian, Trisha Miller, Francesca Di Rienzo
The University of Texas at Austin

R. Jason Lynch
Appalachian State University

Stephen DiDonato
Thomas Jefferson University

ABSTRACT

On January 30, 2020, the World Health Organization (WHO) declared COVID-19 a "Public Health Emergency of International Concern" and characterized it as a pandemic less than two months later (World Health Organization, n.d.). The resulting containment measures led to a financial crisis, emotional isolation, and challenges in the job market, further exacerbating mental health issues, including stress (Brooks et al., 2020; Salari et al., 2020; Sen-Crowe et al., 2020). Our research team conducted a rapid scoping review using the Preferred Reporting Items for Systematic Reviews and Meta-Analyses Extension for Scoping Reviews (PRISMA-ScR) to identify themes, concepts, and knowledge gaps in student stress, coping, and help-seeking

---

Research on College Stress and Coping: Implications From the COVID-19 Pandemic and Beyond, pp. 183–224
Copyright © 2024 by Information Age Publishing
www.infoagepub.com
All rights of reproduction in any form reserved.

during the pandemic (Tricco et al., 2018). The impacts of COVID-19 on students were evident across seven themes, particularly affecting under-represented and minoritized individuals. This review also addresses strategies for educators and administrators that may improve the management of these stressful events moving forward, limitations of our study, and future research directions.

On January 30, 2020, the World Health Organization (WHO) declared COVID-19 a "Public Health Emergency of International Concern," and less than two months later characterized the outbreak as a pandemic (World Health Organization, 2020). As of May 3, 2023, COVID has caused over 6 million deaths globally (WHO, n.d.). Moreover, related containment interventions like lockdowns, quarantine, and social distancing resulted in financial crisis, the physical and emotional absence of family, friends, and formal support systems, and difficulties navigating the job market, which all significantly exacerbated people's mental health problems, including overall stress (Brooks et al., 2020; Salari et al., 2020; Sen-Crowe et al., 2020). Symptoms of stress-related mental disorders increased markedly across all countries and many researchers and healthcare providers feel that it will take years to understand the pandemic's full impact on individual's mental health (Daniali et al., 2023; Łaskawiec et al., 2022).

The COVID-19 pandemic generated considerable research on college student's mental health, and in order to better understand overall findings, a rapid scoping review was conducted with the following study objectives in mind: (1) conduct a systematic search of the published literature regarding college student stress and coping, particularly help-seeking (2) better understand the characteristics and themes of these articles, (3) examine the gaps in this field of literature, and (4) propose future directions for research specific to student's stress and coping during and following a traumatic event, like COVID-19. This literature review will discuss the definition of stress, particularly college students' stress, and the types of coping and help-seeking students engage in, especially during the pandemic. This review will also expand on why our research team chose a rapid scoping review as the methodology for this chapter to accommodate the quick timeframe of the manuscript as well as address gaps in the literature for a rapid, and much needed growing field of research.

Challenges in Defining Stress

The concept of "stress" is ubiquitous but often imprecisely defined in the literature. Historically, stress was defined as either a physiological reaction (i.e., increased heart rate, release of stress hormones such as cortisol (Selye, 1956), or an external event such as moving, losing a job, or the death of someone close (Holmes & Rahe, 1967). Current research emphasizes the psychological nature of stress and derive their definition of stress from one of the two main pillars of stress theory: (1) The transactional model of stress (Lazarus & Folkman, 1984) and (2) The conservation of resources theory (COR; Hobfoll, 1998). The transactional model of stress defines stress as resulting from appraisals about external demands (e.g., does it represent a threat to me?) and appraisals of the sufficiency of resources they have at their disposal to manage or cope with this stressful situation (Lazarus & Folkman, 1984). In contrast, COR theory (Hobfoll, 1989) defines stress in terms of potential threats to resources in one's environmental, cultural, and social contexts (e.g., money, social support, sense of autonomy, etc.) (Hobfoll, 1998).

Our research team was guided by these two frameworks to inform the literature search, but as we started the review, it became apparent that not all researchers used these two frameworks to inform their research and also had varied definitions of stress that overlapped with other related constructs, such as trauma. Our definition of stress continued to expand and shift as we moved through the scoping review process, and the research team met regularly to discuss what should be categorized as "stress." However, the team continued to reference the two frameworks mentioned above in order to influence theme creation and understanding of the literature.

To understand how college students experience stress and deploy coping strategies in general, specifically during the pandemic, we will share a deeper look into the two existing theoretical frameworks of stress, as mentioned above. While the two models of stress are the pillars of this field, they have very different premises. Each theory has also spurred further research and spawned additional theories, as described below.

The Transactional Model of Stress and Coping

The transactional model of stress and coping (Lazarus & Folkman, 1984) emphasizes a two-step evaluation procedure that unfolds when individuals encounter potential obstacles and challenges in their environment (Chang, 2009). This process commences with a "primary appraisal," where individuals evaluate the severity and characteristics of the threat or demand they face. Subsequently, this primary appraisal leads to a secondary assessment in which individuals assess their available resources for dealing with the given challenge. An imbalance between the demands placed on individuals and the resources available to them frequently results in elevated levels of stress (Lazarus & Folkman, 1984).

To apply this model to college students during the pandemic, students first evaluated their situation to determine whether it was a threat or not.

This primary appraisal significantly impacted how students perceived their situation. Second, students engaged in a "secondary appraisal" to assess their available coping skills and resources to manage their threatening situation. The theory posits that students who perceived a major discrepancy between their demands and resources often experienced higher levels of stress during the pandemic.

This basic understanding of the different types of appraisals is helpful for readers to better understand why students had worse or better outcomes from the pandemic compared to their peers. In addition, it helps conceptualize why students leaned toward certain coping strategies and help-seeking tendencies.

Conservation of Resources Theory

The conservation of resources theory (COR; Hobfoll, 1998) is another theoretical framework used to describe and conceptualize stress in the literature. Instead of focusing on the individual's appraisal and ability to cope, COR focuses on a bigger picture of how one's stress and resources co-exist with their environment, culture, and social contexts. Demands placed on individuals can have a cultural component, as can their resources. Individuals use both learning and personal experiences to recognize the specific skills needed to survive or be successful in their culture (i.e. resources). In contrast to the transactional model, Hobfoll (1998) emphasizes how much our resources originate from our culture, family, environment, and societal formal support, and so forth, and how a lack of resources can lead to elevated levels of stress for not only ourselves but our community at large.

When an individual loses resources, it can significantly impact the community's ability to handle ongoing challenges. A community can conserve its resources, leading to favorable outcomes for the community. However, unsuccessful conservation of resources can lead a community, and its individuals, to greater levels of psychological distress (Buchwald & Schwarzer, 2010). Given that college students operate within their community (e.g., their campus), this theoretical framework helps readers conceptualize the mutually beneficial, or detrimental, relationship between an individual, their community, and the balancing of resources that is needed to be successful, or simply cope.

Other Models of Stress

While this study predominately used the transactional model of stress and coping and COR to conceptualize stress, it is important to note the other models of stress used in the broader literature. Most of the subsequent models of stress were adapted and expanded from the transactional model of stress and focused primarily on stress within occupational settings. These include the job demand-control model (Karasek & Theorell, 1990), the job-demands resource model (Bakker & Demerouti, 2007), and the effort-reward imbalance model (Siegrist, 1996). These models highlight the element of "balance" with demands and resources, much like the transactional model. Balance is a way of explaining stress and burnout dependent on the demands of the individual and the resources they have to cope with these demands. More demands and fewer resources often lead to an imbalance and, thus, higher levels of stress and burnout.

The difference between these models is that each addresses unique elements of the demands-resources equation. For example, Karasek's demand-control model of job stress focuses on workers in high-demand jobs with different levels of autonomy (Karasek & Theorell, 1990). From this theory, one can deduce that a worker in a high-demand job with lower autonomy in the workplace would exhibit higher levels of stress. Similarly, the job-demands resource model posits that those with high-demanding jobs and low resources/positives typically experience increased stress and burnout (Bakker & Demerouti, 2007). While this theory focuses on workers at high-demand jobs, similar to the demand-control model of stress, this places less emphasis on the worker's autonomy and more on their resources. Finally, Siegrist's effort-reward imbalance model focuses on effort spent and rewards received at work in comparison to the previous two theories that focused more on job demands (Siegrist, 1996). A worker who exudes a large amount of effort but does not receive rewards (e.g., a pay increase) would hypothetically show greater levels of stress.

While students operate within their campus much like workers operate within their offices, as described in the aforementioned stress models, we decided to use the two main theoretical frameworks of stress (e.g., transactional model of stress and coping and COR) because they are more applicable to different populations outside of occupational settings. For example, the transactional model has been applied to medical settings (Lowenstein et al., 2019) and sports settings (Lim et al., 2023) just to name a few, and has also been applied to school settings (McCarthy et al., 2016). COR has most recently been used in tourism research (Jiang & Tu, 2022) and medical settings (Fu et al., 2023). These limited, but specific, examples give further credence as to why the transactional model of stress and coping and COR can be effectively used to explain stress in many different settings, including higher education settings. Below, we will give greater detail on why college students are an important population to study regarding stress, and how the two frameworks can help us understand how college students appraise their situation and deploy coping skills, including help-seeking.

College Students' Stress

Students are an important sample to study, as they are often regarded as a microcosm of the larger population. It is imperative to understand the effects of COVID-19 on student's stress and coping skills as it can inform directions for future studies regarding groups of people that are (1) closely intertwined, (2) dependent on social support as a coping mechanism, (3) and are all moving toward a common goal (e.g., graduating college).

Stress is more prevalent in the college student population generally, let alone during a global pandemic (Leppink et al., 2016; Wang et al., 2021). Studies have shown that as many as 71% of students experience moderate to high levels of stress and almost half of students seeking counseling and mental health services report stress-related concerns (Ibrahim et al., 2013; LeViness et al., 2019). An abundance of research explores why university students are at increased risk for stress. First, university students are developmentally in transition as they navigate emerging adulthood. Some even categorize this time as the most unstable period throughout one's life (Matud et al., 2020; Reddy et al., 2018). As students use this time of transition to explore their identities, they also create and maintain relationships with friends, significant others, and peers. These connections hold great value, and conflict within those relationships is a common and notable stressor for university students (Hurst et al., 2013). Additionally, university students often feel increased pressure to maintain high academic achievement, which can be especially challenging as students adjust to a new learning environment and expectations (Bedewy & Gabriel, 2015). Many students are also financially responsible for their housing, food, and other activities, as they become less dependent on family financial support (Heckman et al., 2014). This often leads students to seek employment, which can take away from their social and academic needs, further escalating their stress (Robb, 2017).

With the onset of the COVID-19 pandemic, stress levels among college students have increased (Hamaideh et al., 2022; Wang et al., 2021). At the height of the pandemic, students were met with new challenges related to social isolation and online learning that limited social and academic support as mitigators of stress (Fruehwirth et al., 2021). Many students also experienced distress because of loss of employment and other opportunities, such as internships and travel, and experienced an increased uncertainty about the future (Aucejo et al., 2020; Sirrine et al., 2021). Furthermore, students experienced stressors surrounding the health and well-being of themselves and their loved ones. In some cases, students also had to cope with grief and loss (Lee et al., 2021; Mortazavi et al., 2020). Help seeking is an important way in which college students adjust to coping with demands and attempt to reduce stress, and it played a large role in how students dealt with the pandemic. The following section provides a more extensive look at help-seeking behaviors in the collegiate population.

Help-Seeking Behaviors

While there has been an almost 50% increase in college students presenting with a mental health disorder, the number of students who seek help has not increased to that extent (Lipson et al., 2022). Little progress has been made to improve help-seeking behaviors and inequities related to help-seeking have worsened (Lipson et al., 2022). Often, a lack of help-seeking behaviors is attributed to things like feelings of not mattering, perceived stigmatization, and low mental health literacy (Aldalaykeh et al., 2019; Niegocki & Ægisdóttir, 2019; Shannon et al., 2020). However, there is a growing field of literature that supports the use of brief anti-stigma interventions for improving help-seeking behaviors among college students (Shahwan et al., 2020).

Help-seeking during the pandemic was even more restricted given the limited access to counseling centers and community providers, and delays in help-seeking often resulted in "lost opportunities" for college students to access the help needed (Yonemoto & Kawashima, 2023). In one particular study, over half of the participants (i.e., college students) reported not receiving the proper professional care when they needed it (Legros & Boyraz, 2023). In addition, male-identifying students, particularly undergraduate students, were less likely to seek psychological help for emotional difficulties (Burns et al., 2023).

As indicated, college students were significantly impacted by the pandemic, and the levels of help-seeking within this population did not expand at the same rate as those reporting mental health difficulties. With this being said, there are still gaps in how researchers looked at and investigated students' stress and coping skills, particularly help-seeking, during COVID-19. In addition, the two main theoretical frameworks of stress (i.e. transactional model of stress and coping and COR) are beneficial when trying to define and conceptualize stress, however, these frameworks were not always implemented in stress research, leading to an ambiguous understanding of the term "stress." To (1) understand the larger field of research regarding students' stress and coping during the pandemic, and (2) to gain a clearer definition of "stress," a methodological approach needed to be determined. Below, the definition of scoping review will be addressed as well as the reasoning behind why a rapid scoping review was chosen for this particular study.

190   C. H. WEPPNER ET AL.

METHODS

Below we outline our process in determining our methodological approach, the procedure for the rapid scoping review, including reporting protocol, exclusion criteria, research team members, details on each round of review conducted, and theme creation.

Reporting Protocol: Rapid Scoping Review

After years of deliberation regarding the definition and conduction of scoping reviews, the larger research community has come to a consensus on how to define and conduct scoping reviews (Pham et al., 2014). Scoping reviews are often used in situations where a systematic review would not be useful (Munn et al., 2018). Systematic reviews are conducted to answer a specific set of research questions to "inform practice, policy, and further research" (Munn et al., 2018), whereas scoping reviews are predominately used to determine the scope or coverage of a section of literature. The focus is often broader than a systematic review and gives special attention to emerging evidence for specific research questions, and ways in which a field may change its practice or how research is conducted (Munn et al., 2018).

We decided on a rapid scoping review since COVID-19 is a fairly recent event, yet there has been considerable research conducted given its global pervasiveness. A rapid scoping review has similar features to a full scoping review but accelerates the process by "streamlining or omitting specific methods" to present results in an efficient manner (Garritty et al., 2020). We did this by adjusting and narrowing our search terms, which can be found in Appendix A. In order to keep the integrity of the project, we used the Preferred Reporting Items for Systematic Reviews and Meta-Analyses Extension for Scoping Reviews (PRISMA-ScR). The main focus of the PRISMA-ScR, and what we hoped to accomplish in this rapid scoping review, is to identify themes, concepts, and knowledge gaps in data-based studies (Tricco et al., 2018). The limitations and future research implications of this decision are listed below in the discussion section.

Research Team and Inclusion Criteria

Our research team consisted of seven members, including three faculty members and four PhD-level graduate students. All faculty members have extensive expertise in stress research, and one of the faculty members has experience with scoping reviews and the PRISMA model for reporting.

To be included, the articles were judged based on a series of criteria. The peer-reviewed empirical studies needed to: (1) take place in a university setting, (2) focus primarily on college students (not staff, faculty, etc.), (3) include topics related to stress and/or trauma, and (4) conducted during the COVID-19 pandemic (December 12, 2019—December 31, 2022). In addition, the articles needed to be written in English or translated into English, however, there were no exclusion criteria that limited the geographic location of the articles. See Figure 8.1 for inclusion and exclusion at each stage of the review.

Round 1 of Review

The initial step in developing a finalized list of articles for the scoping review involved performing a search in September 2022 on three different databases: APA PsycINFO, ERIC, and Education Source. The search, which is shown in Appendix A, included 16 terms broken into three different categories (1) COVID/pandemic, (2) college or university (3) mental health/well-being (inclusive of stress, anxiety, coping, help-seeking, etc.). The Liaison Librarian for Education and Team Lead for the STEM & Social Science Engagement Team at our university was consulted for the search criterion. Appendix A provides the specific search terms used to produce the articles within the three databases. The three databases were split among three of the graduate students, who then determined whether the articles should be included in the next round of reviews by reviewing the article's title only. Of the 237 articles, 149 were either duplicates or excluded based on their title, resulting in 88 articles.

Round 2 of Review

The second round of reviews (88 articles) was conducted by the same three graduate students as in Round 1 of the review with the addition of the three faculty members. The research team split into three groups of two. Each pair used a spreadsheet to keep track of the article's descriptive qualities, including authors, title, abstract, and inclusion criteria. To aid in the larger selection process (e.g., full-text review of each article), the reviewer teams first analyzed 30 abstracts, first separately and then together, each using the set of inclusion criteria described above in Inclusion Criteria and Research Team: (1) took place in a university setting, (2) focused primarily on college students, (3) discussed topics related to stress and/or trauma, and (4) conducted during the COVID-19 pandemic. Of the 88 articles analyzed, 65 articles proceeded to the next round of reviews. Following this round of reviews, the larger group met to discuss progress and whether there needed to be modifications to the inclusion criteria.

Round 3 of Review

Round 3 of reviews (65 articles) used the same pairs as Round 2, but each group was given only 20 different articles to complete a full-text review of each article. The same inclusion criteria were used to include or exclude articles from the final list. Each pair continued to use a spreadsheet to keep track of the article's descriptive qualities, including authors, title, abstract, and exclusion criteria and then decided whether or not to include the article as they did in round 2 of reviews. If the pair had a discrepancy regarding the inclusion of an article, they first met to discuss. If they were still in disagreement, they shared the article and their different viewpoints with the larger team, who then helped decide on inclusion or exclusion. After this round of edits, 18 articles were excluded and 47 were kept for inclusion in the manuscript (see Figure 8.1).

Theme Creation

We sought to create codes that capture important themes from the 47 articles, which were led by three of the graduate assistants, including the lead researcher. Byrne (2022) identifies three ways to address thematic analysis: (1) coding reliability thematic analysis, (2) codebook approaches to thematic analysis, and (3) the reflexive approach to thematic analysis. We used a reflexive approach to the inductive thematic analysis, given the rapid timing of this chapter. We first focused on the interpretation of individual coding throughout the articles and then focused on the aggregated meaning of each code across the dataset, collapsing codes to create themes with shared meanings (Byrne, 2022). The process is described in greater detail below.

To establish a system of coding, we had to first determine whether the coding of major themes of the articles (i.e. keywords) was consistent amongst the three graduate students. In order to do this, each of the three graduate assistants decided on keywords for the same five articles individually. The keywords ranged from three per article to nine per article and mainly included the keywords used by the authors of the articles and the themes found throughout the results and discussion sections. Once the graduate assistants had individually decided upon keywords for the five articles, the lead researcher compared keywords across graduate assistants to determine whether there were any disagreements or misunderstandings while coding. Since the keywords were relatively consistent across all three graduate assistants, it was determined that there was intercoder reliability, or reliability, across the three coders on how to code the same data. The remaining articles were split evenly among the three researchers to finish the analysis. Each graduate assistant received 14 articles to code. After the

Figure 8.1

Literature Search and Screening Process

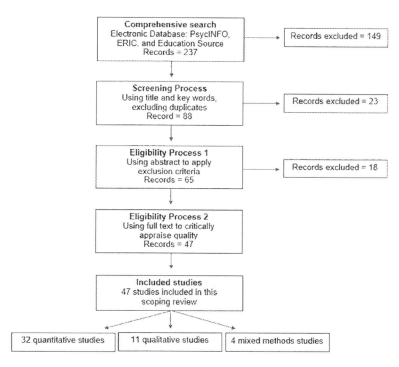

Note. Figure 8.1 was adapted from "A Systematic Review of School-based Positive Psychology Interventions to Foster Teacher Wellbeing" by Duyen T. Vo & Kelly-Ann Allen.

keywords were decided, the lead researcher compiled all the keywords and inductively created themes or interpreted significance and formulated patterns from the data without any preconceived notions, based on the frequency of each keyword (e.g., keywords related to social support appeared in 18 articles) (Page et al., 2021; Tricco et al., 2018).

RESULTS

The section below first addresses the characteristics of the analyzed studies, including the type of study, the timeframe, the population, and where the research for each article took place. Subsequently, we explain why "stress and well-being" was determined to be our overarching theme of the manuscript, and then we discuss in greater depth the seven themes that emerged

194   C. H. WEPPNER ET AL.

from our inductive thematic analysis. Each section includes the number of articles that fell within that theme and explanations of the subjects discussed in the articles that categorized them within that particular theme.

Characteristics of the Studies

To summarize, of the 237 original articles (Figure 8.1) independently and jointly reviewed by the three professors and three graduate students, 47 were included in this scoping review. Thirty-two were quantitative studies (68.10%), 11 were qualitative studies (23.40%), and 4 were mixed methods (8.50%) (i.e., contain a component of both quantitative and qualitative). The type of study and other quantitative summaries of the below characteristics can be found in Figure 8.2.

The research team created two timeframes to better delineate when these studies/articles were conducted/published. The first timeframe, "Beginning," indicates December 12, 2019–December 1, 2020. These dates were decided upon given that December 12, 2019, was when the first patient worldwide was diagnosed with COVID-19, and December 1, 2020, was the start of the vaccination rollouts. The second, or "Middle," timeframe runs from December 2, 2020–December 31, 2022. This indicated the time period from the vaccination rollouts to the start of this study. There were 38 studies conducted at the "beginning" of the pandemic, five conducted in the "middle," two that spanned both timeframes, and two that were unclear from the article when the data was gathered.

While all studies primarily focused on students within a university setting, the majority focused on undergraduate students ($N = 30$). Five articles included only graduate students, 10 looked at both undergraduate and graduate, and a small number of articles ($N = 2$) either focused on both students and staff/faculty or it was unclear what type of student they included in their sample. Twenty-seven studies took place in the United States, while 20 articles focused on the effects of COVID-19 on university students in other parts of the world.

Seven Emergent Themes Regarding Student Stress During the Pandemic

Seven themes were established across the 47 articles, within the overarching theme of stress and well-being: coping strategies, COVID-specific concepts, changes in addiction/usage, physical health concerns, social/cultural difficulties, social support, and educational concepts. The larger theme of "stress and well-being" was mentioned in every article present in

Figure 8.2

A Quantitative Representation of the Included Articles

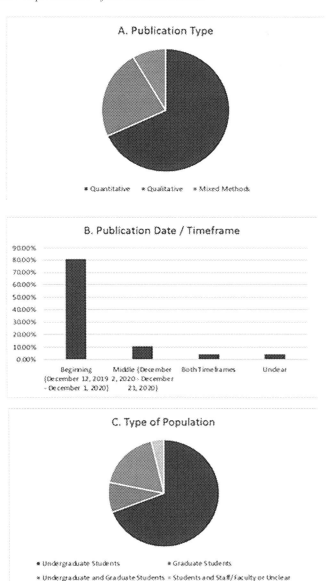

Note. Figure 8.2 describes the publication type, publication date/timeframe, and type of population present in this rapid scoping review.

this scoping review; therefore, it served as the larger umbrella under which the other seven themes fall under. Below, we have included representative findings for each of the themes established. Both transactional theory and the COR heavily influenced the seven themes. The research team used the ideas of demands (e.g., academic achievement, health concerns, etc.) and resources (social support, adaptive coping skills, etc.) as a starting point for keywords when analyzing the literature regarding college students during the pandemic. Stress and well-being is described below and each of the following sections highlight one of the themes and include data and representative findings from articles whose keywords fell into those sections.

Stress and Well-Being

Every article ($n = 47$) addressed college students' stress and well-being during the COVID-19 pandemic. As mentioned in the introduction and literature review, stress is specifically and narrowly defined in some studies, while in others it is broadly defined or not defined at all. The lead researcher used a similarly broad definition to understand what keywords fell into this theme, as the research team used to determine the inclusivity of articles in this scoping review. In some articles, stress was defined as, and was even used synonymously with, other psychological distress terminology like depression, anxiety, and post-traumatic stress disorder. The most common ways in which articles addressed stress were: stress, worry, anxiety, negative psychological distress, fears, and overall psychological well-being. Stress itself was split into numerous categories, including occupational stress, chronic stress, traumatic stress, social stress, academic stress, and pandemic stress. Stress will be referred to as different concepts moving forward, given the terminology of each article.

Fruehwirth and colleagues' (2021) findings are representative of this theme and reported that ¼ of students experienced moderate-severe anxiety and nearly 1/3 experienced moderate-severe depression four months into the pandemic. One of the main limitations that was mentioned throughout this article was that it was difficult to delineate whether the stress, anxiety, depression, trauma, and so forth, that the students were experiencing were above and beyond the normal psychological distress that accompanies the massive transition into collegiate life. Fruehwirth and colleagues determined that the changes they found in anxiety and depression in students were more significant than typical first-year stressors prior to the pandemic.

Across most articles, individuals who endorsed social stressors (e.g., difficulties with friends, struggling relationships with family members, and lack of support from faculty members) were more likely to endorse negative psychological distress, such as depression, anxiety, and PTSD (Camilleri et al., 2022; Gallegos et al., 2021; Rudenstine et al., 2022). In addition, students who reported COVID-19-related stress also reported elevations in constructs like interpersonal disengagement, struggles with motivation, and boredom, all of which are important for the academic and social success of a collegiate student (Das et al., 2021; Popa-Velea et al., 2021; Tasso et al., 2021).

In review, stress is not consistently defined and is often used interchangeably with other negative psychological distress terms (i.e., anxiety, depression, PTSD). With that being said, all articles that discussed the pandemic's impact on students' mental health were included in this section. These articles highlighted the overwhelming negative impact of the pandemic, above and beyond the already stressful transition to adult life. The following section goes into greater depth on how students coped with the significant increase in stress during COVID-19.

Coping Strategies. The second most frequent theme, as determined by the frequency at which the keywords were used when analyzing the articles, was coping strategies ($n = 23$). Within these 23 articles, coping strategies were often separated into either adaptive and maladaptive (or dysfunctional) coping strategies, or they were split up by their focus: Problem-focused and emotion-focused strategies, which is heavily aligned with Lazarus and Folkman's transactional theory. Problem-focused coping strategies work to solve an issue (e.g., find adaptive ways to keep oneself safe during the pandemic) and emotion-focused coping is used to manage emotions and perceptions of the situation (e.g., work on cognitive restructuring to address anxiety regarding catching COVID) (Schoenmakers et al., 2015).

The types of coping strategies had significant effects on students' ability to succeed in college. For example, while negative coping strategies (e.g., denial and substance use) were used less frequently than adaptive coping strategies (e.g., use of humor, acceptance of the situation, and religion), the negative coping strategies had a predictive negative impact on communication with peers, learning abilities, and time management (Johnson et al., 2022; Popa-Velea et al., 2021). This means that those who used negative coping strategies, like substance use, to handle the pandemic had worse communication with peers, less ability to succeed in classes, and worse time management (Popa-Velea et al., 2021; Prowse et al., 2021). Several studies found that levels of stress, anxiety, and depression significantly affected the type of coping used, and higher levels of negative psychological distress were strongly related to the use of maladaptive coping strategies, particularly avoidance strategies, during lockdown (e.g., self-distraction, venting, and self-blaming) and vice versa, the use of maladaptive coping strategies led to higher levels of psychological distress (Apker, 2022; Le Vigouroux et al., 2021).

As for the focus of the coping strategies, problem-focused coping behaviors were used to obtain information and support from peers, while emotion-focused coping techniques were used predominately to obtain emotional support from peers (Apker, 2022). More specifically, problem-focused coping was used by students to directly manage their stress, whereas emotion-focused coping was used to ease distressful feelings. This was especially true in students of under-represented or minoritized populations. Lancaster and Arango (2021) was representative in showing that there was a lower utilization of mental health services seen in people of color, particularly Black and Hispanic students. However, these students seemed more willing to use alternative and complementary mind-body exercises, such as mindfulness, relaxation, yoga, etc.).

Help-seeking as a coping strategy was also mentioned throughout numerous articles. The literature showed that students have very different help-seeking behaviors based on their identities and backgrounds. For example, international students, especially from Asian cultures, exhibit lower help-seeking intentions and behaviors (Sustarsic & Zhang, 2022). Particularly with this population of students, counselors and educators must find alternative methods to address these students' concerns, particularly the stigma surrounding help-seeking (Xiong et al., 2022).

COVID-Specific Concepts. COVID-specific concepts ($n = 16$) were a "catch-all" category for articles that mentioned things like precaution, front-line workers, government action, isolation, "new normal," and so forth. Students' anxiety seemed to increase during the pandemic because of the lack of knowledge about the pandemic (Baloran, 2020; Santosa et al., 2021). These included challenges distinguishing between true and false information, as well as the "incompatible" and "incomplete" information from governments regarding COVID-19 protocols (Santosa et al., 2021). While some government systems were more honest and transparent than others (Baloran, 2020), two specific articles mentioned government action (or inaction) as playing a significant role in the decrease of students' psychological well-being (Stamatis et al., 2021; Tasso et al., 2021).

The majority of articles included in this theme focused on the impacts of isolation on collegiate students' overall mental health (e.g., Cherdymova et al., 2020; Hamza et al., 2021), but each article referred to it slightly differently, with some calling it temporary involuntary isolation and others using the terms lockdown, social distancing, quarantine, and restrictions. Regardless of the terminology, every article was referring to the social and emotional isolation that many students felt during the entirety of the pandemic.

Several studies noted that pre-existing mental health conditions were affected the most by social isolation and, thus, these students experienced an increase in psychological distress (Hamza et al., 2021). In addition, students in underrepresented or minoritized groups felt that the COVID-19 restrictions led to feelings of discrimination (Jones et al., 2022).

Changes in Addiction/Usage. Many students used substance and media use as coping strategies to cope with difficulties during the pandemic, such as isolation, fear of contracting the virus, and elevated academic stress, however, given the frequency at which substance use and media use was used as a keyword, the lead research decided "changes in addiction/usage" should be a section separate from "coping strategies." With that being said, representative findings from the eight articles ($n = 8$) that mentioned "changes in addiction/usage" are discussed below.

Substance use was often mentioned in tandem with overdose and drug misuse, while other articles discussed behavior changes related to media use (TV and social media), as well as alcohol consumption. Seven articles discussed substance use (including drugs and alcohol) while four articles focused specifically on media use (i.e., TV and social media). Overall, changes in substance use were a significant predictor of many negative psychological difficulties, such as PTSD, anxiety, and depression (Bountress et al., 2022). In addition, there is a significant interaction between the severity of COVID-19 pandemic stressor exposure and alcohol consumption even among those students with prior mental health difficulties pre-pandemic (Cusack et al., 2022).

Both TV and video game usage increased in college students from pre-pandemic to post-pandemic, which could have resulted because of the increase in unexpected confinement and quarantine. More TV usage seemed to increase students' concern for society, which might have been tied to the elevated viewing of deaths during the pandemic. In addition, increasing social media use significantly affected students' concerns over their future when they endorsed low levels of anxiety pre-pandemic, and increased students' concerns for society for students who endorsed an already higher level of depression (Fraser et al., 2022).

Physical Health Concerns. Aside from health concerns specific to COVID, this theme captured a relatively small number of articles ($n = 8$). The common words used in articles to describe overall physical health concerns were: sleep/sleep disturbances, pain, exhaustion, and energy. As for COVID-specific, many articles discussed COVID exposure, COVID diagnosis, and hospitalization. One article in particular, by Lancaster and Arango (2021), examined the health and emotional well-being of college students in the era of COVID-19. Interestingly, they found that their sample population scored high on physical health and physical functioning compared to significantly low scores on emotional well-being and social functioning. However, they did note that the students included in the study endorsed significant loss of sleep, which might be because of the high rates of unemployment during COVID (Lancaster & Arango, 2021).

Cusack and colleagues (2022) focused more heavily on physical health as it relates to COVID, particularly COVID exposure. In those who have experienced previous trauma, COVID-19 pandemic exposure worry was significantly related to levels of PTSD post-COVID. In addition, students that endorsed higher levels of worry regarding COVID-19 exposure reported drinking less during the pandemic, which might be because they had higher levels of physical health concerns that prevented them from spending time with friends and peers in a social environment that might include drinking (Cusack et al., 2022).

Social/Cultural Difficulties. The social and cultural difficulties that students experienced during the COVID-19 pandemic were included in n = 15 articles and coded into three categories: (1) discrimination against students of Asian ethnicity, (2) immigration-related uncertainties (i.e., visa processing delays, U.S. Immigration and Customs Enforcement (ICE) proclamation barring international students from taking online courses in the Unted States), and (3) systemic racism, particularly affecting Black and Hispanic students. Since the race-driven social unrest pre-pandemic significantly affected the ability of students of minoritized and under-represented groups to cope with the pandemic, they would be termed "cascading collective trauma." Cascading collective trauma refers to one traumatic event that has unforeseen complications and consequences with the events that follow (Silver et al., 2021).

Students of Asian descent, especially international students, were often found in the studies reviewed to report higher discrimination at the beginning of the pandemic compared to their white counterparts. These increased levels of discrimination led to higher levels of anxiety and depression and significantly lower levels of academic engagement (Inman et al., 2021; Xiong et al., 2022). A qualitative study conducted by Burt & Eubank (2021), discussed optimism, resilience, and other health factors during the pandemic that predominately affected Black, Indigenous, and People of Color (BIPOC) students. They found that essential healthcare workers in many hospitals were a role predominately held by those in the BIPOC community, which resulted in an increased perception of the continuous threat of COVID-19. In addition, because of systemic racism, many BIPOC students often live in inter-generational housing, which caused an increase in stress and worry about their parents and grandparents catching the virus (Burt & Eubank, 2021). However, BIPOC students did demonstrate higher levels of optimism than their white peers, which might have led to a higher level of resilience seen in these populations during the COVID-19 pandemic (Burt & Eubank, 2021).

Social Support. Social support was included in many articles (n = 16) and referred to relationships with not only peers but also professors, advisors, mentors, family members, etc. Articles discussed the positives of social support (e.g., social cohesion, social confidence) as well as the negatives (e.g., social maladaptation), much of which was influenced by the rules and regulations set forth by the government in response to the pandemic (i.e., quarantine and social distancing). With quarantine rules and social distancing, many students found that it was harder to maintain relationships with friends and family. However, others felt that their social support systems were a protective factor against mental distress (e.g., anxiety, stress, depression) during the pandemic.

On the other hand, studies found that the pandemic increased feelings of social isolation and disconnection, usually through the negative impact COVID had on communication and the challenges of sustaining distant relationships (Das et al., 2021). Since the transition was so rapid from living in residence halls or with numerous roommates to being sent home to live with family, many students were not able to adapt and cope with the social interaction being stripped away (Das et al., 2021). All of these significant changes created an elevated risk of emotional distress in students, particularly those early in their college years (Das et al., 2021).

Andal and Wu (2021) studied doctoral students' experiences during the pandemic. Interestingly, there seemed to be a "shared unfamiliarity" with doing doctoral work during a pandemic, that included not only the experience of the students but also supervisors and faculty members (p. 634). This means that the doctorate students, and their professors, were experiencing the pandemic for the first time together, sharing in the similar stress associated with a traumatic event. Along similar lines, research showed that students in a "cohort" system (e.g., doctoral students, honors college, etc.) seemed to fare better during the pandemic since it offered the students trusted peer support and shared connections as opposed to being a singular student at a large university (Brochu et al., 2021).

Educational Concepts. Several subthemes coded as "Educational Concepts" included online/blended learning (Baloran, 2020; Giannoulas et al., 2021; Hadar et al., 2020; Jaradat & Ajlouni, 2021; Kourea et al., 2021; Popa-Velea et al., 2021; Santosa et al., 2021; Sustarsic & Zhang, 2022), student support/communication (Giannoulas et al., 2021), academic engagement changes (Inman et al., 2021), and academic performance (Son et al., 2020) and were included in $n = 20$ articles. The transition from in-person learning to online learning, with some schools opting for a hybrid version of learning, made it difficult for some students to excel both academically and personally. Popa-Velea and colleagues (2021) found that college students had a preference for classical teaching, which is supported by anecdotal evidence regarding education during the pandemic, followed by hybrid and online learning formats. They also found that online learning, while not the preference of most students, offered more opportunities for advancement in time management and information seeking. Interestingly, online learning was preferred by male college students in urban environments (Popa-Velea et al., 2021).

Giannoulas and colleagues (2021) indicated that online learning had negative repercussions for students and teachers. Students felt that online learning technical difficulties prevented proper communication between students and teachers and between peers, 74.5% of students and 57.5% of students, respectively. In addition, 47.5% of students felt like the online lectures were too long with too many PowerPoint slides (Giannoulas et al., 2021). With this being said, many students said they would consider continuing some online classes (Giannoulas et al., 2021).

Summary of Themes

The pandemic had a significant effect on the mental health of college students, resulting in elevated levels of anxiety and depression among a large majority (Fruehwirth et al., 2021). Students that deployed maladaptive coping strategies (e.g., substance use) performed worse in their classes and displayed difficulties in their social relationships compared to those who used more adaptive coping strategies (e.g., acceptance) (Popa-Velea et al., 2021). Furthermore, substance use was a significant predictor of PTSD, anxiety, and depression (Bountress et al., 2022).

Throughout the literature, social isolation seemed to play a large role in the mental well-being of college students, particularly those in underrepresented or minoritized groups (Hamza et al., 2021). While social support significantly waned during the pandemic, those that had strong peer and family dynamics stated that these relationships were protective forces against the negative impacts of the pandemic (Andal & Wu, 2021; Das et al., 2021). Since most students found classical training, where they are in classrooms with their peers and professors, favorable, the transition to online or hybrid learning had a very negative impact on the stress levels and overall well-being of collegiate students (Giannoulas et al., 2021; Popa-Velea et al., 2021).

These representative findings separated into larger themes play an important role in the scoping review. They lend the reader a broad understanding of the literature in a digestible way and lead the researcher to decide upon limits to the study, future research directions, and potential practice and policy changes. In the next section, key takeaways from each representative findings will be explained, as will limitations and next steps regarding student stress during a major traumatic event such as COVID-19.

DISCUSSION

This scoping review aimed to address the following objectives: (1) conduct a systematic search of the published literature regarding college student stress and coping, particularly help-seeking, (2) better understand the characteristics and themes of these articles, (3) examine the gaps in this field of literature, and (4) propose future directions for research specific to student's stress and coping during and following a traumatic event, like COVID-19. Specifically, we will discuss how the empirical studies defined stress and what roles, if any, the stress theories played in the understanding and interpretation of stress. In addition, the below discussion section addresses what the literature shows regarding the coping strategies of university students during the pandemic and how that might impact changes needed to the higher education system as a whole. We will conclude by describing the limitations of this study and future research directives to address the gaps in literature seen throughout this scoping review.

Defining Stress

As mentioned throughout this chapter, stress is imprecisely defined. We only included the term "stress" within the literature search but, given the ambiguity of the word, the team acknowledged that stress is often used synonymously or in tandem with other words, such as trauma. This was taken into account when analyzing the empirical literature and determining the final group of articles to code. In fact, the code for "stress" included so many different ways of interpreting this mental health phenomenon, that the researchers decided to include "Stress and Well-Being" as a larger "umbrella theme" which the other seven themes fell under.

In addition, the relationship between a stressful event and its impact on mental health is complex. This is due mainly to the differential nature of events and how the individual perceives the stressful event. This is not too dissimilar to the appraisal line of thought in Lazarus and Folkman's transactional theory of stress (1984), interestingly, however, very few articles cited one of the above theories (e.g., transactional theory of stress or COR) to explain their interpretation or understanding of stress. Regardless, a major takeaway from the articles is that one's interactions with their environment significantly affect their ability to cope with certain stressors. The appraisal of the situation determines the behavioral and cognitive coping responses that a person uses to manage the situation (Lazarus & Folkman, 1984). This ambiguity of how people experience stress makes it very difficult to define and expand on the concept of stress, which is evidenced by the gaps in the literature regarding students' stress during the pandemic.

From what is explained in the literature, the pandemic, especially the increase in isolation, negatively affected students' mental health and well-being above and beyond the typical collegiate experience (Fruehwirth et al., 2021; Rudenstine et al., 2022). Numerous factors played a significant role in the increase of stress, anxiety, and depression, especially worry about their health. Prasath (2021) and colleagues state that psychoeducation and strategies to lower levels of worry and promote activities that combat loneliness might help curb these negative impacts on mental health during a traumatic event, such as COVID-19.

Coping Strategies Moving Forward

Coping, a critical element of transactional theory, was another major focus throughout this scoping review. Articles that were analyzed explored the difference between adaptive and maladaptive coping strategies as well as problem-focused versus emotion-focused coping. Apker (2022) stated that problem-focused coping was used directly to manage stress, specifically through self-help behaviors. Conversely, emotion-focused coping was used to ease distressful feelings using things like self-soothing behaviors (Apker, 2022). These types of coping strategies were often contingent on the student's demographics, as described below.

Research shows that there is a lower utilization of mental health services seen in people of color, particularly Black and Hispanic students (Poma et al., 2021). Students from minority groups are more likely to use alternative and complementary mind-body exercises (e.g., mindfulness, relaxation, yoga, etc.) versus typical mental health services like using the university counseling center. In addition, peer and social support played a large role in what coping strategies were chosen as well. While social support is important for the larger student body, it is especially important for under-represented and minoritized groups of students since it is a place to reflect on culturally relevant events and receive support in light of recent social issues (Fruehwirth et al., 2021; Jones et al., 2022).

Key Takeaways and Implications From the Scoping Review

Overall, this review showed that students as well as professors were poorly prepared for e-learning and hybrid learning at the start of the pandemic. There was no precedence over how higher education institutions should handle a universal shutdown of schools. In addition to technological difficulties, many students, staff, and faculty were managing personal, family, institutional, and community barriers that elevated levels of psychological distress (Gallegos et al., 2021; Lancaster & Arango, 2021; Kourea et al., 2021). Even when universities allowed students to come back in person, anxiety levels were still elevated because of social distancing rules and hybrid learning, which, once again, both students and professors were poorly prepared for (Giannoulas et al., 2021). Moving forward, it would be helpful for higher education institutions to provide training for hybrid and online learning to at least the faculty if not everyone at the university. This will better prepare individuals if there were to be another institutional shutdown where they had to continue classes online for a period of time (e.g., environmental disaster).

In addition to technological training for future online and hybrid learning instances, it is important for universities, including staff and faculty, to understand the effect social isolation has on students, especially marginalized and under-represented groups. Social gatherings are spaces that allow culturally relevant celebrations, validation, and support, as well as a safe space to explore and address social issues, therefore social isolation can lead to decreased psychological well-being. In tandem with online learning/hybrid training, universities should include psychological training and preparation, especially for those in marginalized and under-represented groups, on how to combat isolation and mental distress. This is especially important to offer in groups that can act as a support system even if a university needs to switch to online/hybrid learning.

By sharing the above information regarding coping strategies moving forward, it is important to acknowledge larger shifts that are needed within higher education as a whole. Given the generational impacts on wellbeing (McCarthy & Lambert, 2023), institutions must go beyond one-off programming targeted toward wellness and well-being. Instead, there must be a strategic and collaborative effort among all student-facing areas of the institution to create a co-curriculum that helps students build skillsets that help cultivate and maintain a healthy sense of well-being. Institutions may look to co-curricular models spearheaded by organizations such as the American College Personnel Association (ACPA). In addition, limited resources might prompt institutions to invest in peer-support resources to bolster professional counseling and wellness offerings, which is especially important for those in minority groups as mentioned above (Hamza et al., 2021). Last but not least, institutions should explore ways in which trauma-informed practices or care may be infused throughout the organization, for example, the Integrative Trauma and Healing Framework (McGlynn-Wright, 2021) focuses on how organizational leaders view their policies and practices through the lens of safety, belonging, agency, and dignity. Furthermore, using frameworks such as those expanded on in Lynch and Wojdak's (2023) "An exploration of trauma inclusive pedagogy and students' perceptions of academic success," faculty development professionals can help instructors balance academic rigor with instructional practices that reduce harm and bolster. The aforementioned training for hybrid and online learning, as well as trauma-informed support for students, should be influenced by the growing literature regarding these topics (e.g., Bennett et al., 2021; Hitchcock et al., 2021; Sherwood et al., 2021).

Limitations of this Scoping Review

While this scoping review provided a comprehensive overview of the breadth of literature predominately focused on students' stress and coping during the COVID-19 pandemic, there are limitations that are important to acknowledge. The largest limitation, and one that required many meetings by the research team to come to consensus on, was their lack of definition for stress among researchers. This was a challenge for the inclusion teams to decide whether articles fit the criteria or not to be included in this study as well as making it difficult to write the theme that encompassed "stress." Stress is often used interchangeably with other mental health concepts, such as anxiety, depression, and PTSD, thus deciding whether the theme focused solely on "stress" or the larger mental health and well-being took much consideration.

Another limitation of this study was that the coding team did not use a codebook. Codebooks are often used to assist in the credibility and reliability of a qualitative study (Roberts et al., 2019). While the team checked for intercoder reliability, the team took a collaborative reflexive approach to inductive thematic analysis. This means that the three research assistants worked together to code the articles, and the lead researcher then created themes by clustering together similar codes. While this system may not have provided the highest level of coder reliability, it did allow the research team the ability to evolve the codes throughout the process, split or collapse codes, and redraw the boundaries of codes to highlight the most important concepts in the included articles.

Future Directions for Understanding and Addressing Stress in Higher Education

While the impacts of COVID were clear throughout the articles, especially the decrease in students' mental well-being and the negative impact of social isolation on under-represented and minoritized individuals, the strategies for addressing COVID impacts were less clear. This includes both the sense of remediation for current students as well as prevention for future traumas that have similar impacts as COVID (e.g., natural disasters). Another aspect that was unclear was the definition of stress within the psychological community. Moving forward, future research should focus on defining proper coping skills for students and faculty in higher education institutions during traumas, like COVID, as well as refining the definition of stress in order to make research more focused.

Even as the world comes out on what seems to be the other side of the pandemic, hybrid learning has not fully phased out, nor will that aspect of learning ever go back to the exact way it operated before the pandemic. There is a paucity of research regarding the impacts of online learning and how best to prepare faculty and staff for offering the best education and social support system for students that are not taking classes in person. The potential negative effects of online and hybrid learning can especially be seen with the transfer student population as well as the marginalized or under-represented groups. Research moving forward needs to be heavily focused on how best to offer support to these students in order to decrease psychological distress.

Conclusion

This scoping review provided a comprehensive lens through which to understand the literature published in the field regarding collegiate students' stress and coping during the pandemic. Throughout the literature, there were seven themes that emerged that highlighted the impacts COVID had on students' overall mental health and well-being, including stress, as well as the importance of preparation regarding hybrid learning moving forward. In addition, the research indicated there are special considerations in regard to individuals from under-represented and minoritized groups regarding the impacts of social isolation that are needed should there be another traumatic event like COVID. Students reported using both adaptive (e.g., cognitive restructuring) and maladaptive (e.g., substance use) techniques in order to cope with the significant impacts of such a traumatic event.

While this scoping review lacked a specific definition of stress and the research team did not use a structured codebook, it shed light on insightful potential research questions, such as: (1) What exactly IS stress? (2) What specific strategies are best used to counteract the negative impacts of a traumatic event, such as COVID (3) How should faculty and staff be prepared for hybrid or online teaching moving forward in this new age of teaching? (4) How should students, especially those from under-represented and minoritized groups, be supported throughout certain situations where

208   C. H. WEPPNER ET AL.

social isolation is a major concern? It is the hope of this research team that this scoping review provides future researchers with a greater understanding of the studies conducted during the pandemic and offers a springboard for future research directions.

Table 8.1

A List of Included Articles With the Author, Year Published, Title, Location Of Sample, Type Of Study, Timeframe, and Sample Type

Author and Year Published	Title	Location	Type of Study	Time-frame	Sample
Andal and Wu (2021) [1]	Doctoral journey during COVID-19: Reflections from a collaborative auto-ethnography	International	Qualitative	Middle	Graduate Students
Ang et al. (2022) [2]	First-year college students' adjustment during the CO-VID-19 pandemic: The protective roles of hope and gratitude	United States	Quantitative	Beginning	Undergraduate Students
Apker (2022) [3]	College student accounts of coping and social support during COVID-19 impacted learning	United States	Qualitative	Middle	Undergraduate Students
Arora et al. (2021) [4]	Impact of coronavirus and online exam anxiety on self-efficacy: The moderating role of coping strategies	International	Quantitative	Beginning	Undergraduate and Graduate Students
Baloran (2020) [5]	Knowledge, attitudes, anxiety, and coping strategies of students during CO-VID-19 pandemic	International	Quantitative	Middle	Undergraduate Students
Bountress et al. (2022) [6]	The COVID-19 pandemic impacts psychiatric outcomes and alcohol use among college students	United States	Mixed Method	Beginning	Undergraduate Students

(Table continued on next page)

A Rapid Scoping Review of Collegiate Students' Stress   209

Table 8.1 (Continued)

A List of Included Articles With the Author, Year Published, Title, Location Of Sample, Type Of Study, Timeframe, and Sample Type

Brochu et al. (2021) [7]	Redefining roles: Female scholars' reflections and recommendations for coping during the COVID-19 pandemic	United States	Qualitative	Unclear	Graduate Students
Burt and Eubank (2021) [8]	Optimism, resilience, and other health-protective factors among students during the COVID-19 pandemic	International	Qualitative	Beginning	Undergraduate Students
Camilleri et al. (2022) [9]	The impact of COVID-19 and associated interventions on mental health: A cross-sectional study in a sample of university students	United States	Quantitative	Beginning	Undergraduate Students
Cherdymova et al. (2020) [10]	Peculiarities of math students' adaptation to temporary forced isolation or quarantine	International	Quantitative	Beginning	Undergraduate Students
Cusack et al. (2022) [11]	A longitudinal investigation of resilience as a protective factor during the COVID-19 pandemic	United States	Quantitative	Beginning	Undergraduate Students
Das et al. (2021) [12]	Understanding the impact of the COVID-19 pandemic on honors college students: A qualitative content analysis	United States	Qualitative	Beginning	Undergraduate Students
El-Monshed et al. (2022) [13]	University students under lockdown, the psychosocial effects and coping strategies during COVID-19 pandemic: A cross sectional study in Egypt	International	Quantitative	Beginning	Undergraduate Students

(Table continued on next page)

Table 8.1 (Continued)

A List of Included Articles With the Author, Year Published, Title, Location Of Sample, Type Of Study, Timeframe, and Sample Type

Erekson et al. (2021) [14]	Responding to the COVID-19 pandemic at a university counseling center: Administrative actions, client retention, and psychotherapy outcome	United States	Quantitative	Beginning	Unclear
Evans et al. (2021) [15]	Social work doctoral student well-being during the COVID-19 pandemic: A descriptive study	United States	Quantitative	Beginning	Graduate Students
Fraser et al. (2021) [16]	College students' media habits, concern for themselves and others, and mental health in the era of COVID-19	United States	Quantitative	Beginning	Undergraduate Students
Friehat (2021) [17]	Psychological stress and coping strategies among private university students in Amman Governorate during the corona pandemic	International	Quantitative	Beginning	Unclear
Fruehwirth et al. (2021) [18]	The COVID-19 pandemic and mental health of first-year college students: Examining the effect of COVID-19 stressors using longitudinal data	United States	Quantitative	Beginning	Undergraduate Students
Gallegos et al. (2022) [19]	COVID-19 pandemic stresses and relationships in college students	United States	Quantitative	Beginning	Undergraduate Students
Giannoulas et al. (2021) [20]	How greek students experienced online education during COVID-19 pandemic in order to adjust to a post-lockdown period	International	Quantitative	Beginning	Undergraduate Students

(Table continued on next page)

A Rapid Scoping Review of Collegiate Students' Stress   211

Table 8.1 (Continued)

A List of Included Articles With the Author, Year Published, Title, Location Of Sample, Type Of Study, Timeframe, and Sample Type

Hadar et al. (2020) [21]	Rethinking teacher education in a VUCA world: Student teachers' social-emotional competencies during the COVID-19 crisis	International	Qualitative	Beginning	Graduate Students
Hamza et al. (2021) [22]	When social isolation is nothing new: A longitudinal study on psychological distress during COVID-19 among university students with and without preexisting mental health concerns	International	Quantitative	Beginning	Undergraduate Students
Hunt et al. (2021) [23]	Gender diverse college students exhibit higher psychological distress than male and female peers during the novel coronavirus (COVID-19) pandemic.	United States	Quantitative	Beginning	Undergraduate and Graduate Students
Inman et al. (2021) [24]	Discrimination and psychosocial engagement during the COVID-19 pandemic	United States	Qualitative	Beginning	Undergraduate and Graduate Students
Jaradat and Ajlouni (2021) [25]	Undergraduates' perspectives and challenges of online learning during the COVID-19 pandemic: A case from the University of Jordan	International	Quantitative	Beginning	Undergraduate Students
Johnson et al. (2022) [26]	Resilience to stress-related sleep disturbance: Examination of early pandemic coping and affect	United States	Quantitative	Beginning	Undergraduate Students
Jones (2022) [27]	The impact of COVID-19 on Black college students' mental health	United States	Qualitative	Beginning	Undergraduate and Graduate Students

(Table continued on next page)

212 C. H. WEPPNER ET AL.

Table 8.1 (Continued)

A List of Included Articles With the Author, Year Published, Title, Location Of Sample, Type Of Study, Timeframe, and Sample Type

Kourea et al. (2021) [28]	Voices of undergraduate students with disabilities during the COVID-19 pandemic: A pilot study	International	Qualitative	Middle	Undergraduate Students
Lancaster and Arango (2021) [29]	Health and emotional well-being of urban university students in the era of COVID-19	United States	Quantitative	Beginning	Undergraduate Students
Le Vigouroux et al. (2021) [30]	The psychological vulnerability of french university students to the COVID-19 confinement	International	Quantitative	Beginning	Undergraduate and Graduate Students
Madrigal and Blevins (2021) [31]	I hate it, it's ruining my life': College students' early academic year experiences during the COVID-19 pandemic	United States	Qualitative	Beginning	Undergraduate and Graduate Students
Mayorga et al. (2022) [32]	Evaluating the interactive effect of COVID-19 worry and loneliness on mental health among young adults	United States	Quantitative	Unclear	Undergraduate Students
Mohammed and Mudhsh (2021) [33]	The effects of COVID-19 on EFL learners' anxiety at the University of Bisha	International	Quantitative	Beginning	Undergraduate Students
Poma et al. (2022) [34]	How are you coping with the COVID-19 pandemic? Survey of undergraduate dental students' well-being during an unexpected global event	International	Quantitative	Beginning	Undergraduate Students

(Table continued on next page)

Table 8.1 (Continued)

A List of Included Articles With the Author, Year Published, Title, Location Of Sample, Type Of Study, Timeframe, and Sample Type

Popa-Velea et al. (2021) [35]	Teaching style, coping strategies, stress, and social support: Associations to the medical students' perception of learning during the SARS-CoV-2 pandemic	International	Quantitative	Both Timeframes	Undergraduate Students
Prasath et al. (2021) [36]	University student well-being during COVID-19: The role of psychological capital and coping strategies	United States	Quantitative	Beginning	Undergraduate and Graduate Students
Prowse et al. (2021) [37]	Coping with the COVID-19 pandemic: Examining gender differences in stress and mental health among university students	International	Quantitative	Beginning	Undergraduate Students
Roman (2020) [38]	Supporting the mental health of teachers in COVID-19 through trauma-informed educational practices and adaptive formative assessment tools	United States	Mixed Method	Both Timeframes	Undergraduate Students
Rudenstine et al. (2022) [39]	Examining the role of material and social assets on mental health in the context of COVID-19 among an urban public university sample	United States	Quantitative	Beginning	Undergraduate Students
Santosa et al. (2021) [40]	A description and factors causing student anxiety during the COVID-19 pandemic in Indonesia	International	Mixed Method	Beginning	Undergraduate Students
Son et al. (2020) [41]	Effects of COVID-19 on college students' mental health in the United States: Interview survey study	United States	Mixed Method	Beginning	Undergraduate Students

(Table continued on next page)

Table 8.1 (Continued)

A List of Included Articles With the Author, Year Published, Title, Location Of Sample, Type Of Study, Timeframe, and Sample Type

Stamatis et al. (2022) [42]	A longitudinal investigation of COVID-19 pandemic experiences and mental health among university students	United States	Quantitative	Beginning	Undergraduate Students
Sustarsic and Zhang (2022) [43]	Navigating through uncertainty in the era of COVID-19: Experiences of international graduate students in the United States	United States	Qualitative	Beginning	Graduate Students
Sveinsdottir et al. (2021) [44]	Predictors of university nursing students' burnout at the time of the COVID-19 pandemic: A cross-sectional study	International	Quantitative	Beginning	Undergraduate and Graduate Students
Tasso et al. (2021) [45]	COVID-19 disruption on college students: Academic and socioemotional implications	International	Quantitative	Beginning	Undergraduate and Graduate Students
Wolfe (2021) [46]	Dispositional gratitude affects college student stress and depression from COVID-19 pandemic: Mediation through coping	United States	Quantitative	Beginning	Undergraduate Students
Xiong et al. (2022) [47]	A mindfulness-based well-being group for international students in higher education: A pilot study	United States	Quantitative	Middle	Undergraduate and Graduate Students

A Rapid Scoping Review of Collegiate Students' Stress 215

Table 8.2

A Summary of the Seven Themes Identified Through the Included Articles (Appendix B): Coping Strategies, COVID-Specific Concepts, Changes In Addiction/Usage, Physical Health Concerns, Social/ Cultural Difficulties, Social Support, and Educational Concepts

Themes	Related Publications
Coping Strategies	1, 3, 4, 7, 9, 12, 13, 17, 19, 21, 26, 27, 30, 31, 33, 35, 36, 37, 40, 41, 43, 46, 47
COVID-Specific Concepts	5, 6, 10, 11, 12, 13, 14, 18, 28, 30, 31, 34, 40, 42, 43, 45
Changes in Addiction/Usage	6, 9, 11, 16, 19, 22, 37, 42
Physical Health Concerns	9, 18, 23, 26, 30, 31, 41, 45
Social/Cultural Difficulties	1, 5, 7, 8, 12, 15, 23, 24, 27, 28, 31, 33, 34, 43, 47
Social Support	1, 3, 7, 8, 9, 10, 12, 14, 15, 17, 19, 29, 35, 37, 39, 40
Educational Concepts	1, 5, 7, 12, 14, 20, 21, 24, 25, 28, 31, 34, 35, 37, 38, 40, 41, 42, 43, 44

REFERENCES

Aldalaykeh, M., Al-Hammouri, M. M., & Rababah, J. (2019). Predictors of mental health services help-seeking behavior among university students. *Cogent Psychology, 6*(1). https://doi.org/10.1080/23311908.2019.1660520

Aucejo, E. M., French, J., Araya, M. P., Zafar, B. (2020). The impact of COVID-19 on student experiences and expectations: Evidence from a survey. *Journal of Public Economics, 191.* https://doi.org/10.1016/j.jpubeco.2020.104271

Bakker, A. B., & Demerouti, E. (2007). The job demands-resources model: State of the art. *Journal of Managerial Psychology, 22*(3), 309–328. https://doi.org/10.1108/02683940733115

Bedewy, D., & Gabriel, A. (2015). Examining perceptions of academic stress and its sources among university students: The Perception of Academic Stress Scale. *Health Psychology Open, 2*(2). https://doi.org/10.1177/2055102915596714

Bennett, B., Ross, D., & Gates, T.G. (2021). Creating spatial, relational, and cultural safety in online social work education during COVID-19. *Social Work Education, 41*(8), 1660–1668. https://doi.org/10.1080/02615479.2021.1924664

Brooks, S. K., Webster, R. K., Smith, L. E., Woodland, L., Wessely, S., Greenberg, N., & Rubin, G. J. (2020). The psychological impact of quarantine and how to reduce it: Rapid review of the evidence. *The Lancet, 395*(10227), 912–920. https://doi.org/10.1016/S0140-6736(20)30460-8

Buchwald, P., & Schwarzer, C. (2010). Impact of assessment on students' test anxiety. *International Encyclopedia of Education, 3*, 498–505. https://doi.org/10.1016/B978-0-08-044894-7.00304-3

Burns, D., Dagnall, N., & Denovan, A. (2023). Predictors of help-seeking behaviour in UK university students during the COVID-19 pandemic. *Journal of Further and Higher Education, 47*(6), 727–739.

https://doi.org/10.1080/0309877X.2023.2226598

Byrne, D.A. (2022). A worked example of Braun and Clarke's approach to reflexive thematic analysis. *Quality and Quantity, 56*, 1391–1412. https://doi.org/10.1007/s11135-021-01182-y

Chang M.L. (2009). An appraisal perspective of teacher burnout: Examining the emotional work of teachers. *Educational Psychology Review, 21*(3), 193–218.

Daniali, H., Martinussen, M., & Flaten, M. A. (2023). A global meta-analysis of depression, anxiety, and stress before and during COVID-19. *Health Psychology, 42*(2), 124–138. https://doi.org/10.1037/hea0001259

Fu, S., Cai, Z., Lim, E., Liu, Y., Tan, C., & Lin, Y. (2023). Unraveling the effects of mobile application usage on users' health status: Insights from Conservation of Resources Theory. *Journal of the Association for Information Systems, 24*(2), 452–489. https://doi.org/10.17705/1jais.00808

Garritty, C., Hamel, C., Hersi, M., Butler, C., Monfaredi, Z., Stevens, A., Nussbaumer-Streit, B., Cheng, W., & Moher, D. (2020). Assessing how information is packaged in rapid reviews for policy-makers and other stakeholders: a cross-sectional study. *Health Research Policy and Systems, 18*, 112. https://doi.org/10.1186/s12961-020-00624-7

Hamaideh, S., Al-Modallal, H., Tanash, M., & Hamdan-Mansour3, A. (2022). Depression, anxiety, and stress among undergraduate students during COVID-19 outbreak and "home-quarantine." *Nursing Open, 9*(2), 1423–1431. https://doi.org/10.1002/nop2.918

Heckman, S., Lim, H., & Montalto, C. (2014). Factors related to financial stress among college students. *Journal of Financial Therapy, 5*(1), 19–39. https://doi.org/10.4148/1944-9771.1063

Hitchcock, L.I., Báez, J. C., Sage, M., Marquart, M., Lewis, K., & Smyth, N.J. (2021). Social work educators' opportunities during COVID-19: A roadmap for trauma-informed teaching during crisis. *Journal of Social Work Education, 57*(1), 82–98. https://doi.org/10.1080/10437797.2021.1935369

Hobfoll, S. E. (1998) *Stress, culture, and community: The psychology and physiology of stress*. http:// doi.org/10.1007/978-1-4899-0115-6

Holmes, T. H., & Rahe, R. H. (1967). The Social Readjustment Rating Scale. *Journal of Psychosomatic Research, 11*(2), 213–218. https://doi.org/10.1016/0022-3999(67)90010-4

Hurst, B., Wallace, R., & Nixon, S. B. (2013). The impact of social interaction on student learning. *Reading Horizons: A Journal of Literacy and Language Arts, 52*(4). https://scholarworks.wmich.edu/reading_horizons/vol52/iss4/5

Ibrahim, A. K., Kelly, S. J., Adams, C. E., & Glazebrook, C. (2013). A systematic review of studies of depression prevalence in university students. *Journal of Psychiatric Research, 47*(3), 391–400. https://doi.org/10.1016/j.jpsychires.2012.11.015

Jiang, Z., & Tu, H. (2022). Does sincere social interaction stimulate tourist immersion? A conservation of resources perspective. *Journal of Travel Research, 62*(2), 469–487. https://doi.org/10.1177/00472875211067549

Karasek, R., & Theorell, T. (1990). *Healthy Work: Stress, productivity, and the reconstruction of working life*. Basic Books.

Lancaster, M., & Arango, E. (2021). Health and emotional well-being of urban university students in the era of COVID-19. *Traumatology, 27*(1), 107–117. https://doi.org/10.1037/trm0000308

Łaskawiec, D., Grajek, M., Szlacheta, P., & Korsonek-Szlacheta (2022). Post-pandemic stress disorder as an effect of the epidemiological situation related to the COVID-19 pandemic. *Healthcare (Basel), 10*(6), 975. https://doi.org/10.3390/healthcare10060975

Lazarus, R. S., & Folkman, S. (1984). *Stress, appraisal, and coping.* Springer.

Lee, J., Solomon, M., Stead, T., Kwon, B., & Ganti, L. (2021). Impact of COVID-19 on the mental health of US college students. *BMC Psychology, 9*(1), 1–95. https://doi.org/10.1186/s40359-021-00598-3

Legros, D. N., & Boyraz, G. (2023). Mental health and help-seeking among college students during the COVID-19 pandemic: Roles of campus mental health climate and institutional support. *Journal of American College Health.* https://doi.org/10.1080/07448481.2023.2227716

Leppink, E., Odlaug, B., Lust, K., Christenson, G., & Grant, J. (2016). The young and the stressed: Stress, impulse control, and health in college students. *The Journal of Nervous and Mental Disease, 204*(12), 931–938. https://doi.org/10.1097/NMD.0000000000000586

LeViness, P., Bershad, C., Gorman, K., Braun, L., & Murray, T. (2019). *The association for university and college counseling center directors annual survey.* https://www.aucccd.org/assets/documents/Survey/2019%20AUCCCD%20Survey-2020-05-31-PUBLIC.pdf

Lim, T., Thompson, J., Tian, L., & Beck, B. (2023). A transactional model of stress and coping applied to cyclist subjective experiences. *Traffic Psychology and Behavior, 96*, 155–170. https://doi.org/10.1016/j.trf.2023.05.013

Lipson, S.K., Zhou, S., Abelson, S., Heinze, J., Jirsa, M., Morigney, J., Patterson, A., Singh, M., & Eisenberg, D. (2022). Trends in college student mental health and help-seeking by race/ethnicity: Findings from the national healthy minds study, 2013–2021. *Journal of Affective Disorders, 306*, 138–147. https://doi.org/10.1016/j.jad.2022.03.038

Lowenstein, K., Barroso, J., & Phillips, S. (2019). The experiences of parents in the Neonatal Intensive Care Unit: An integrative review of qualitative studies within the Transactional Model of Stress and Coping. *The Journal of Perinatal & Neonatal Nursing, 33*(4), 340–349. https://doi.org/10.1097/JPN.0000000000000436

Lynch, R. J., & Wojdak, K. (2023). An exploration of trauma-inclusive pedagogy and students' perceptions of academic success. *A Journal of Educational Development, 42*(2). https://doi.org/10.3998/tia.2634

Matud, M. P., Diaz, A., Bethencourt, J. M., & Ibáñez, I. (2020). Stress and psychological distress in emerging adulthood: A gender analysis. *Journal of Clinical Medicine, 9*(9), 2859. https://doi.org/10.3390/jcm9092859

McCarthy, C. J., & Lambert, R. G. (Eds.). (2023). *Research on stress and coping in K–12 Education: Implications for the COVID-19 pandemic and beyond.* Information Age Publishing.

McCarthy, C. J., Lambert, R. G., Lineback, S., Fitchett, P., & Baddouh, P. G. (2016). Assessing teacher appraisals and stress in the classroom: Review of the classroom appraisal of resources and demands. *Educational Psychology Review, 28*, 577–603. https://doi.org/10.1007/s10648-015-9322-6

McGlynn-Wright, T. (2021, March 30). *Integrative trauma and healing framework: In the works.* https://intheworksllc.squarespace.com/inflections/2021/3/30/integrative-trauma-and-healing-framework

Mortazavi, S., Assari, S., Alimohamadi, A., Rafiee, M., & Shati, M. (2020). Fear, loss, social isolation, and incomplete grief because of COVID-19: A recipe for a psychiatric pandemic. *Basic and Clinical Neuroscience, 11*(2), 225–232. https://doi.org/10.32598/bcn.11.covid19.2549.1

Munn, Z. Peters, M. D. J., Stern, C., Tufanaru, C., McArthur, A., & Aromataris, E. (2018). Systematic review or scoping review? Guidance for authors when choosing between a systematic or scoping review approach. *BMC Medical Research Methodology, 18*(143). https://doi.org/10.1186/s12874-018-0611-x

Niegocki, K.L., & Ægisdóttir, S. (2019). College students' coping and psychological help seeking attitudes and intentions. *Journal of Mental Health Counseling, 41*(2), 144–157. https://doi.org/10.17744/mehc.41.2.04

Page, M. J., McKenzie, J. E., Bossuyt, P. M., Boutron, I., Hoffmann, T. C., Mulrow, C.D., Shamseer, L., Tetzlaff, J.M., Akl, E.A., Brennan, S.E., Chou, R., Glanville, J., Grimshaw, J. M., Hróbjartsson, A., Lalu, M. M., Li, T., Loder, E. W., Mayo-Wilson, E., McDonald, S., ... Moher, D. (2021). The PRISMA 2020 statement: An updated guideline for reporting systematic reviews. *Systematic Reviews, 10*(89). https://doi.org/10.1186/s13643-021-01626-4

Pham, M. T., Rajić, A., Greig, J. D., Sargeant, J. M., Papadopoulos, A., & McEwen, S. A. (2014). A scoping review of scoping reviews: Advancing the approach and enhancing the consistency. *Research Synthesis Methods, 5*(4), 371–385. https://doi.org/10.1002/jrsm.1123

Reddy, K. J., Menon, J. R., Thattil, A. (2018). Academic stress and its sources among university students. *Biomedical and Pharmacology Journal, 11*(1). http://biomedpharmajournal.org/?p=19485

Robb, C. (2017). College student financial stress: Are the kids alright? *Journal of Family and Economic Issues, 38*(4), 514–527. https://doi.org/10.1007/s10834-017-9527-6

Roberts, K., Dowell, A., & Nie, J. (2019). Attempting rigour and replicability in thematic analysis of qualitative research data; a case study of codebook development. *BMC Medical Research Methodology, 19*(66). http://doi.org/10.1186/s12874-019-0707-y

Salari, N., Hosseinian-Far, A., Jalali, R., Vaisi-Raygani, A., Rasoulpoor, S., Mohammadi, M., Rasoulpoor, S., & Khaledi-Paveh, B. (2020). Prevalence of stress, anxiety, depression among the general population during the COVID-19 pandemic: A systematic review and meta-analysis. Globalization and Health, *16*(1), 57. https://doi.org/10.1186/s12992-020-00589-w

Schoenmakers, E. C., van Tilburg, T. G., & Fokkema, T. (2015). Problem-focused and emotion-focused coping options and loneliness: How are they related? *European Journal of Ageing, 12*(2), 153–161. https://doi.org/10.1007/s10433-015-0336-1

Selye, H. (1956). *The stress of life.* McGraw-Hill.

A Rapid Scoping Review of Collegiate Students' Stress   219

Sen-Crowe, B., McKenney, M., & Elkbuli, A. (2020). Social distancing during the COVID-19 pandemic: Staying home save lives. *The American Journal of Emergency Medicine, 38*(7), 1519–1520.
https://doi.org/10.1016/j.ajem.2020.03.063

Shannon, A., Flett, G.L., & Goldberg, J.O. (2020). Feelings of not mattering, perceived stigmatization for seeking help, and help-seeking attitudes among university students. *International Journal of Mental Health and Addiction, 18*, 1294–1303. https://doi.org/10.1007/s11469-019-00138-6

Shahwan, S., Lau, J. H., Goh, C. M .J., Ong, W. J., Tan, G. T. H., Kwok, K. W., Samari, E., Lee, Y. Y., The, W. L., Seet, V., Chang, S., Chong, S. A., & Subramaniam, M. (2020). The potential impact of an anti-stigma intervention on mental health help-seeking attitudes among university students. *BMC Psychiatry, 20*, 562. https://doi.org/10.1186/s12888-010-02960-y

Sherwood, D., VanDeusen, K., Weller, B., & Gladden, J. (2021). Teaching note—Teaching trauma content online during COVID-19: A trauma-informed and culturally responsive pedagogy. *Journal of Social Work Education, 57*(1), 99–110. https://doi.org/10.1080/10437797.2021.1916665

Siegrist, J. (1996). Adverse health effects of high-effort/low-reward conditions. *Journal of Occupational Health Psychology, 1*(1), 27–41.
https://doi.org/10.1037/1076-8998.1.1.27

Silver, A. M., Elliott, L., & Libertus, M.E . (2021). Parental math input is not uniformly beneficial for young children: The moderating role of inhibitory control. *Journal of Educational Psychology, 114*(5), 1178–1191.
https://doi.org/10.1037/edu0000679

Sirrine, E., Kliner, O., & Gollery, T. (2021). College student experiences of grief and loss amid the COVID-19 global pandemic. *Omega: Journal of Death and Dying.* https://doi.org/10.1177/00302228211027461

Tricco, A. C., Lillie, R., Zarin, W., O'Brien, K. K., Colquhoun, H., Levac, D., Moher, D., Peters, M. D. J., Horsley, T., Weeks, L., Hempel, S., Akl, E. A., Chang, C., McGowan, J., Stewart, J., Hartling, L., Aldcroft, A., Wilson, M. G., Garritty, C.,... Straus, S. E. (2018). PRISMA extension for scoping reviews (PRISMA—ScR): Checklist and explanation. *Annals of Internal Medicine, 169*(7), 467–473. https://doi.org/10.7326/M18-0850

Sustarsic, M., & Zhang, J. (2022). Navigating through uncertainty in the era of COVID-19: Experiences of international graduate students in the United States. *Journal of International Students, 12*(1), 61–80.
https://doi.org/10.32674/jis.v12i1.3305

Wang, C., Wen, W., Zhang, H., Ni, J., Jiang, J., Cheng, Y., Zhou, M., Lan, Y., Feng, Z., G., Zhongjun, Luo, H., Wang, M., Zhang, X., & Liu, W. (2021). Anxiety, depression, and stress prevalence among college students during the COVID-19 pandemic: A systematic review and meta-analysis. *Journal of American College Health*, 1–8. https://doi.org/10.1080/07448481.2021.1960849

WHO Coronavirus (COVID-19) Dashboard. (n.d.). Retrieved May 5, 2023, from https://covid19.who.int

Yonemoto, N., & Kawahima, Y. (2023). Help-seeking behaviors for mental health problems during the COVID-19 pandemic: A systematic review. *Journal of Affective Disorders, 323*(15), 85–100. https://doi.org/10.1016/j.jad.2022.11.043

APPENDIX A

Database Search Terms

Date of Search: September 13, 2022
Database Searched: APA PsycINFO, ERIC, and Education Source

Line 1 search terms: COVID OR coronavirus OR pandemic
Line 2 search terms: "higher education" OR SU(college OR universities)
Line 3 search terms: SU (stress OR anxiety OR "mental health" OR "well being")
Line 4 search terms: "stress management" OR coping OR "help seeking" OR "seek* help" OR counseling OR therapy
Limits: peer reviewed from 2020

APPENDIX B

Literature Included in the Rapid Scoping Review

1. Andal, A. G., & Shuang Wu. (2021). Doctoral journey during Covid-19: reflections from a collaborative autoethnography. *International Journal of Doctoral Studies, 16*(1), 633–656. https://doi.org/10.28945/4871
2. Ang, J. Y.-Z., Monte, V., & Tsai, W. (2022). First-year college students' adjustment during the COVID-19 pandemic: The protective roles of hope and gratitude. *Translational Issues in Psychological Science*. https://doi.org/10.1037/tps0000320
3. Apker, J. (2022). College student accounts of coping and social support during COVID-19 impacted learning. *Communication Quarterly, 70*(3), 296–316. https://doi.org/10.1080/01463373.2022.2051574
4. Arora, S., Chaudhary, P., & Singh, R. K. (2021). Impact of coronavirus and online exam anxiety on self-efficacy: The moderating role of coping strategy. *Interactive Technology and Smart Education, 18*(3), 475–492. https://doi.org/10.1108/ITSE-08-2020-0158
5. Baloran, E. T. (2020). Knowledge, Attitudes, anxiety, and coping strategies of students during COVID-19 Pandemic. *Journal of Loss & Trauma, 25*(8), 635–642. https://doi.org/10.1080/15325024.2020.1769300
6. Bountress, K. E., Cusack, S. E., Conley, A. H., Aggen, S. H., Vassileva, J., Dick, D. M., & Amstadter, A. B. (2022). The COVID-19 pandemic impacts psychiatric outcomes and alcohol use among college students. *European Journal of Psychotraumatology, 13*(1). https://doi.org/10.1080/20008198.2021.2022279
7. Brochu, K. J., Bryant, T. R., Jensen, A. J., Desjardins, D. R., Robinson, R. M. M., & Bent, L. G. (2021). Redefining Roles: Female Scholars' Reflections and Recommendations for Coping during the COVID-19 Pandemic. *Impacting Education: Journal on Transforming Professional Practice, 6*(2), 54–60.

A Rapid Scoping Review of Collegiate Students' Stress   221

8. Burt, K. G., & Eubank, J. M. (2021). Optimism, Resilience, and Other Health-Protective Factors among Students during the COVID-19 Pandemic. *Journal of Effective Teaching in Higher Education, 4*(1), 1–17.

9. Camilleri, C., Fogle, C. S., O'Brien, K. G., & Sammut, S. (2022). The impact of COVID-19 and associated interventions on mental health: A cross-sectional study in a sample of university students. *Frontiers in Psychiatry, 12*. https://doi.org/10.3389/fpsyt.2021.801859

10. Cherdymova, E. I., Masalimova, A. R., Khairullina, E. R., Vasbieva, D. G., Ismailova, N. P., Kurbanov, R. A., & Tyazhelnikov, A. A. (2020). Peculiarities of Math Students Adaptation to Temporary Forced Isolation or Quarantine. *EURASIA Journal of Mathematics, Science and Technology Education, 16*(11).

11. Cusack, S. E., Bountress, K. E., Denckla, C. A., The Spit for Science Working Group, Vassileva, J., Dick, D. M., & Amstadter, A. B. (2022). A longitudinal investigation of resilience as a protective factor during the COVID-19 pandemic. *Traumatology, 28*(3), 403–410. https://doi.org/10.1037/trm0000397

12. Das, B. M., Walker, C., Hodge, E., Christensen, T., Darkenwald, T., Godwin, W., & Weckesser, G. (2021). Understanding the impact of the COVID-19 pandemic on honors college students: A qualitative content analysis. *Journal of the National Collegiate Honors Council, 22*(1), 169–181.

13. El-Monshed, A. H., El-Adl, A. A., Ali, A. S., & Loutfy, A. (2022). University students under lockdown, the psychosocial effects and coping strategies during COVID-19 pandemic: A cross sectional study in Egypt. *Journal of American College Health, 70*(3), 679–690. https://doi.org/10.1080/07448481.2021.1891086

14. Erekson, D. M., Bailey, R. J., Cattani, K., Fox, S. T., & Goates-Jones, M. K. (2021). Responding to the Covid-19 pandemic at a university counseling center: Administrative actions, client retention, and psychotherapy outcome. *Counselling Psychology Quarterly, 34*(3/4), 729–743. https://doi.org/10.1080/09515070.2020.1807914

15. Evans, K. E., Holmes, M. R., Prince, D. M., & Groza, V. (2021). Social work doctoral student well-being during the Covid-19 pandemic: *A Descriptive Study. International Journal of Doctoral Studies, 16*(1), 569–592. https://doi.org/10.28945/4840

16. Fraser, A. M., Stockdale, L. A., Bryce, C. I., & Alexander, B. L. (2021). College students' media habits, concern for themselves and others, and mental health in the era of COVID-19. *Psychology of Popular Media*. https://doi.org/10.1037/ppm0000345

17. Friehat, R. H. (2021). Psychological stress and coping strategies among private university students in Amman Governorate during the corona pandemic. *Review of International Geographical Education Online, 11*(5), 4600–4613. https://doi.org/10.48047/rigeo.11.05.337

18. Fruehwirth, J. C., Biswas, S., & Perreira, K. M. (2021). The Covid-19 pandemic and mental health of first-year college students: Examining the effect of Covid-19 stressors using longitudinal data. *PLoS ONE, 16*(3). https://doi.org/10.1371/journal.pone.0247999

19. Gallegos, M. I., Zaring-Hinkle, B., & Bray, J. H. (2022). COVID-19 pandemic stresses and relationships in college students. *Family Relations, 71*(1), 29–45. https://doi.org/10.1111/fare.12602

20. Giannoulas, A., Stampoltzis, A., Kounenou, K., & Kalamatianos, A. (2021). How Greek students experienced online education during COVID-19 pandemic in order to adjust to a post-lockdown period. *Electronic Journal of E-Learning, 19*(4), 222–232.

21. Hadar, L. L., Ergas, O., Alpert, B., & Ariav, T. (2020). Rethinking teacher education in a VUCA world: Student teachers' social-emotional competencies during the Covid-19 crisis. *European Journal of Teacher Education, 43*(4), 573–586.

22. Hamza, C. A., Ewing, L., Heath, N. L., & Goldstein, A. L. (2021). When social isolation is nothing new: A longitudinal study on psychological distress during COVID-19 among university students with and without preexisting mental health concerns. *Canadian Psychology/Psychologie Canadienne, 62*(1), 20–30. https://doi.org/10.1037/cap0000255

23. Hunt, C., Gibson, G. C., Vander Horst, A., Cleveland, K. A., Wawrosch, C., Granot, M., Kuhn, T., Woolverton, C. J., & Hughes, J. W. (2021). Gender diverse college students exhibit higher psychological distress than male and female peers during the novel coronavirus (COVID-19) pandemic. *Psychology of Sexual Orientation and Gender Diversity, 8*(2), 238–244. https://doi.org/10.1037/sgd0000461

24. Inman, E. M., Bermejo, R. M., McDanal, R., Nelson, B., Richmond, L. L., Schleider, J. L., & London, B. (2021). Discrimination and psychosocial engagement during the COVID-19 pandemic. *Stigma and Health, 6*(4), 380–383. https://doi.org/10.1037/sah0000349

25. Jaradat, S., & Ajlouni, A. (2021). Undergraduates' perspectives and challenges of online learning during the COVID-19 pandemic: A case from the University of Jordan. *Journal of Social Studies Education Research, 12*(1), 149–173.

26. Johnson, K. T., Williams, P. G., Aspinwall, L. G., & Curtis, B. J. (2022). Resilience to stress-related sleep disturbance: Examination of early pandemic coping and affect. *Health Psychology, 41*(4), 291–300. https://doi.org/10.1037/hea0001169

27. Jones, M. K. (2022). The impact of COVID-19 on Black college students' mental health. *Journal of College Student Development, 63*(3), 239–254. https://doi.org/10.1353/csd.2022.0021

28. Kourea, L., Christodoulidou, P., & Fella, A. (2021). Voices of undergraduate students with disabilities during the COVID-19 pandemic: A pilot study. *European Journal of Psychology Open, 80*(3), 111–124. https://doi.org/10.1024/2673-8627/a000011

29. Lancaster, M., & Arango, E. (2021). Health and emotional well-being of urban university students in the era of COVID-19. *Traumatology, 27*(1), 107–117. https://doi.org/10.1037/trm0000308

30. Le Vigouroux, S., Goncalves, A., & Charbonnier, E. (2021). The psychological vulnerability of French university students to the COVID-19 confinement. *Health Education & Behavior, 48*(2), 123–131.

A Rapid Scoping Review of Collegiate Students' Stress   223

31. Madrigal, L., & Blevins, A. (2021). "I hate it, it's ruining my life": College students' early academic year experiences during the COVID-19 pandemic. *Traumatology*. https://doi.org/10.1037/trm0000336

32. Mayorga, N. A., Smit, T., Garey, L., Gold, A. K., Otto, M. W., & Zvolensky, M. J. (2022). Evaluating the interactive effect of COVID-19 worry and loneliness on mental health among young adults. *Cognitive Therapy and Research, 46*(1), 11–19. https://doi.org/10.1007/s10608-021-10252-2

33. Mohammed, G. M. S., & Mudhsh, B. A. D. M. (2021). The effects of COVID-19 on EFL learners' anxiety at the University of Bisha. *Arab World English Journal*, 209–221.

34. Poma, M., Al Amri, F., Tawse-Smith, A., & Ma, S. (2022). How are you coping with the COVID-19 pandemic? Survey of undergraduate dental students' well-being during an unexpected global event. *European Journal of Dental Education, 26*(3), 459–467. https://doi.org/10.1111/eje.12721

35. Popa-Velea, O., Pristavu, C. A., Ionescu, C. G., Mihailescu, A. I., & Diaconescu, L. V. (2021). Teaching Style, Coping Strategies, Stress and Social Support: Associations to the Medical Students' Perception of Learning during the SARS-CoV-2 Pandemic. *Education Sciences*, 11.

36. Prasath, P. R., Mather, P. C., Bhat, C. S., & James, J. K. (2021). University student well-being during COVID-19: The role of psychological capital and coping strategies. *Professional Counselor, 11*(1), 46–60.

37. Prowse, R., Sherratt, F., Abizaid, A., Gabrys, R. L., Hellemans, K. G. C., Patterson, Z. R., & McQuaid, R. J. (2021). Coping with the COVID-19 pandemic: Examining gender differences in stress and mental health among university students. *Frontiers in Psychiatry, 12*. https://doi.org/10.3389/fpsyt.2021.650759

38. Roman, T. (2020). Supporting the mental health of teachers in COVID-19 through trauma-informed educational practices and adaptive formative assessment tools. *Journal of Technology and Teacher Education, 28*(2), 473–481.

39. Rudenstine, S., Bhatt, K., Schulder, T., McNeal, K., Ettman, C. K., & Galea, S. (2022). Examining the role of material and social assets on mental health in the context of COVID-19 among an urban public university sample. *Psychological Trauma: Theory, Research, Practice, and Policy*. https://doi.org/10.1037/tra0001307

40. Santosa, H., Widyastuti, D. A., Basuki, A., Kasman, R., Buchori, S., & Fitria, N. (2021). A description and factors causing student anxiety during the COVID-19 pandemic in Indonesia. *Cypriot Journal of Educational Sciences, 16*(4), 1917–1925.

41. Son, C., Hegde, S., Smith, A., Wang, X., & Sasangohar, F. (2020). Effects of COVID-19 on college students' mental health in the United States: Interview survey study. *Journal of Medical Internet Research, 22*(9). https://doi.org/10.2196/21279

42. Stamatis, C. A., Broos, H. C., Hudiburgh, S. E., Dale, S. K., & Timpano, K. R. (2022). A longitudinal investigation of COVID-19 pandemic experiences and mental health among university students. *British Journal of Clinical Psychology, 61*(2), 385–404. https://doi.org/10.1111/bjc.12351

43. Sustarsic, M., & Jianhui Zhang. (2022). Navigating through uncertainty in the era of COVID-19: experiences of international graduate students in the United States. *Journal of International Students, 12*(1), 61–80. https://doi.org/10.32674/jis.v12i1.3305

44. Sveinsdóttir, H., Flygenring, B. G., Svavarsdóttir, M. H., Thorsteinsson, H. S., Kristófersson, G. K., Bernharðsdóttir, J., & Svavarsdóttir, E. K. (2021). Predictors of university nursing students burnout at the time of the COVID-19 pandemic: A cross-sectional study. *Nurse Education Today, 106*, N.PAG-N.PAG. https://doi.org/10.1016/j.nedt.2021.105070

45. Tasso, A. F., Hisli Sahin, N., & San Roman, G. J. (2021). COVID-19 disruption on college students: Academic and socioemotional implications. *Psychological Trauma: Theory, Research, Practice, and Policy, 13*(1), 9–15. https://doi.org/10.1037/tra0000996

46. Wolfe, W. L. (2021). Dispositional gratitude affects college student stress and depression from COVID-19 pandemic: Mediation through coping. *North American Journal of Psychology, 23*(4), 723–740.

47. Xiong, Y., Prasath, P. R., Zhang, Q., & Jeon, L. (2022). A mindfulness-based well-being group for international students in higher education: A pilot study. *Journal of Counseling & Development, 100*(4), 374–385. https://doi.org/10.1002/jcad.12432

CHAPTER 9

CONCLUSION

HIGHER EDUCATION IN THE AFTERMATH

R. Jason Lynch
Appalachian State University

Christopher McCarthy
University of Texas, Austin

Stephen DiDonato
Thomas Jefferson University

In the wake of the chaos brought by the COVID-19 pandemic, academic communities worldwide found themselves at the center of an unprecedented challenge. Whether dips in enrollment (Copely & Douthett, 2020; Sutton, 2021), retention of employees (Bichsel et al., 2022), or worsening of the student mental health crisis (Lee et al., 2021), colleges and universities will continue to face a myriad of escalating crises in the years to come. The stories contained within this volume, spanning multiple campus stakeholders, paint a vivid picture of an academic world fraught with unique intersectional challenges. From linguistic racism and visa-related hurdles to gender-based adversities, the challenges were multifaceted. Yet, intertwined with these accounts of struggle, there were powerful stories of resilience. As we reflect on these themes, it becomes clear that the real work lies ahead. Institutions must actively champion a shift from the traditional "business model" mindset, transcending the view of students as mere

---

Research on College Stress and Coping: Implications From the COVID-19 Pandemic and Beyond, pp. 225–232
Copyright © 2024 by Information Age Publishing
www.infoagepub.com
All rights of reproduction in any form reserved.

226   R. J. LYNCH, C. McCARTHY, AND S. DiDONATO

customers and staff as dispensable cogs in the higher education machine. They must see them as multi-faceted individuals with needs and pressures external to the institution. This pandemic has shown us that a more humanized higher education approach isn't just preferable—it is imperative. Below, we offer a few key takeaways from this volume, grounded in the themes and recommendations of contributing scholars.

Double Down on Educational Equity

Inequities based on race, gender, ability, and socioeconomic status within higher education existed well before the onset of the COVID-19 pandemic. Authors in this volume showcased the ways in which these circumstances were only magnified as campuses scrambled to balance campus safety and operations. Additionally, we would be remiss if we did not acknowledge the impact of state sanctioned racial violence and subsequent national demonstrations in the wake of the murder of George Floyd (Eichstaedt et al., 2021), as well as the surge of anti-Asian sentiment as government leaders used China as a scapegoat for the pandemic (Bresnahan et al., 2023). Combined, the onset of the pandemic era foreshadowed the continued erosion of safety and belonging for students, staff, and faculty at historically White institutions.

Unfortunately, since 2020, there is little evidence that college and university leaders have learned from these lessons. The allure of "organizational amnesia," where institutions, in their haste to move forward, forget the lessons of the past, has been potent. Yet, the call to "return to normal" must be resisted, for the "normal" was fraught with many systemic issues that became increasingly clear. Instead of plastering over these visible cracks, institutions must delve deep, addressing them at their roots to build a more inclusive and equitable academic environment.

Embrace 21st Century Technologies

The onset of the pandemic highlighted the strengths and weaknesses of our digital infrastructure. While online learning presented challenges ranging from diminished motivation (Marler et al., 2021; Wester et al., 2021) to feelings of detachment (Marler et al., 2021), it also unveiled a world of opportunities. Faculty who had never considered teaching within the online environment were forced to rethink their pedagogical approaches to limit interruption of students' time to degree. At the same time, student affairs professionals sought to provide community, support, and guidance to students who found their college experiences completely upended. Although these circumstances led to significant stress for both faculty and students, as highlighted in this volume, much of this stress centered on the fact that the transition to digital operations occurred in an unpredictable and rapid fashion with little training or direction. Knowing the power of technology, higher education leaders can and should harness the power of technology, emphasizing flexible learning and work environments that cater to diverse student, staff, and faculty needs. Of course, this will mean continued and substantial investment in technology and ensuring that faculty and staff have adequate support from information technology specialists.

From a faculty perspective, such innovations may include incentivizing instructors to develop their skills in building community-oriented and meaningful online learning communities. Conversely, as online learning becomes an increasingly popular option among students, campuses must be strategic in how they are attending to issues of community, belonging, and well-being for these populations. Whether increasing virtual mental health services or using technology to increase access to other student services, campus leaders must be strategic and intentional in their institution's evolution to meet the needs of the 21st century student.

Finally, as many campuses face issues with deferred maintenance and issues with office space (Carlson, 2023), human resource professionals should work with supervisors to provide increased opportunity for fully remote or hybrid work. Numerous studies have demonstrated how such flexible work arrangements increase employee well-being (Shiri et al., 2022), and ultimately higher levels of performance (Jiang et al., 2023). As Lynch et al. (2023) point out in an earlier chapter, the demands on caregivers (parents and otherwise) within the higher education community are only increasing. Providing more flexibility through use of technology can only help aid caregivers juggling life and work.

Reframe Co-Curriculum to Prioritize Well-Being

Although this volume highlights the ways in which the global pandemic challenged the health and well-being of campus stakeholders, particularly students, campus leaders must look toward future years in anticipation of a generation of pandemic-impacted students that will be seeking postsecondary education. College leaders must recognize that learning extends beyond academic curricula to encompass holistic development. In addition to creating campus environments that promote well-being, leaders in student affairs must also focus on developing an intentional and cross-campus collaborative co-curriculum (i.e., activities that work together with those inside the classroom to enhance students' learning) focused on building students' ability to build and maintain their well-being. Beyond traditional workshops or seminars, it should integrate life skills, emotional intelligence training, stress management techniques, and opportunities for self-reflection. These components can empower students to navigate the multifaceted challenges of college life and beyond.

Additionally, campuses must ensure that the environments in which students learn and live are conducive to maintaining well-being. This involves creating spaces that foster social connections, encourage physical activity, and promote mental rest and recovery. Whether it is through dedicated wellness centers, serene outdoor spaces, or interactive community-building events, the physical and psychological aspects of the campus environment play a pivotal role in students' well-being. In essence, the goal should be an integrative approach where the co-curriculum and the campus environment harmoniously work together, ensuring that students not only learn about well-being but also are supported in the ability to maintain it.

Embedding Care in Campus Communities

Depending on a student's positionality, campus climates can range from warm and welcoming to cold and distant. Campus leaders should take stock of how policy, practice, and culture communicate, or fail to communicate, an ethic of care within their institutions. Kwan (2023) conceptualizes care ethics as:

> A morally rich and generative notion that should be at the heart of ethical thinking and decision-making.... In so doing, care ethics emphasizes the value of people's relationships, the universality of human dependence on others, the significance of emotions and the body, and the context-sensitive nature of ethical deliberation.

By prioritizing care, campus leaders can foster a nurturing and supportive learning environment for students, but also instill in students the values of empathy, compassion, and responsibility. Moreover, an ethic of care can enhance the overall well-being of the campus community through promoting mental and emotional health, reducing stress; these concepts are directly linked to student retention (Eisenberg et al., 2016). To achieve this, colleges and universities can implement a variety of strategies. They should prioritize mental health resources, offer counseling services, and promote a culture of open communication and transparency. Faculty and staff should receive training in promoting student well-being, and policies should be designed with empathy and equity in mind. Additionally, curricula can be enriched with ethical and compassionate components (Lynch & Wodjak, 2023) to educate students about the importance of care in their future endeavors. In essence, embedding an ethic of care into higher education institutions not only benefits individuals but also contributes to the betterment of society as a whole.

CONCLUSION

In a pivotal moment for higher education, our lessons learned can illuminate a path forward. As we contemplate the rich tapestry of experiences and challenges faced by our academic communities, we are compelled to act, not just with reflection, but with a commitment to change. To the leaders of our colleges and universities, we urge you to champion a fundamental shift in mindset. The imperative of a more humanized approach to higher education cannot be overstated; it is no longer preferable—it is essential. As we close this chapter on one of the most challenging periods in modern academic history, let hope be our guiding force. By taking intentional action, we can shape a brighter, more empathetic future for higher education. It is time to act—to re-ground ourselves in our institutional missions and values for the public good. The future of higher education awaits our leadership and our resolve.

REFERENCES

Bichsel, J., Fuesting, M., Schneider, J., & Tubbs, D. (2022, July). *The CUPA-HR 2022 higher education employee retention survey: Initial results.* College & University Professional Association for Human Resources. https://www.cupahr.org/surveys/research-briefs/higher-ed-employee-retention-survey-findings-july-2022/

Bresnahan, M., Zhu, Y., Hooper, A., Hipple, S., & Savoie, L. (2023). The negative health effects of anti-Asian stigma in the U.S. during COVID-19. *Stigma and Health, 8*(1), 115–123. https://doi.org/10.1037/sah0000375

Carlson, S. (2023, March 31). The backlog that could threaten higher ed's viability: A big bill for deferred maintenance is coming due. *The Chronicle of Higher Education.* https://www.chronicle.com/article/the-backlog-that-could-threaten-higher-eds-viability

Copley, P., & Douthett, E. (2020). The enrollment cliff, mega-universities, COVID-19, and the changing landscape of U.S. college. *The CPA Journal, 90*(9), 22–27.

Eichstaedt, J. C., Sherman, G. T., Giorgi, S., Roberts, S. O., Reynolds, M. E., Ungar, L. H., & Guntuku, S. C. (2021). The emotional and mental health impact of the murder of George Floyd on the US population. *Proceedings of the National Academy of Sciences of the United States of America, 118*(39). http://doi.org/10.1073/pnas.2109139118

Eisenberg, D., Lipson, S. K., & Posselt, J. (2016). Promoting resilience, retention, and mental health. *New Directions for Student Services, 156*, 87–95. http://doi.rog/10.1002/ss

Jiang, L., Pan, Z., Luo, Y., Guo, Z., & Kou, D. (2023). More flexible and more innovative: The impact of flexible work arrangements on the innovation behavior of knowledge employees. *Frontiers in Psychology, 14*. http://doi.org/10.3389/fpsyg.2023.1053242

Kwan, J. (2023, May 5). *Care ethics*. Markkula Center for Applied Ethics at Santa Clara University. https://www.scu.edu/ethics/ethics-resources/ethical-decision-making/care-ethics/care-ethics.html

Lee, J., Solomon, M., Stead, T., Kwon, B., & Ganti, L. (2021). Impact of COVID-19 on the mental health of US college students. *BMC Psychology, 9*(95). https://doi.org/10.1186/s40359-021-00598-3

Lynch, R. J., & Wojdak, K. P. (2023). An exploration of trauma inclusive pedagogy and students' perceptions of academic success. *To Improve the Academy: A Journal of Educational Development, 42*(2). http://doi.org/10.3998/tia.2634

Marler, E. K., Bruce, M. J., Abaoud, A., Henrichsen, C., Suksatan, W., Homvisetvongsa, S., & Matsuo, H. (2021). The impact of COVID-19 on university students' academic motivation, social connection, and psychological well-being. *Scholarship of Teaching and Learning in Psychology*. Advance online publication. https://doi.org/10.1037/stl0000294

Shiri, R., Turunen, J., Kausto, J., Leino-Arjas, P., Varje, P., Väänänen, A., & Ervasti, J. (2022). The effect of employee-oriented flexible work on mental health: A systematic review. *Healthcare, 10*(5), 883. https://doi.org/10.3390/healthcare10050883

Sutton, H. (2021, April). Recent research shows dismal outcome for community college enrollment after COVID-19. *Recruiting & Retaining Adult Learnings, 23*(7), 1–9. http://doi.org/10.1002/nsr

Wester, E. R., Walsh, L. L., Arango-Caro, S., Callus-Duehl, K. L., Donald Danforth Plant Science Center. (2021). Student engagement declines in STEM undergraduates during COVID-19 driven remote learning. *Journal of Microbiology & Biology Education, 22*(1), 1–11. http://doi.org/10.1128/jmbe.v22i1.2385

ABOUT THE AUTHORS

EDITORS

Chris McCarthy is a professor in the Department of Educational Psychology at the University of Texas at Austin. Dr. McCarthy's professional specialization is in Counselor Education and Counseling Psychology. His research focuses on extending basic research on stress and coping to educational settings, particularly in understanding the stress that educators and counselors experience.

R. Jason Lynch, PhD (he/him), is an assistant professor of higher education at Appalachian State University and the Executive Editor for the Journal of Trauma Studies in Education. His teaching, research, and service center the ways in which trauma manifests and impacts various stakeholders in higher education. Specifically, he is interested in issues of trauma-informed leadership, organizational trauma, and systemic interventions to prevent or mitigate the impact of trauma for higher education stakeholders.

Stephen DiDonato, PhD, LPC, is an Associate Professor in the Jefferson College of Nursing (JCN) and is a psychologist and a licensed professional counselor. Dr. DiDonato has spent his career as a clinician, educator, and researcher. Clinically, Dr. DiDonato's focus has been on children and families who have experienced the intersection and complexity of exposure to trauma and social injustice. Dr. DiDonato has been an educator in higher

232   ABOUT the AUTHORS

education for psychology, counseling, and nursing training programs with a specialty in trauma-informed education and educational practices. Dr. DiDonato's research covers focuses on higher education program evaluation and research, and global child welfare systems. Dr. DiDonato is an Associate Editor for the *Journal of Trauma Studies in Education*.

AUTHORS

Megan Adkins, PhD, is the associate dean of graduate studies and academic innovation at the University of Nebraska at Kearney, where she is also a professor in the health and physical education program. Dr. Adkins's research interests include pedagogy, teacher preparation, XR technology advancements, online educational practices, and STEM. Prior to joining the university, she taught middle school physical education and coached.

Nuchelle L. Chance, PhD, is an applied social psychologist and leadership scholar-practitioner at Fort Hays State University. Her focus lies at the intersection of sex and gender, women's studies, race, learning, perceptions and attitudes, and leadership development. As a junior faculty and early career researcher, she examines how these factors influence individuals' experiences in both academic and professional environments. Dr. Chance utilizes her academic platform as a means to highlight and dismantle injustice.

Libby Clary (she/her) serves as the Tutoring Coordinator for University Tutorial Services at Appalachian State University. As a higher education professional passionate about researching trauma, resilience, and prevention science, she seeks to bring awareness to the ongoing relationship between high ACE scores and levels of academic success. As an adult with a high ACE score, it is very important to her to be a voice for those still finding theirs.

Cassandra R. Davis is an Assistant Professor of Public Policy at the University of North Carolina at Chapel Hill. Dr. Davis has researched environmental disruptions, specifically the impact of hazards on low-income schooling communities of color. Dr. Davis aims to support community leaders, educators, and policymakers to improve responses, mitigation strategies, preparedness, and recovery in areas with the highest need.

Jan DeWaters is an Associate Professor at the Institute for STEM Education at Clarkson University, in Potsdam, NY. An environmental engineer by training, she teaches mainly in the school of engineering where her

About the Authors   233

approach is to expose students to the complex relationship between the technological work of engineers and technical professionals, and the social and natural environments in which those technologies are used. Her research focuses on developing and assessing effective, inclusive teaching and learning strategies in a variety of settings, typically integrating environmental topics such as energy and climate into STEM settings.

Francesca Di Rienzo is a third-year student in the Counseling Psychology PhD program at UT Austin. Prior to commencing her doctoral studies, she worked in the humanitarian-development sphere for six years, where she specialized in psychosocial health and migration. She is further developing this background as a PhD student, while also expanding her research interests to include student mental health in higher education and comparative analyses of psychotherapeutic approaches.

Tricia M. Farwell, PhD, is an associate professor in the School of Journalism and Strategic Media at Middle Tennessee State University. Her research focuses on pedagogy relating to advertising and public relations classes, and academic mentoring and productivity. She is the associate editor for the *Journal of Advertising Education*. She is the author of Love and Death in Edith Wharton's Fiction. Prior to academics, Dr. Farwell worked in corporate communication in the industrial sector.

Knut Inge Fostervold is a licensed psychologist and a professor in Psychology at the University of Oslo. His research interests include the relationship between the physical environment, psychological factors, and personality, as well as the effects of modern work life on workers' health and well-being. He has extensive experience as a lecturer and supervisor in both scientific methods and work and organizational psychology. Fostervold is appointed as a Fellow of the International Ergonomics Association for his contribution to the field of ergonomics and human factors.

Ben Galluzzo is an associate professor of mathematics at Clarkson University. Dr. Galluzzo's area of research concentrates on developing new strategies and best practices for bringing innovation and active learning into K–16 STEM classrooms, with a particular emphasis on mathematical modeling. Dr. Galluzzo also has an extensive background in creating and teaching professional development for K–12 STEM teachers.

Bethany Gonzalez (she/her) is the Associate Director for Military Affiliated Services at Appalachian State University. She earned her bachelor's in Family Consumer Science and Master's in Higher Education, College & University Leadership, both from Appalachian State University.

234   ABOUT the AUTHORS

Katie Kavanagh is the Director of the Institute for STEM Education and an Applied Mathematics Professor at Clarkson University. Dr. Kavanagh's research interests primarily focus on environmental problems using simulation-based optimization and modeling. She also has an extensive background in providing professional development for STEM teachers and directing large-scale K–12 outreach programs.

Rex Long is a doctoral candidate at Texas State University in the Department of Anthropology. Long's research interests include examining the socio-emotional impacts of natural hazards, such as extreme weather events and infectious diseases.

Sten Ludvigsen, PhD, is a Professor in the Department of Education at the University of Oslo. For the past 30 years, he has conducted research on how to promote social and cognitive skills through the use of digital learning resources in various knowledge domains within the educational sector. Ludvigsen has extensive experience in academic leadership and research education, as well as teaching and supervision both nationally and internationally. He has served as editor-in-chief for the *International Journal of Computer-Supported Collaborative Learning* and is a fellow in the International Society of the Learning Sciences.

Trisha Miller is a third-year counseling psychology doctoral student at the University of Texas at Austin. She received her bachelor's degree in Applied Learning and Development from the University of Texas and worked as an elementary school teacher for five years. Her current research interests include stress, coping, help-seeking, and suicide prevention in college students and emerging adults.

Shannon C. Mulhearn, PhD, is an assistant professor in health and physical education at the University of Nebraska at Kearney. She also serves as the director of the center for teaching excellence. Dr. Mulhearn's research interests connect to holistic wellness and coping skills and how these competencies can be taught throughout the K–12 and higher educational journey with a particular focus on movement and physical education opportunities.

Stefanie Neal, EdS, MsEd, NCC, LMHP, RRT, LMT, is currently the mental health provider for Holdrege Public Schools in Nebraska. She also serves as a Registered Respiratory Therapist and Exercise Physiologist in her community. Stefanie utilizes a progressive and holistic approach in her practices through which she combines multiple forms of therapy with art, music, physical education, special education, school counseling

About the Authors 235

and academic wellness to form a collaborative approach towards optimal physical, mental and educational wellness for students. Her research interest includes identifying best practices for mental health in a school setting.

Chelsea Pratt, PhD (she/her), is a former student affairs practitioner and current student affairs and higher education scholar. Her work focuses on the intersection of trauma, supervision, and higher education, and seeks to envision more liberatory higher education practices that center the wisdom of minoritized student affairs staff. She holds a MEd in Higher Education from Merrimack College, and a PhD in Higher Education and Student Affairs from The Ohio State University.

Mike Ramsdell is an associate professor of physics at Clarkson University. Dr. Ramsdell's research interests include physics education research, laboratory curriculum development and design. Dr. Ramsdell has focused on the implementation and assessment of the physics team design program for the calculus-based introductory Mechanics, Electricity, and Magnetism courses. Dr. Ramsdell also has an extensive background in developing and running STEM professional development and STEM camps for middle and high school students.

Megan K. Rauch Griffard is an Assistant Professor of Educational Policy and Leadership at the University of Nevada, Las Vegas. Her research focuses on disruptions to schooling, including both large-scale events such as climate disasters and pandemics and individual events such as student hospitalizations.

Silje Endresen Reme is a professor of health psychology at the University of Oslo, and a clinical pain psychologist at Oslo University Hospital. She completed her educational and doctoral studies at the University of Bergen, followed by a postdoctoral fellowship at Harvard University. Prior to joining the University of Oslo, Dr. Reme worked as a senior researcher at Uni Research Health, where she co-headed the research group Stress, Health and Rehabilitation. Dr. Reme currently leads the Mind-Body Lab Oslo, where her research focuses on chronic pain treatment, chronic post-surgical pain prevention, chronic fatigue, stress, and work disability.

Seema Rivera a is an Associate Professor of STEM Education at Clarkson University in New York State. Dr. Rivera's research focuses on STEM pedagogy in both secondary schools and higher education, with a particular focus on equity. Dr. Rivera is also involved in outreach, bridging STEM pro-

236   ABOUT the AUTHORS

gramming between secondary schools and higher education. Prior to higher education, Dr. Rivera taught high school chemistry in public schools.

Helge I. Strømsø is a professor of higher education in the Department of Education at the University of Oslo, Norway. His main research interests are teaching and learning in higher education, digital literacy, and thinking and reasoning about socioscientific issues.

Yijie ("Teresa") Tian is a counseling psychology doctoral student at the University of Texas at Austin. She earned her bachelor's degree in Biology and Psychology from Bucknell University. Her research focuses on investigating the relationship between teacher stress and school leadership.

Preethi Titu is an Assistant Professor of Science Education in the Department of Elementary and Early Childhood Education at Bagwell College of Education, Kennesaw State University, Georgia. Her research focuses on how both preservice and in-service teachers meaningfully integrate STEM pedagogy into classroom practice. Additionally, her work addresses issues of diversity, equity and identity at the K–12 level and in higher education settings.

Caroline Weppner is a fourth-year counseling psychology doctoral student at the University of Texas at Austin. She graduated in 2021 with a master's degree in Psychological Sciences from the Catholic University of America in Washington, DC., and has continued to pursue her research interests in stress, coping, and predictors of peak performance, particularly in the educational setting with educators and students.

Printed in the United States
by Baker & Taylor Publisher Services